D1521667

CULTURE WAR
AND
ETHICAL THEORY

Richard F. Von Dohlen

University Press of America, Inc.
Lanham • New York • London

Copyright © 1997 by
University Press of America,® Inc.
4720 Boston Way
Lanham, Maryland 20706

3 Henrietta Street
London, WC2E 8LU England

Library of Congress Cataloging-in-Publication Data

Von Dohlen, Richard F.
Culture war and ethical theory / Richard F. Von Dohlen.
p. cm.
Includes bibliographical references and index.
1. Ethics. 2. Applied ethics. 3. Culture conflict--Moral and ethical
aspects. 4. Culture conflict--United States--History--20th century. 5.
United States--Moral conditions. 6. Rawls, John, 1921-. 7.
MacIntyre, Alasdair C. 8. United States--Intellectural life--20th
century. I. Title.
BJ1012.V66 1996   171--dc21   96-46342 CIP

ISBN 0-7618-0616-4 (pbk: alk. ppr.)

♾™ The paper used in this publication meets the minimum
requirements of American National Standard for information
Sciences—Permanence of Paper for Printed Library Materials,
ANSI Z39.48—1984

Contents

Preface

Culture War and Ethical Theory has been some years in writing and grows out of my desire to make the discussion of ethical theory relevant to my students most of whom are taking a first course in philosophy. As such, it is an introduction to ethical theory that relates theory to the contemporary debate about the so called 'culture wars' rather than a book on the culture wars debate as such. I compare each theory discussed with the explicit or implicit response of both fundamentalism and secular humanism in order to illustrate the relevance of the theory to a polemical contemporary debate with which most moderately well informed students will be at least somewhat familiar. This goal defines both the strengths and limitations of the book It is an introduction to ethical theory that treats cultural relativism, emotivism, egoism, hedonism, utilitarianism, Kant, John Rawls and Alasdair MacIntyre. It is hardly a systematic survey of the field of ethics. Furthermore, although I have tried to be fair and accurate when referring to fundamentalism and secular humanism, this is not an introduction to either movement. I have chosen to discuss these two movements because they are so diametrically opposed in the popular mind and each other's eyes. This makes them especially useful in setting forth the implications of various positions in stark relief.

I have not tried to conceal my own Christian presuppositions but this is not a work in Christian apologetics or defense of the faith. I have deliberately tried to be non-polemical in my treatment of issues and positions that are most frequently treated polemically. Whether I have succeeded or not I cannot say. My hope, however, is that this book might be read by both fundamentalists and secular humanists without the perception that their respective positions had been caricatured or distorted. I have tried to avoid bashing either position in the conviction that there has already been to much of that already. I believe that civil, reasoned discourse is necessary if we are to make progress in resolving cultural conflict.

I think that my treatment of Rawls and MacIntyre, at least at this point in time, may be somewhat unique in making these thinkers accessible to the introductory student. There are any number of introductory works that treat of relativism, emotivism, hedonism, utilitarianism and Kant. Despite their importance on the contemporary scene, however, I am not aware of any good reasonably short expositions that make both Rawls and MacIntyre available to the first time student of philosophy. I hope to have been of special, if modest, service to the philosophical community in this regard. Although I have sought to be accurate in my treatment of both Rawls and MacIntyre, I have not limited myself to simple exposition but have endeavored to critique both thinkers.

Another feature of this book that should prove useful is the comparison of the various positions with each other that is developed throughout. Each new position considered is compared with all the previous positions, so that emotivism is contrasted with cultural relativism, utilitarianism with both emotivism and relativism, and so forth throughout. MacIntyre's position is compared and contrasted with all of the previous thinkers studied, including Rawls. I think this enhances the clarity of the exposition and is pedagogically sound, providing the first time student of philosophy with a framework that would not be available if each position were presented independently.

To assist the student in assessing whether or not he or she has grasped the essential distinctions of the various concepts and theories introduced, I have included a study guide that includes three different types of help. The glossary included in the back of the book contains key concepts that are introduced in the various chapters. Secondly, I have included a set of objective questions that are designed to test the student's grasp of these concepts. Finally, there are essay questions designed to be considered after the careful study of each chapter. I have also prepared a bank of test questions that contains approximately five hundred objective questions similar to those included in the study guide. These questions in both hard copy and diskette are available to instructors by writing to the author at Lenoir-Rhyne College, Hickory, North Carolina, 28601. Objective tests cannot give the student practice in dialogue on philosophical issues or writing philosophical essays which are, of course, the most important goals in a philosophy course. They can test whether the student has grasped and is able to compare and contrast various theories and thinkers. An added benefit is practice in taking the sort of tests that are given on exams like the SAT, GRE, LSAT, NTE, etc.

I teach and have written with the conviction that philosophy can and ought to be relevant to the solution of problems that concern ordinary people in their day-to-day existence. Clarification of the most fundamental assumptions we as humans make about ourselves and our social order will not in itself resolve our problems and insure justice and the common good. It can, however, make a significant contribution to these worthy goals. This book is written with the conviction that cultural conflict is both inevitable and frequently extremely constructive. Culture wars, I believe, are not inevitable and are all to frequently, like wars of physical combat, very destructive. Philosophy has not the power, by itself, to turn swords in plowshares. It can, however, contribute significantly to the more modest goal of turning cultural 'war' into cultural 'conflict.' It is my hope that this book will contribute to that end.

CHAPTER I

THE RELATIONSHIP OF CULTURE WAR TO ETHICAL THEORY

The Use of the Term 'Culture War'

'Culture war' or frequently the plural 'culture wars' has become headline news in recent years.[1] Why is this? What does the phrase mean and what has caused its use to come into vogue? 'War' usually means violent conflict usually between nation states or politically organized entities. 'Culture' in this context refers to fundamental values, commitments and patterns of behavior of a social order.

One might expect, therefore, that the term 'culture war' would refer to violent conflict carried on by organized political entities and directed at destroying or defending the fundamental, values, commitments and behaviors of a particular social order. This is what one might expect. As a matter of fact, however, the term is used much more loosely to describe various means for carrying on conflict and less radical ends than the destruction of a social order. Wars occur when persuasion, negotiation, and compromise have failed. Wars are directed to the end of subjugation or the resistance to subjugation. In extreme cases, wars are directed to the end of total annihilation of the enemy. A stalemate in a war may result in a reversion to negotiation, compromise and even persuasion, but this occurs when one or both of the parties to the war fail at their original end. Wars are usually accompanied by the conviction that the other side has violated the basic rights of one's community. In extreme cases, one or both sides take the position that the other has no moral standing at all.

Of course, one may take the position that the individual persons who comprise a nation state or a political community have moral standing, and that it is only the community itself that has no moral standing. A less radical position is that both the persons that comprise a community and the community itself have moral standing, but that the particular goals that are being sought by the community have no moral standing.

An example may be helpful here. World War II certainly qualifies as an example of a war. Over fifty million people were killed. The position of the allies, however, was not that individual Germans or Japanese had no moral standing. The goal was not to annihilate all Germans, Italians and Japanese.[2] The goal was not to prevent the Germans or the Japanese from having a nation state. It was only the nation state in its particular form that was the object of war.

Was World War II a culture war? It would seem to qualify by any definition. Hitler's Germany attempted to annihilate the Jews. Hitler argued not only that Jewish culture was inferior, but that it was corrupt and corrupting. He argued further, that the culture was borne by race. Therefore, destruction of Jewish culture required the destruction of all Jews. The allies, for their part, regarded themselves in a war to save democracy. They further regarded democratic government and freedoms as central to their cultures and the essence of Western civilization. In short, they regarded themselves to be in a war to save Western culture. It was not simply a war about land, wealth or even power. After the war, the allies attempted to eradicate those cultural influences in Germany and Japan that had promoted the war. They did not, however, attempt to eradicate all German or Japanese history and culture. They certainly did not attempt to annihilate all Germans and Japanese.

Was the 'cold war' between the democracies and communist block a real war? The main difference between a 'hot war' and a 'cold war' is that a 'cold war' substitutes the threat of violence for actual violence. There was always the threat of the outbreak of actual violence that was prevented mainly by a policy of mutual deterrence. Both sides were convinced that they could not win a hot war at a price that they were willing to pay.

If the cold war was a real war, was it a culture war? The cold war had to do with basic political, economic, and religious values--democracy versus dictatorship, extensive civil liberties versus totalitarianism, capitalism versus communism, state mandated atheism versus religious liberty in a civilization deeply indebted to the Judeo-Christian ethic. It would seem to clearly qualify as a culture war.

What about the American Revolution? This was certainly a war, but was it a culture war? Historians may differ on this point but the answer to me seems clearly to be in the negative. The two warring groups were the same religiously, ethnically, and linguistically and for the most part agreed on the nature of basic civil liberties and good political institutions.

The American Civil War is more ambiguous than any of the other examples given above. It was a terribly violent war. Fifty thousand died in just three days at Gettysburg. It was in large measure about basic values--the issue of slavery. Most of the combatants, however, were from the same ethnic and linguistic group. Both sides believed in democracy. There were, however, important political, economic and regional differences as well as basic cultural differences. It was a total war. It does not seem, however, to have been a total culture war. From the Northern point of view, at least, it was an effort to reform the culture and not an effort to destroy a totally alien culture.

The American Indian wars, on the other hand, seem to clearly be examples of culture wars. There was organized violence by political entities. The wars involved political, economic, and social structures. They included different linguistic and ethnic groups and different religious beliefs.

Is war the only kind of possible conflict? Most of us would answer: certainly not! Democracy assumes the values of pluralism (including religious and cultural pluralism), dialogue, persuasion, compromise, accommodation, sharing and peaceful coexistence. It also assumes the possibility of evolutionary change as an alternative to dramatic violent revolution.   Why then all this rhetoric about culture war in our contemporary political debate?

There are a number of reasons both in our historical traditions and in the contemporary situation that account for the emphasis on culture war. *In the first place, many wars including W.W.II and the Cold War do qualify as culture wars.* If one grants the appropriateness of referring to the Cold War as an example of a real war that was not (for the most part) violent, then it is possible to have a non-violent cultural war. Thus, we have recent historical precedent for referring to non-violent war. Wars furthermore, whatever the real motives behind them, are usually promoted as culture wars. The reasons for this are obvious. Violent wars require motivating people to kill and maim and to be killed or maimed. Perhaps the only way to motivate large numbers of people to do this is to convince them that the war has to do with the most fundamental values of society. There is thus a natural tendency to promote wars as conflicts between absolute good and absolute evil.

Secondly, the idea of a culture war is deeply embedded in the Judeo-Christian tradition that has so significantly influenced Western culture. Except for the reign of Solomon, the Old Testament reads like the history of a people who are almost always on the verge of political, religious, cultural and ethnic extinction. It may not be an exaggeration to say that the history of Israel is the history of one long cultural war. The New Testament images are no less stark. The cross, light versus darkness, good versus evil, heaven versus hell, the works of the flesh versus the fruits of the spirit, the spirit against the flesh, the Kingdom of God versus mammon are all images that permeate the New Testament. Constantine's consolidation of the Roman Empire under the sign of the cross, Charlemagne's Holy Roman Empire, the Crusades, the 100 Years War following the Protestant and Catholic Reformations are also part of a rich heritage of cultural warfare on the behalf of Judeo/Christian values.

This heritage has its secular roots as well. Marxism perceives capitalism as grounded upon an economic structure that determines the social, intellectual, cultural and religious values of the population. The bourgeoisie uses these structures to make virtual warfare on the proletariat. The struggle between capitalism and communism is in its deepest roots a culture war.

Thirdly, there are the radical social, economic, and technological changes that have occurred in this century. This has put enormous strain on the collective psyche. We have never in human history had as much technological control over our world. Actual technological control, however, has not been accompanied by a proportionate psychological sense of control. Whether one is committed to the application of traditional values to a changing situation or to the creation of new values to help us adapt to the changing situation, the task is enormous. Rapid change, the breakdown of moral consensus, and the psychological sense of things being out of control tend to produce the conviction that "we" are not in control. We often conclude, therefore, that "they" must be in control and that "they" are trying to destroy our culture. In short, we must be at war.

Fourthly, there is the phenomenon of the decline of rational discourse with respect to ethics. This decline has both philosophical and sociological implications. Chapter III will be devoted to the ethical position known as emotivism which is an example of this decline. Emotivism (ironically because of a commitment to the rational discourse of science) asserts that rational discourse regarding ethical assertions is impossible. According to the emotivist, normative statements--all statements about what is good or bad or concerning what ought or ought not to be done--are cognitively meaningless and are mere expressions of emotions. They are neither true nor false. If the emotivist position is correct, all the language that passes for rational arguments about what is good or bad or right or wrong is really not rational at all but an attempt to manipulate the emotions of those toward whom it is directed. Moral discourse cannot be an attempt at rational persuasion but is entirely reduced to propaganda of one sort or another. As we shall discover in Chapter III, emotivism and its theory of language has been largely discredited in philosophical circles.

Emotivism as a sociological phenomenon, however, is another matter. It is one thing to argue that discourse about values is not necessarily merely an expression of emotions. One may still argue, however, that in our society discourse about values is for the most part not rational but simply an attempt to manipulate emotions. In other words, rational discourse about values may be theoretically possible but still not be widely practiced in our society. There is plenty of evidence that much political, religious, ethical and cultural debate is discourse directed at the manipulation of the emotions rather than grounded on attempts at rational persuasion. It also seems that the advertising industry--whether selling soap, political candidates or cultural values--is founded not on the dissemination of factual information and a commitment to rational persuasion but on the unabashed manipulation of emotions.

What has this to do with culture wars? To the extent, for example, that fundamentalists and secular humanists believe that the other side is either not practicing, not committed to or even incapable of rational discourse, dialogue between the two groups becomes impossible. Both sides are perceived by the other as engaged exclusively in propaganda and manipulation. Propaganda and manipulation are, of course, almost universally used as instruments of warfare.   Thus, the other side is perceived as engaging not in fair rational discourse devoted to helping members of society make free rational decisions but in a form of cultural warfare.

Finally, there is the motivational appeal to give money, time and energy to cultural wars. People are more easily motivated to devote their wealth and energy to combat absolute evil as opposed to combating the second best.   We are more ready to commit our resources when basic values are believed to be at stake as opposed to situations when peripheral values or concerns are at risk. This presents a great temptation to present one's opponents in the guise of a threat of absolute evil and to present one's own position as a defense of absolute good. Its simply good fundraising strategy.

The Benefits of Ethical Theory and Systematic Reflection

It is possible to disagree about ethics without engaging in rational reflection but disagreement about ethics that includes rational reflection forces us to think *systematically* about right behavior, the good and just society, and what it means to be a good person. One goal of this book is to introduce the reader to the problems associated with thinking in a systematic way about ethics.   Ethics is concerned with questions concerning how one ought to live, to act and to be. Anyone able to read these words has been introduced to many of the problems associated with these questions a long time ago. We have all thought a great deal about how we ought to live, to act and to be almost since the time we were able to think about anything at all.

We have not, however, all necessarily thought about ethics in a *systematic* manner. Some of us, of course, may have been brought up in a religious tradition or homes with fairly clear and precisely defined sets of principles and rules. Having been confronted with an organized system of obligations at an early age we may have been forced to reflect on at least one ethical system, namely, the one in which we were raised.

Others may have been confronted with a particular ethical problem like the following; should I, or someone who is seeking my advice, have an abortion, or engage in extramarital sex, or accept military service in a war that many people are claiming is unjust, etc.? Under the pressure of deciding what to do in a difficult situation where we are receiving conflicting signals from our society, we may have been forced to consider reasons pro and con for a particular course of action. We may have been therefore encouraged to carefully rethink some of our most basic assumptions about what is real, true and good, at least with respect to this particular decision.

Many books and discussions on ethics capitalize on this experience that many have had and are organized around problems in ethics such as abortion, euthanasia, just war, poverty, extramarital sex, homosexuality, capital punishment, etc. Other books are directed to the consideration of ethical issues related to particular professions or social phenomena. Thus, we have books, texts, and college and university courses in business ethics, medical ethics, sports ethics, media ethics, legal ethics, etc. This type of focus is valuable in at least two ways. It does force one to think carefully and systematically about ethical issues. Secondly, such approaches have the value of being "relevant". They direct us to issues with which we are familiar and about which we are concerned.

There are, however, some drawbacks to this approach as an introduction to the discipline of ethics in particular and to a discussion of the relationship of ethics and cultural conflict in general. Frequently, participants in a discussion of these issues disagree with one another not because they differ in their view of the relevant facts but because they make different assumptions about the nature of reality, the nature of personhood, the ways in which we come to know the truth (at least ethical truth) or about the very way one should go about systematically exploring issues from an ethical perspective. In other words, they disagree about the whole theoretical approach to ethics. They implicitly or explicitly have different theories about the way one should go about dealing with ethical issues. Frequently this disagreement is based on different fundamental assumptions about the meaning of life.

Failure to recognize this fact results in considerable confusion as people talk past each other rather than to each other.

Recognizing the relationship between cultural conflict, ethical theory and specific disagreements about right and wrong, and good and bad will not *necessarily* result in the resolution of either ethical conflicts or broader cultural conflicts. It will tend to make meaningful dialogue possible and more likely. Making such dialogue possible is one of the important goals of this book.

It is my conviction that an introduction to ethical theory can be extremely useful in helping people to focus on central issues in contemporary ethical discourse and to avoid a great deal of confusion and irrelevant discussion. In order to help the reader see the relevance of each theory to contemporary problems, I will attempt to indicate how a person holding each theory might approach various problems which concern us in everyday life such as euthanasia, extramarital sex, poverty, social justice, the problem of just war, etc. I will not, however, try to deal adequately or systematically with these problems. The problems will be introduced to illustrate the various ethical theories discussed, rather than for their own sake.

A second benefit that can come from an understanding of ethical theory is that it enhances the ability of an individual to understand his or her own presuppositions and assumptions about the nature of reality, the nature of the knowing process, and what it means to be a good person and to act morally. Everyone who discusses ethical issues in an intelligent manner has such assumptions, but we are not always clear with respect to what the assumptions are and the impact they have on our thinking and behavior. If we understand our assumptions, we are able to articulate them more clearly to others and to think and act in a manner more consistent with those assumptions. We are also in a better position to change both our assumptions and our behavior should we choose to do so.

Ethics and Other Branches of Philosophy

Ethical theories may be described as different views concerning the proper way to think systematically about how one ought to live and act, and what type of person one ought to be. Usually ethical theories are associated with theories about the nature of the universe, the nature of the knowing process, and the nature of persons. Philosophers refer to these areas as 'ontology,' 'epistemology,' and 'philosophical anthropology.' These are probably unfamiliar terms to those who have had no previous work in philosophy. Perhaps a brief lesson in philology will help. These are all 'ology' words which we encounter frequently, as in 'biology,' 'sociology,' 'psychology,' 'theology,' etc. The Greek word 'logos' literally means 'word' but is often translated 'theory of.' Since 'bios' in Greek means life, we derive the word 'biology' or the theory of living things. 'Theos' is Greek for God and 'theology' refers to theories about the nature of God. 'Ontos' is Greek for being. Thus, 'ontology' is theory of being or theory about the ultimate nature of reality. 'Episteme' is one of the Greek words for knowledge. Hence, 'epistemology' is theory of knowledge. 'Anthropos' is Greek for man. Thus, 'anthropology' is theory of human nature. So much for our brief lesson in philology. 'Philology,' by the way, comes from the Greek 'phileo' (love) and 'logos' which as we have said means 'word.' Hence, 'philology' literally means love of words but has come to mean simply the study of words.

To those encountering philosophy for the first time this may seem both abstract and irrelevant. But as a matter of fact, probably everyone has thought about an ontology, epistemology and anthropology in relationship to some ethical principle. Let us take a couple of examples. Hedonism is the ethical theory which asserts that pleasure is the ultimate and only good. One hedonist in the history of thought (Epicurus) was an egoistic hedonist who asserted that everyone ought to affirm and live according to the precept that his or her own pleasure is the ultimate and only good. Epicurus further asserted that reason is the only guide to life (epistemology), that reason taught that there is no God, in the Judeo-Christian sense of that term, (theology) and that the universe held no meaning beyond the individual (ontology). Furthermore, human beings are composed completely of material atoms and have no immortal souls. They are also not capable of selfless love (anthropology). Thus, they cannot have any goals or ideals that transcend their own selfish interests. Therefore, individual pleasure is the only possible reasonable basis for ethics.

Christianity makes different assumptions about the nature of being. For example it asserts the existence of a loving God who created the universe (ontology). This God, according to most Christians, can be known in part by reason, but revelation is also both available and necessary (epistemology). Human beings are made in the image of this loving God and have existence beyond this life. They are not just material atoms but have immortal souls. (anthropology). Therefore, the highest ethical goal for men and women is to live a life that manifests a selfless love toward God and fellow human beings.

Of course, things are frequently not as simple as the examples given above might indicate. Not all hedonists are egoistic. There have been Christian philosophers who have maintained that pleasure is the good. Christians are not the only ones who have asserted the ultimate value of selfless love. Those who assert that love is the ultimate goal have different theories concerning how this should be implemented and hedonists have differed among themselves as well. We will deal with some of these differences later on. The point I wish to make here is that most people who have thought about right and wrong have done so in the context of some assumptions (if not a well worked out theory) about the nature of the universe, the nature of persons, and the nature of knowledge.

Positions and Theories Considered in this Book

There are several different theoretical approaches and issues which we will consider in this book. These have been chosen both because of their historical importance in the history of ethical discussion and for their contemporary relevance. *Cultural relativism* is the view that there are no values or ethical obligations which transcend the particular cultures in which they are affirmed. *Emotivism* is the view that statements pretending to assert ethical obligation are merely expressions of emotion and not cognitively meaningful statements at all. *Hedonism*, as has been noted above, is the view that pleasure is the ultimate and indeed the only good. *Utilitarianism* is the ethical position that what is right and wrong action is to be determined solely on the basis of the contribution of the action to the greatest good of the greatest number. An *ethics of duty* as represented by Immanual Kant and the contemporary philosopher John Rawls affirms that right action is based not entirely on its consequences for either oneself or the greatest number but that the good and justice must be defined in terms of obligations which exist (in Rawls' case, at least in part) regardless of consequences. There has been much recent discussion concerning an ethics of virtue which is contrasted with an ethics of duty. Philosophers affirming an ethics of virtue are maintaining that in our discussion and practice of ethics, we should concentrate first on *being the right kind of person* and only secondarily on *doing the right sorts of things* rather than the other way around.   Cultural relativism, emotivism, hedonism, utilitarianism, and the debate between an ethics of duty and an ethics of virtue by no means exhaust the topics to which ethical theorists have devoted themselves in the history of thought. Exploration of these positions and issues, however, will perhaps be sufficient to constitute at least an introduction to ethical theory and its relationship to contemporary cultural conflict.

Use of the Terms 'Christian,' 'Fundamentalist,' and 'Secular Humanist'

At this point it is appropriate to indicate my choice of Christianity, secular humanism and fundamentalism in its Christian variety to illustrate the relevance of ethical theory for cultural conflict. Why not Christianity, Islam, Buddhism, Hinduism, and Confucianism and the fundamentalistic variations of these religions?   There are several reasons.

In the first place, this book is intended to be an introduction to ethical theory which demonstrates the relevance of ethical theory to the analysis of cultural conflict. It is not intended to be a comprehensive treatment of cultural conflict, fundamentalism, or secular humanism.

Secondly, in the contemporary American political scene, the most prominent form of fundamentalism associated with the so-called religious right is that associated with Protestant fundamentalism. This, of course, is not the whole story. Pat Buchanan, the most prominent political representative of the religious right in the 1994 presidential race is a Roman Catholic. In the 1992 Republican convention, he gave the term 'culture wars' a prominence in political rhetoric that it had not had previously. With respect to many issues related to cultural conflict, Orthodox Jews and conservative Protestants and Roman Catholics have more in common with each other than they have with the more liberal wings of their own religious groups.

The term 'Islamic fundamentalism' is frequently used by the media but it has become almost a synonym for terrorism. When the media bothers to give a somewhat more detailed description, Shiite Muslims are identified with fundamentalism while Sunnite Muslims are identified as more moderate.   Unfortunately, this translates to an

American public largely ignorant of Islamic thought as a distinction between good Muslims (read moderate and Sunnite) and bad Muslims (read extremist/fundamentalist and Shiite). This is not only not fair. It is also over simplified, unsophisticated and unhelpful. Superficial demonization of a particular group may sell papers, boost television ratings, garner votes, raise money, or give short-term emotional satisfaction. It does not, however, encourage understanding or peaceful coexistence. Doubtless a book that attempted to relate Ayer, Kant, Mill, Rawls, MacIntyre, etc., to Islamic thought, including Islamic fundamentalism, would be useful. It would be most useful, however, to an audience more familiar with Islamic culture than most of my readers. It would also need to be written by someone more conversant with Islamic thought and culture than myself.

In the third place, Protestant fundamentalism has a specific historical tradition started by individuals who identified themselves by the term 'fundamentalism.' Contrary to the situation in contemporary portrayals in the media where the term 'fundamentalism' is most often derogatory, fundamentalists originally chose this designation as a complementary one. They regarded themselves as continuing to subscribe to the fundamentals of Christianity as over against 'liberals' whom they regarded as having abandoned that which was fundamental to the faith. This makes careful definition, if not easy, at least more nearly possible.

Finally, a similar point may be made with regard to secular humanism. There are people who proudly identify with the term 'secular humanism' and who make sophisticated attempts to articulate its meaning and implications. This group has its own magazine (Free Inquiry), its own publishing house (Prometheus), and its own declaration of principles, one might say its own list of fundamentals (The Humanist Manifesto).

My reasons for choosing to illustrate the relevance of these various theories to fundamentalism and secular humanism will, I trust, become more obvious as we go along. Let me say for now, that these two positions are considered in the popular mind to be two dichotomous perspectives which can have nothing in common. To many, they represent opposite extremes in the cultural conflict debate. One result of this is that the terms are often used, one may say most often used, in a heated polemical fashion. In many contexts they are used by critics as terms of opprobrium and derision. Nevertheless, both of these positions claim numerous adherents and both the adherents and the positions are worthy of more than slander. One goal that I have in using them to illustrate the theories considered is to promote genuine dialogue where there is, all too often, simply name calling and shouting matches.

Secondly, I think that the comparison can be a useful pedagogical tool to those of us who might not identify with either camp. Just because they are and are perceived to be so far apart, asking "What would a fundamentalist say about this theory?" or "What would a secular humanist say about this theory?" can be useful in understanding the theories themselves. This will provide us with a way of mapping various ethical perspectives using guideposts with which many of us have some familiarity.

To lessen the possibility of misunderstanding it will be useful here to define terms at least as I intend to use them in this text. By the term "Christian," unless I indicate otherwise, I intend a broad use embracing a wide range of believers which would include Pope John Paul II and the Reverend Jerry Falwell. By "fundamentalists" I intend those Christians who either call themselves fundamentalists or tend to exhibit doctrines and attitudes associated with those who do call themselves fundamentalists.

For our purposes, it is sufficient to define fundamentalists as follows. (1) Fundamentalists attempt to define those doctrinal affirmations which are *necessary and sufficient* for one to be identified as a Christian. These conditions are the so-called 'fundamentals' of the faith which usually include the deity and virgin birth of Christ, the Trinity, the bodily resurrection of Christ, the second coming, the creation and fall of man, the substitutionary atonement, the inspiration and inerrancy of scripture, etc. (2) In addition to the inerrancy of scripture which perhaps more than any other doctrinal affirmation tends to divide fundamentalists from other Christians, there is a tendency for fundamentalists to be more likely to give a literal interpretation of scripture than is true for non-fundamentalist Christians. (3) Fundamentalists are also less likely to view certain scriptural passages as being relative to the culture in which they were first uttered. Thus, fundamentalists are more likely to see passages of scripture referring to the status of women as normative for the present as well as ancient times, whereas other Christians might view these passages as pastoral advice applicable only to the specific context of the first century.   (4) Fundamentalists are also more likely to be alienated from secular culture, particularly academic culture than non-fundamentalists. They tend to see less need to attempt to enrich the Christian perspective by study of explicitly non-Christian sources. They also correspondingly see more danger in such sources and less possibility for accommodation with non-Christian perspectives.[3]

Especially with respect to literal interpretation of the scripture, the tendency to apply all scriptural passages to present circumstances, and alienation from the secular culture, one has to speak of tendencies rather than absolute positions. Fundamentalists do not interpret all passages of scripture literally, do not think all passages apply to our present situation and do not reject all of secular culture. Conversely, those Christians who would not call themselves fundamentalists interpret some passages of scripture literally, affirm that some theological and ethical pronouncements apply in the present as well as in ancient times, and are alienated from or at least critical of some aspects of secular culture, and believe that at some points accommodation is impossible.   Furthermore, the overwhelming majority of those Christians who reject inerrancy accept the Bible as authoritative revelation with respect to some issues and to some degree. Fundamentalists differ among themselves with respect to these issues. Non-fundamentalist Christians differ with respect to these issues and also differ on their views concerning the nature and authority of scripture.

The term 'humanism' has been used in a number of differing ways. Therefore, it may be useful to distinguish some of the senses of the term which are not intended in this book. By 'secular humanists' I do not mean to refer to those who teach or may be trained in one of those disciplines like philosophy, history, English, foreign languages, etc., which come under the heading of the humanities. Neither do I refer to the historical period known as the Renaissance and the particular group of scholars known as Renaissance Humanists.

Secular humanism certainly goes back to ancient Greece but as a self-conscious movement it is fairly recent and may be defined by: (1) the rejection of belief in God and the supernatural, (2) belief in the value of human nature, the good of all humanity and the possibility of human progress, (3) confidence in reason, and the scientific method as the means for achieving human happiness, (4) the rejection of supernatural revelation of any sort and rejection of the authority of traditional religion, and (5) belief in the value of individual autonomy, democracy and world community.[4]

As we shall see, many thinkers who might identify with the statements made above can and do differ on numerous other important questions. Thus, to speak of secular humanists as a single unified group is probably more of a distortion than to speak of all Christians as though they agreed on all major issues. It is certainly a distortion to suppose that secular humanists are engaged in some self-conscious unified conspiracy. Thus, when I refer to them in order to illustrate a particular theoretical perspective in ethics, I will often indicate that some humanists will agree while others may disagree. Furthermore, I will often say things like "humanists would *tend* to agree or disagree" or "Christians would be *likely* to accept or reject certain views." Such statements will, I trust, serve the purpose of clarifying the theories under consideration and also indicate that sometimes things may be more complicated than polemicists on either side of the issue would suppose. It is my conviction that there is both a dearth of and a great need for *reasoned* debate in this area, and it is my hope that this book will contribute to that end. Although I have no intention of concealing my own views, frequently I will neither come to, nor seek to come to, closure with respect to problems that will be raised. I wish to think with my readers, not for them. The sometimes complicated nature of cultural and ethical debate can be clarified by attention to some distinctions that will be made below. I will illustrate those distinctions by analyzing a possible debate between a fundamentalist and a secular humanist.

Bases, Principles, Rules, and Cases

Arthur E. Holmes makes a distinction between *bases, principles, rules,* and *cases* in ethical theories.[5] We can illustrate these distinctions by the following hypothetical arguments that might be offered by a fundamentalist and a humanist in dialogue with each other.

The fundamentalist might argue as follows. *(1) A loving God has created us in His own image. (2) This means that we are obligated to love our fellow man. (3) Loving one's fellow man entails the rule that murder is wrong. (4) All abortion is murder and therefore it is wrong for Suzy to have an abortion and for anyone to assist her in having an abortion.*

The humanist might respond in the following manner. *(1) Human nature is the ultimate value in the universe. (2) This means that we are obligated to treat our fellow human beings with respect and justice. (3) Justice entails the rule that no human being should ever be denied a legitimate freedom. (4) Suzy has a legitimate freedom to have an abortion and it is therefore right for anyone to assist her in obtaining this legitimate freedom.*

Our hypothetical fundamentalist and humanist obviously disagree but at what point? They disagree on the basis of their entire ethical systems. The fundamentalist affirms God as the ultimate ground or foundation of his ethics, while the humanist affirms that respect for humanity is the foundation of all ethical behavior.

It may appear that they disagree on principles. The fundamentalist is arguing in this particular argument from the principle of love while the humanist is arguing from the principle of justice. It may, of course, be the case that the fundamentalist has love as his only principle and sees justice as a derivative or secondary principle. It may be the case that the humanist affirms justice as his only ethical principle while viewing love as good but not as an appropriate principle which should be related to his ethical theory. But this need not necessarily be the case. It is quite possible that both the fundamentalist and the humanist would be quite willing to affirm both love and justice as ethical principles. They simply chose to argue from different principles in this particular case. What about the rules "murder is wrong" and "no human being should ever be denied a legitimate freedom"? It is very doubtful that either one would have a problem in wholeheartedly affirming both of these rules. Where then do they differ? They obviously differ at the level of the fundamental basis of their ethical systems and at the level of application to this particular *case*, namely, whether or not Suzy's abortion is morally acceptable. They do not, however, necessarily differ at the principle and rule level of ethical discourse.

What are the implications of this observation for ethical debate and cultural conflict? One possible implication is that on other issues or with respect to other case applications, the fundamentalist and secular humanist may find themselves in agreement. We cannot, therefore, assume that disagreement at the base level universally leads to disagreement at the rule, principle, and case application level. We cannot assume that disagreement on the case application level in one instance necessarily implies disagreement regarding other cases.

Of course, although disagreement at the base level does not necessarily lead to disagreement at other levels, frequently disagreement at the base level is at the root of deep disagreements at other levels. Ontology, epistemology, and anthropology have profound implications for the way we view the world as it actually is and as it ought to be. Thus, they significantly affect our perspective on the whole cultural enterprise. Furthermore, different conceptions of culture often lead to significant differences in behavior and our conceptions of right and wrong. Some of the ways in which this occurs will be explored in subsequent chapters.

War versus Conflict

This book will deal throughout with the relationship of the various ethical theories under consideration to the so called 'culture wars.' It will, however, do so critically. The term 'culture war' is sometimes appropriate. At other times, however, we may be dealing with 'cultural conflict' or 'cultural evolution.' To a significant extent philosophical discourse is predicated on the assumption that persuasion is possible and that the coercion implied by the term 'war' is not always necessary. Of course, persuasion may not always be possible. Rational discourse may be found to have its limits. These limits may not always be due to a lack of good will. There may be deep seated epistemological grounds that prevent rational discourse from bringing us to a resolution of conflict. Before we conclude that this is the case, or that it is the case in a particular situation, however, the possibility of rational discourse as an option deserves a thorough investigation. This book is dedicated to enhancing the ability of its readers to explore this possibility in their own lives and concrete situations.

Notes

[1] See for example: James Davison Hunter, *Culture Wars: The Struggle to Define America* and *Before the Shooting Starts: Searching for Democracy in America's Culture War.* See also Joe Loconte: "The Battle to Define America Turns Violent," *Christianity Today*, 25 October 1993, 74-77; John D. Woodbridge, "Culture War Casualties: How Warfare Rhetoric is Hurting the Work of the Church," *Christianity Today*, 6 March 1995; The cover story of *Time Magazine,* Jeffrey H. Birnbaum "The Right Hand of God: The Gospel According to Ralph," *Time*, 15 May 1995.

[2] This is not to deny that some individuals who were part of the conflict didn't have such a goal. The official goal of the allied powers, however, was to bring about the defeat of the axis powers.

[3] The literature on fundamentalism is extensive. Two helpful works are George M. Marsden, *Understanding Fundamentalism and Evangelicalism* and Norman J. Cohen, ed., *The Fundamentalist Phenomenon, A View From Within, A Response From Without.*

[4] For a clear, brief and authoritative statement of secular humanism see *A Secular Humanist Declaration,* drafted by Paul Kurtz and endorsed by 58 prominent scholars and writers (Reprinted From *Free Inquiry* Magazine, Vol. 1 #1, Winter, 1980).

[5] Arthur F. Holmes, *Ethics: Approaching Moral Decisions,* pp. 49-56.

CHAPTER II

CULTURAL RELATIVISM

Cultural Relativism: A Preliminary Definition

Cultural relativism does not refer only to the case application level. Cultural relativism is the ethical theory that holds that *all* values are relative to the culture in which they reside. This may be stated negatively by saying that there are *no* universal values. There are no values that transcend all cultures and to which human beings may appeal to determine what is right and wrong, or good and bad. A consequence of this position is that judgments about what is good or bad about a culture cannot come from outside that culture. It is possible to make judgments about whether or not a given practice is consistent with the values of a culture. It is not possible to make judgments about whether those values themselves are good or bad.

The words 'all' and 'no' are important. The cultural relativist is not simply asserting that with respect to *some* issues right and wrong varies from culture to culture. The cultural relativist is making the very strong claim that there are no universal rules or principles that ought to be applied to all cultures at all times in all places. To use the distinctions we introduced in the last chapter, this is not an assertion of relativism only at the level of case application. Most, if not all, universalists would agree that values are relative to cultures at the case application level. The cultural relativist affirms that relativity extends to the level of rules and principles.

Cultural relativism is an ethical philosophical and not simply an historical or sociological position. The cultural relativist is making an ethical (sometimes an epistemological judgment) and not simply a sociological or a historical judgment. The cultural relativist is not simply observing that different cultures at different times and different places have as a matter of fact affirmed different ethical values. That would be a factual claim that most universalists would agree with. The universalist, however, asserts that although cultures have differed regarding what they have affirmed as morally right, that there are some universal standards that they *ought* to have affirmed (whether or not any or all have affirmed them) and that all cultures may be evaluated by these universal standards. The cultural relativist is denying the existence of these standards.

'Universalism' and 'absolutism,' and the opposite of relativism: Generally I will use the word 'universalism' to refer to the position that contradicts relativism rather than the word 'absolutism.' Frequently, however, the word 'absolutism' is used to connote the opposite of relativism and on occasion I will use that term. 'Universalism' is often preferable for several reasons. 'Absolutism' has taken on negative connotations that may interfere with understanding the nature of the debate.   In particular, 'absolutism' has come to mean without qualification, ambiguity, or lack of clarity. As a matter of fact two universalists may believe that love is an absolute or culturally universal value and that it by implication forbids murder. This means that neither is a cultural relativist. They may disagree, however, regarding many issues. Is abortion murder? Is war always murder and therefore wrong? Is capital punishment murder by the state? Was Jones' killing of Smith a justifiable homicide or was it murder? Did gladiators in the very different culture of ancient Rome have a right to kill their opponents since their only alternative was to die themselves? Would a culture that made provision for active euthanasia for terminally ill citizens be morally superior or inferior to our own? Two universalists might disagree or simply be uncertain regarding one or more of these questions. This disagreement, however, would not mean that either one was a cultural relativist. Thus, universalism frequently is accompanied by ambiguity and lack of clarity.

Cultural relativists believe that all values are particular to some culture. Cultural universalists believe that there is at least one value that ought to be applied universally to all cultures. Some values, or at least one value, is absolute and not simply relative to time, place and circumstance.

The distinction between cultural relativism and individual relativism: Individual relativism is the position that all values are relative to the individual. Critics of cultural relativism often maintain that cultural relativism breaks down into individual relativism and individual relativism leads to chaos and the destruction of all social order. Whether or not one believes that these claims are justified, it should be recognized that individual relativism is not the position of the cultural relativist. Cultural relativists are not denying either the existence or desirability of communal norms. They are simply denying the existence (and usually the desirability of affirming the existence) of norms that transcend cultural communities.

Cultural relativism, individual relativism, and individualism: Although individual relativism seems necessarily associated with some form of individualism, cultural relativism is not necessarily associated with either individualism or its opposite of collectivism. Some cultures, like contemporary Western culture have a strong emphasis on the value of individualism or autonomy. Others do not. Cultural relativism seems only to preclude the position that individualism is as a value that transcends all cultures. In other words, individualism cannot be a universal value. Furthermore, there are a number of forms of individualism, that are not associated with individual relativism. For example, someone may maintain that the individual is greater in value than the community and that this is a universal value that should be observed by all cultures. This is the position associated with the Enlightenment with its faith in reason and autonomy. The Enlightenment is thus a form of individualism associated with universalism.

Fundamentalism, secular humanism, and cultural relativism: Fundamentalists are universalists. They affirm what they regard as truths that are 'fundamental' to all cultures and should be observed by them. Thus, fundamentalists regard their position as antithetical to cultural relativism.

People who regard themselves as secular humanists *may* in addition regard themselves as cultural relativists but this is not necessarily the case. Frequently, fundamentalists and others accuse the secular humanist of being a cultural relativist. Secular humanists, however, need not be relativists and, as a matter of fact, relativism of any type seems inconsistent with the secular humanist position. Secular humanists claim as the base for their ethical theory that human nature is the highest value in the universe. They are thus in a position to affirm that cultures that support this value to a higher degree than others are morally superior to the extent this is so. Secular humanists disagree with fundamentalism and with all other theistic perspectives because they regard them as denigrating human nature. This makes theism, in their eyes, a morally inferior position and cultures that are dominated by one sort or another of theism are regarded as morally inferior to the ideal professed by the secular humanist.

Thus, it seems that both fundamentalists and secular humanists are universalists who believe in some culturally transcendent moral values. They simply disagree frequently on what those values are and on the ontological and epistemological foundation of those values.

Cultural Conflict and Cultural Relativism

Does cultural relativism lead to cultural conflict? Like so many issues, the answer to this question depends upon to whom you talk. Proponents of universal moral values frequently argue that cultural relativism provides no basis for social order and that its widespread adoption leads to the breakdown of social order, social chaos, and destructive conflict. Proponents of cultural relativism argue that cultural relativism leads to a more tolerant perspective that tends to reduce social conflict. They argue that, on the contrary, it is the universalist or moral absolutist that by encouraging totalitarianism and intolerance tends to produce destructive conflict.

This looks like it should be a straight forward empirical or factual question capable of being resolved by objective historical and sociological research. Unfortunately, things are probably not this uncomplicated. Most of us, regardless of our particular philosophical perspective, would affirm that some cultural conflict is good and leads to good consequences. We would probably also be willing to affirm that generally there are both good and bad consequences from most cultural conflict. For instance, the American Civil War produced many consequences that most of us would regard as good but at a terrible price in terms of lives lost and maimed, and property destroyed. Any judgment regarding whether or not the war was on balance a good thing would appear to be not simply a judgment about the facts. It includes judgments of value that make assumptions about the ultimate meaning of human existence.

Does cultural conflict lead to cultural relativism? The answer to this question is sometimes, but not necessarily. Cultural conflict often leads to the questioning of values that would otherwise be held uncritically since there is little encouragement from a totally conflict free culture to critically examine them. The questioning of basic values *can* lead to cultural relativism. But obviously not everyone who has ever questioned their most basic values has come to regard them as not universal. Sometimes questioning of values leads to a stronger reaffirmation of the original values than was true in the beginning. Sometimes individuals change their values but adopt a new set of values that they regard as universal.

These remarks are intended to indicate that the relationship of cultural conflict and cultural relativism is complex. We will deal with these questions in subsequent sections. The goal will be to clarify the issues without pretending to completely resolve them.

Basic Claims of Cultural Relativism: Point-Counter Point

What sorts of claims does the cultural relativist make? I will examine below some of the most basic claims made by cultural relativists. All cultural relativists do not necessarily make all of the claims listed below nor am I maintaining that to be a consistent cultural relativist one must necessarily make all of these claims. The claims with which we will deal are, however, sufficiently representative to enable us to get an adequate picture of the nature, strengths and weaknesses of cultural relativism as an ethical position.

Cultural relativists argue that there are no values which are common to all cultures. We will begin by examining the first assertion made by cultural relativists, namely, that there are no values common to all cultures. On the face of it, this seems to be an empirical thesis about the nature of social reality. Different cultures have different values. This seems so obviously true that it is difficult to see why anyone would want to dispute it. In order to test empirical theses, however, it is necessary to define with some care what it is one is testing. Is the cultural relativist simply saying that cultures differ in their application of values at the case level. This is certainly true but as we have observed even our fundamentalist would agree to a certain amount of cultural relativity in the *application* of principles and rules.

Philosophers who affirm cultural relativism are quite well aware that they are not merely affirming cultural relativity in the application of values. They are also aware that the empirical fact that values are applied in different ways at the case level does not constitute evidence for the thesis that values are relative at the level of rules or principles. This awareness is not always so prevalent in dormitory bull sessions, however, where one often hears examples of disagreement at the level of specific application offered as proof that there are no absolutes.

Let us take for example the rule "honor thy father and mother." In primitive Eskimo culture the aged, when they reached the stage when they could no longer contribute to the economic well being of the tribe, were taken out to the edge of an ice flow and encouraged to walk off into the freezing water to their deaths. Is this an example of a culture which does not affirm the rule "honor thy father and mother?" Richard Brandt, a philosopher who is himself a cultural relativist, introduces this example in his writing and admits that it may not be evidence for cultural relativism.[1] In a society living on the very margin of existence, where the continued existence of the grandparents might threaten the very lives of their grand children the best way to honor one's parents may be to provide them with a "death with dignity." Indeed, there may be more "dignity and honor" in such a death then the continued existence in sub-standard nursing homes which is so common in our own society.

This one example does not, of course, prove that rules are not relative to cultures. I merely cite it to illustrate the point that the empirical thesis that there are no common rules is not *obviously* true and the proof for such a thesis needs to be worked out with some care. But even if there are no *rules* which are common to all cultures this would not constitute conclusive evidence against ethical universalism. There might be no rules which are common to all cultures but still be commonalty at the level of *principles*. Principles such as love or justice might be common to all cultures while the way in which these principles are embodied in rules and concrete cases are relative to the particular culture.

It is on the basis of arguments such as the above that critics of cultural relativism argue that the thesis that there are no values common to all cultures is not only not an obvious fact proven by the study of anthropology but that it is in fact false.

Cultural relativists argue from what they regard as the fact that there are no values that all cultures have in common to the ethical assertion that there are no values that all cultures ought to have in common. We have argued above that this supposed 'fact' of lack of common values is not as obviously true as the cultural relativist might suppose. Suppose, however, that we grant the cultural relativist the point that there are no values that all cultures *do* hold in common. Does it follow from this assertion that there are no values that all cultures *ought* to hold?

The debate about the evidence for a lack of cross-cultural consensus is illustrated by the arguments given below. The proponents off cultural universalism might argue the following.

Let us suppose that the empirical thesis that there are no rules or principles which are common to all cultures is true. This still doesn't prove that there are no rules or principles which ought to be common to all cultures. If all cultures agreed that slavery was morally acceptable it would not follow from that fact that we should accept slavery as morally acceptable. There is no logical contradiction in asserting that all cultures are wrong. But if there is no logical contradiction in asserting that all cultures are wrong on some issue, there would seem to be no logical contradiction in asserting that some cultures, for instance those which have asserted or do assert that slavery is morally right, are wrong. Thus, if some or even all cultures hold that slavery is justified, we may still reasonably affirm the universal principle that slavery is wrong.

The defender of cultural relativism might respond to this argument in the following manner.

It is true that there is no logically necessary relationship between the empirical thesis that there are no values which are common to all cultures and the normative thesis that there are no values that ought to be common to all cultures. Nevertheless, this lack of common agreement constitutes evidence for cultural relativism.. This is because it is probable that if there were some values that all cultures ought to agree upon that over time they would have reached agreement. This failure to agree, therefore, makes the cultural relativist thesis more probable and at the very least the burden of proof is on the ethical universalist to show why the existence of universal norms has not led to universal agreement.

The proponent of ethical universalism might respond to argument of the cultural relativist along the following lines.

Just because cultures do not agree on universal values, it is not necessarily probable that there are no universal values. Alternative explanations (both fundamentalist and humanist) for this lack of agreement are possible. There are any number of explanations to show why universal norms have not lead to universal agreement among cultures.

For example, the fundamentalist and other Christians (who agree with the empirical thesis that there are no values which all cultures hold in common) might argue that this lack of agreement is due to man's fallen nature and the pervasiveness of sin in the world. Humanity in the depth of its being has a tendency to reject God and the moral law not only in practice but to reject the very recognition of God and the law of God. This rejection over time has pervasive effects on the cultures in which it occurs and prevents universal norms from even being recognized.

A secular humanist who believes in universal moral norms might have a different explanation.

Certain values, the humanist might argue, are both good and rational but for most of history, humanity has been in the grasp of ignorance and superstition (the very kind of ignorance and superstition represented by the fundamentalist). The pervasive effect of this anti-rational ignorance and superstition has prevented common agreement among cultures on the nature of the good and rational. In short, there are some values upon which all cultures ought to agree but ignorance and superstition have prevented them from being recognized.

I will not take the time here to analyze either of these possible explanations further. I merely want to point out that even if the empirical thesis about ultimate disagreement among cultures is true, there are other explanations of this supposed fact than those offered by the cultural relativist.

Cultural relativists claim that all values are creations of a specific culture. They are either created by the culture in which they occur or they were adopted from another culture which originally created them. If all values are derived some culture then they cannot be derived from other sources.   Thus, revelation from the Judeo-Christian God is excluded as a source of values.   Thus, not only fundamentalists but most persons who would   consider themselves to be either Jews or Christians would be wrong about the source of values.   But it is not the Judeo-Christian God alone who is excluded.   Islamic, Hindu, and Buddhist cosmologies with their views of a culturally transcendent ground for values are also excluded.   Philosophical perspectives that affirm a culturally transcendent universal law of reason are also excluded.   This exclusion would seem to embrace Plato, Aristotle, the Stoics, the Epicureans, Aquinas, Kant, the framers of the Declaration of Independence and the Constitution, and many who would consider themselves to be secular humanists.   All of those referred to above make claim to some culturally transcendent source of values.   They disagree with each other.   They are often quite willing to admit that their values have been mediated by a culture, are imperfectly understood, have even been distorted by the culture in which they have been nurtured.   They nonetheless affirm that their values have a basis that transcends their own and all other cultures.

Even the early Sartre who is an atheistic existentialist would seem to hold a position excluded by the cultural relativist.   The early Sartre may be viewed either as a radical individual relativist or as affirming that radical individual freedom is the one universal value.[2]

So called proponents of 'Situation Ethics,' at least of one popular variety, are also excluded by the affirmation that all values are derived from some culture.   In the sixties a very popular book with the title *Situation Ethics* appeared.   It was written by a professor of social ethics at Harvard University Divinity School by the name of Joseph Fletcher.   Fletcher affirmed that all the ethical rules found in the *Bible*, including the Ten Commandments, could not be taken as morally binding but were merely rules of thumb.   They could be ignored or over-ridden in the interests of the higher *New Testament* value of agape love.   Fletcher was viewed at the time as radical and a relativist, especially among Christian ethicists.   Radical and relativist he may have been but he was not a cultural relativist in the sense we are discussing here.   In the first place, Fletcher affirmed that right and wrong behavior are relative to the situation both across and within cultures, not that right and wrong behavior is relative to the culture.   Secondly, and more importantly, he affirmed the value of one culturally transcendent norm based on the revelation of agape love in Christ. He was thus a relativist with respect to rules but not a relativist with respect values. The principle of agape love, for Fletcher, is culturally transcendent.

Affirming that all values are not derived ultimately from some culture does not mean that one must deny the importance of culture in the mediation of values. Fundamentalists, whatever others may think of them, consider themselves to represent the mainstream of orthodox Christianity. As such they have a high regard for history. Revelation for them comes through historical revelation. It is important for them to affirm that Jesus really was born, lived, died, and was resurrected in a particular time, place, and culture. They are also concerned to maintain the historical importance of the entire Biblical record. Thus, truth is mediated through a particular cultural context. Fundamentalists typically do not have as much concern for the history of the church since the end of Biblical times as do, for instance, Roman Catholics and other Protestants. Catholics affirm that it is also through the history of "The Church" that God's culturally transcendent truth is mediated. The point I make here with these illustrations is that orthodox Christianity broadly defined has always maintained that culturally transcendent truth, although not *derived from* culture is *necessarily mediated through* particular historical cultures. Thus, they not only admit that there is an important relationship between values and culture, they insist upon it.

Some liberal Protestants, secular humanists and a number of the philosophers and positions named above have been less concerned with the relationship of truth and history. They, however, are not constrained by their positions to deny that knowledge and values are *transmitted* through cultures. The admission that values are transmitted through cultures, however, does not constitute an admission that all values can only be the *creation* of cultures.

The examples given above are offered as a criticism of position of the cultural relativist. They demonstrate that it is a position that contradicts not only fundamentalism but virtually all of the worlds great religions and the positions held by most secular philosophers. The fact that cultural relativism is such an extreme minority position does not disprove cultural relativism but it does suggest that the *burden of proof* rests on the cultural relativist rather than the other way around.

What would it take for the cultural relativist to satisfy this burden of proof concerning the derivation of values? In asserting that all values are derived from some culture, the cultural relativist seems to be asserting a cultural determinism, at least with respect to values. That is to say that culture determines everything. What would it take to prove cultural determinism? At the very least, a sociological theory of enormous predictive power. What is being claimed seems to be something like the following: For any given value V, it is possible to state the necessary and sufficient cultural conditions Cc that explain the existence of that value V. In the absence of such a powerful sociological theory *we must at least leave open the possibility* that biological factors, the universal law of reason, man's free creative choice and even revelation from God may be a partial determinant of our values. All of this does not disprove cultural relativism. It does, I think, indicate that at this point in the development of the social sciences the firm believer in cultural relativism must "walk by faith and not by sight".

Cultural relativists frequently argue that since all values are derived from the culture and have no culturally transcendent ground, there are no morally binding obligations on the individual. This position is not universally held by cultural relativists and as we shall see shortly is incompatible with an assertion that we will consider below. Furthermore, the cultural relativist might object that what is really being asserted is that *since all values are derived from the culture and have no culturally transcendent ground that there are no morally binding obligations on the individual which are morally binding in an absolute or universal sense.* This second way of phrasing the issue seems to follow clearly from the cultural relativist position. If there are no universal moral standards, it would seem to follow that there are neither universal moral obligations or universal moral rights. When confronted with a belief in a moral obligation or a moral right--to oppose abortion or to affirm the right of every women to have control over her own body--to defend one's country or to affirm pacifism--to be faithful to one's spouse or to assert one's right to live a life that maximizes pleasure--the cultural relativist would seem to be in the position of being able to say that the belief in all of these values is culturally derived and that none of these supposed rights and obligations are absolutely binding.

But on what grounds then shall our cultural relativist make a decision on critical questions such as these? The cultural relativist cannot affirm with the atheistic existentialist Sartre that it doesn't matter what choice is made as long as the individual self-consciously embraces the responsibility of his or her own absolute freedom in the world. For after all, if the cultural relativist is right, Sartre's belief in the absolute freedom of the individual and the moral obligation to accept that freedom is relative to the culture in which Sartre originated. It cannot be asserted that one therefore has a right to do what one pleases, if by that is meant that one has an universal culturally transcendent moral right to do what one pleases. For if the cultural relativist is right, then the belief that one has a moral right to do what one pleases is itself culturally derived. Thus, it would seem that if cultural relativism is true, that it can neither establish that the individual has an absolute or universal obligation to act in a certain way or refrain from acting in a certain way nor that the individual has a universal right to act in a certain way or to refrain from acting in a certain way.

Cultural relativists are accused of maintaining that since all values are derived from the culture and have no culturally transcendent ground, the individual is obligated to obey the norms of the culture in which he or she resides. This claim has perhaps been more often made about cultural relativists than by them. If true as it stands, it would seem to bind the cultural relativist to a conservative stance with respect to cultural critique and change. Cultural relativists would doubtless like to reject the conservative implications of their position as defined by this assertion. It seems to me that strictly speaking, we cannot say that the cultural relativist is obligated to obey the norms of the culture in which he or she resides. This would only be true if there were some *absolute* or universal ethical truth such as the following: *Since there are no absolute values which transcend culture, one must always treat as absolute the values and norms of the culture in which one resides.* This, of course, would be contradictory, since the cultural relativist would be asserting that there are no absolutes and that there is at least one absolute or universal. This absolute would be the universal obligation to treat the culturally relative values of one's culture as if they were universal. This would be contradictory and there seems to be no reason why the cultural relativist would or should affirm it.

Why then has the cultural relativist been accused of affirming this contradictory position. This is doubtless because critics of cultural relativism have assumed that the practical (though not logical) implications of cultural relativism lead to social conservatism and the treating of one's own culture *as if* it embodied absolute ethical truth. If there are no universal values which transcend culture, then there would seem to be no basis for criticizing the values and norms of a given culture. Thus, if the cultural relativist resides in a culture that condones slavery, racism, the subjugation of women, pedophilia or anything else, the relativist may not be obligated to accept these beliefs and practices but also has no consistent ethical basis for rejecting them. This may lead *by default* to treating the values and norms of the culture *as if* they are absolute.

The practical implications of the cultural relativist position for cultural conflict are somewhat ambiguous. Clearly the cultural relativist is not in a position to address conflict between cultures. If one accepts the relativist position, it cannot consistently be affirmed that one culture is superior to another.

What about conflicts within a culture? With regard to conflicts within a culture, the cultural relativist can enter into the debate about whether a particular case application is consistent with the rules or principles that the culture has adopted. The cultural relativist can also enter into the debate about whether rules of a culture are consistent with principles of that culture. This is because at this level the debate is not about the validity of those values but simply about the degree to which a culture is consistent in the application of its own values.

But what about those situations where the rules or principles within a culture conflict or those situations where the consensus within a culture is breaking down? The cultural relativist can attack the position of social conservatives who defend their conservatism on the basis of universal transcendent norms. In this case, the relativist functions as a radical or liberal. The relativist attack, however, cannot consistently be based on the affirmation of universal values counter to the prevailing ones in the culture. It can merely be a negative attack on the supposed universal grounds of those prevailing values whatever they are. This places certain limits on radicalism. The cultural relativist cannot consistently be either a Marxist or a prophet of the Lord.

In those case where basic principles of the culture are in conflict or cultural consensus is breaking down the consistent cultural relativist would seem to have little to offer. The relativist can be neither a conservative or a liberal but rather must function as a participant observer. Cultural relativists can, of course, make a plea for tolerance--provided they reside in a culture in which tolerance is an important value. This last comment leads us to a consideration of the next affirmation frequently made by cultural relativists.

Cultural relativists have maintained that ethical universalism tends to reinforce a predisposition to tyranny, totalitarianism and intolerance. Ethical relativism tends to reinforce a predisposition to democracy, pluralism, and tolerance. Therefore ethical absolutism has socially and morally evil consequences while ethical relativism has socially and morally good consequences. This affirmation could be treated as a strictly empirical thesis. If it is an empirical thesis, we would test it by turning the problem over to a team of sociologists, social historians (with some sophistication regarding the history of ideas) and asking them to determine whether or not it is an historical fact that relativists have tended to promote democracy, pluralism and tolerance and an historical fact that universalists have tended to promote its opposite.

In all probability, however, the cultural relativist is not simply committed to some empirical thesis concerning the consequences of universalism and relativism but also thinks that there is something in the *logic of the universalist position* which leads a *consistent* universalist to promote tyranny, totalitarianism and intolerance while there is something in the *logic of the relativist position* which leads a *consistent* relativist to promote, democracy pluralism and tolerance.

We will try to deal here with both the empirical and the logical thesis. In the first place, with respect to the empirical thesis, it seems clear that both throughout human history and on the contemporary scene it is an historical fact that there are numerous examples of moral universalists who have used their belief in moral absolutes to promote tyranny, totalitarianism, intolerance and a host of other evils. It is also an historical fact, however, that there are also numerous counter examples: Socrates, Jesus, Ghandi and Martin Luther King Jr., to name a few.

Furthermore, many of the proponents of tolerance argued that the logic of their beliefs in universals (and the beliefs that their opponents held to be universal) required tolerance. Martin Luther King Jr., for example challenged the racist values of his culture in terms of some other values he found in his culture, equality, justice, etc., which he and his contemporaries (even many of his racist contemporaries) considered to be universal.

But before we go much further we need to define what we mean by 'tolerance.' Cultural relativists have encouraged Westerners, including social scientists, business men and women, politicians and Christian missionaries to be critical of the naive assumption that Western culture is superior in every way to non-Western cultures (sometimes referred to as 'primitive', sometimes as 'economically undeveloped' nations and cultures). This has doubtless helped Westerners to be somewhat more tolerant of non-Western cultures. For this contribution we should be grateful to cultural relativist however much we may disagree with their ethical theory and final conclusions. But some of those cultures are tyrannical, totalitarian, racist, sexist and (by our Western cultural standards) intolerant. Tolerating intolerance either in other nations and cultures over which we may have some influence (like South Africa) or among sub-cultures in our own country may not be a good thing. Clearly cultural relativists do not want us to tolerate every thing. Nor do they wish to defend their theory by insisting that it encourages the tolerance of everything. If tolerance is a virtue of cultural relativism then it must be because it encourages us to tolerate those things that *ought to be tolerated* and does not encourage us to tolerate those things that *ought not to be tolerated.* But it seems clear that cultural relativists have no criteria for distinguishing between these two. They can only tell us what our culture or some other culture thinks ought to be tolerated and ought not to be tolerated, not whether our culture or some other culture is right or good in so doing. Ethical universalists, on the other hand, can at least ask whether abortion, war, ordination of women, smoking in public places or nude bathing beaches ought or ought not to be allowed in our culture. They may come up with stupid, destructive, contradictory and ambiguous answers to these questions (as many have) but they can at least consistently ask the questions. Cultural relativists cannot consistently ask these questions. Are democracy and pluralism better than tyranny and totalitarianism? Our culture asserts that they are morally better. Is our culture right in so asserting? Universalists can debate the issue. Cultural relativists, if they are consistent, must remain silent before such questions.

Many cultural relativists are relativists with respect to ethics but are absolutists or universalists with respect to scientific method. Other cultural relativists deny not only that there are universal ethical principles but also hold that the principles of scientific method affirmed by the West are not absolute but only an expression Western culture.

Cultural relativists obviously have maintained that ethical values are relative to the culture and there are no culturally transcendent universals with respect to personal ethics, aesthetics, and social justice. What about the sciences? Are there any culturally transcendent universals with respect to either factual truths or methodological criteria? If there are culturally transcendent universals, are they confined to the natural sciences or do they extend to the social sciences? If there are culturally transcendent universals and they extend to the social sciences, do some of the criteria that apply to the social sciences also apply to what we call humanistic studies like language, literature, art and music, and history? What about curricula and professional enterprises that do not fall clearly in either the humanities or the sciences like communication, business, law, and education?

To understand the implications of these questions it is necessary to consider the position that has been maintained for most of this century that has been termed the 'fact/value' distinction. On this view, science deals with facts and is capable of giving us truth. This so called truth may be revised in the light of subsequent discoveries but nonetheless it is assumed that in scientific method we have a reliable method of grasping reality that is superior to all non-scientific methods of grasping reality. Science, on their view, deals with physical reality or, in some cases, social facts. It does not deal with the truth or falsehood of values. Thus, with respect to 'facts' we can have objective scientific truth. With respect to 'values' we can have only subjective non-scientific opinion. This form of cultural relativism can be viewed as only a partial relativism. Science is not relative. Its criteria are universal. It is only values that are relative to the culture. There are several problems with this view that we will explore below.

The first problem with maintaining the fact/value distinction is that we are faced with the question of whether a culture that espouses scientific values is superior to a culture that makes assumptions that exclude these values. The people in the forefront of espousing cultural relativism tended to be not exclusively or even primarily philosophers but social scientists, particularly anthropologists. The presumption is that anthropology is a scientific discipline and its findings (methodological assumptions?) about social reality are made on the basis of science. We are asked to believe that the findings of anthropology are true (and therefore we ought to accept them) and that acceptance of the truths of anthropological studies leads to increased tolerance (and therefore there are good moral consequences from the acceptance of these truths). This may not be clearly articulated or consistently held by all anthropologists who are cultural relativists but it is difficult to hold that we do not have a moral obligation to seek and believe the truth when this is attainable. It is also difficult to maintain that a culture that supports institutions that enable its members to discover truth is not superior to one that does not support these institutions or does so to a lesser degree.

There is a second problem. Most cultures are founded on the assumption that their most fundamental values are true or at least more nearly true than alternative cultures. So basic is the assumption of moral universalism for most cultures that it is hard to imagine how a culture might adopt both scientific rationalism and cultural relativism without abandoning the very basis of the culture which defines their existence. I do not mean to imply that all experts in the *academic discipline* of cultural anthropology assume the *philosophical position* of cultural relativism. This is not the case. I am merely asserting that those cultural anthropologists that assume cultural relativism or regard the findings of their discipline as proof for cultural relativism are holding a position that if adopted by members of the cultures that they are studying would in most cases destroy the very cultural entities that are the object of their study.

A third major problem for the historical position of cultural relativism that purports to found its position on scientific fact is that recent philosophical discussions have tended to undermine the so called 'fact/value' distinction.[3] This distinction has been problematic in the social sciences for a long time. For example, critics of the fact/value distinction maintain that different social science theories define what counts as 'fact' differently. The concepts of ego, super-ego, and id appear in Freudian theory but do not appear in various versions of behaviorism. This vocabulary is simply absent. Existential social science theories define the problem of interpreting human behavior in large part in terms of human choice. Behavioral theories such as B.F. Skinner's assume within the very framework of the theory that genuine human choice is impossible. Thus, prescientific fundamental assumptions about the nature of human beings and social reality are built into the theories that are supposed to give objective scientific information about social reality. "Values" are not and cannot be divorced from 'facts.'

This view of the nature of the scientific enterprise is not confined to the social sciences. Thomas Kuhn in his *The Structure of Scientific Revolutions* argues that natural science theories are theoretical frameworks that define what counts as a fact prior to any empirical testing of reality. Thus all scientific theorizing presupposes certain assumptions. 'Facts' are entities that appear within frameworks. This is true not only for the social sciences but for the natural sciences as well.

The point is not that these views of the nature of science disprove relativism. They in fact, to a significant degree, assume relativism. But this view of science does undermine the argument for cultural relativism that asserts that an *objective and universal* scientific analysis of the facts can prove the *subjective cultural relativity* of values.

One recent and prominent movement in philosophy, literary theory, and Biblical studies is known as *deconstructionism*. Deconstructionism is a relativistic perspective but it is not cultural relativism. Deconstructionists affirm that a particular text whether it be the Pauline writings, the Constitution of the United States or one of Shakespeare's plays cannot have a single meaning. The meaning of the text is always founded on the interplay of the reader, the interpreter, and the text. We never get at what St. Paul really meant, or Shakespeare, or the writers of the Constitution. We cannot think like people in their times thought. We cannot even think like other persons in our own times. We interact with the text and meaning emerges in the very process of our interaction. Thus, on this view, meaning does not just very from culture to culture, but from sub-culture to sub-culture, and from person to person. Interpretative meanings that have been taught and handed down from previous generations are constructs. They are not meanings that are found but meanings that are made up. To understand the text we must deconstruct the constructs. This process of deconstruction does not, however, enable us to arrive at the true meaning that the author intended. There is no such meaning and if there were we could never find it. Thus, if deconstrutionism is adopted, it becomes impossible to achieve a coherent grasp of the meaning and values of any particular culture.

This is not the place to engage in a full blown discussion of deconstructionism. There are obviously problems with this position.

One problem is that the presuppositions of the deconstructionist raise the question of how it would be possible for anyone to understand what the deconstructionist means. Furthermore, if we or anyone else could understand what is meant, what would it mean to say that what deconstructionism means is true? What this discussion does point out is that the epistemology of a radical individual relativism like deconstructionism poses almost as many problems for cultural relativism as it does for those perspectives that affirm culturally transcendent universals. It is of course not compatible with fundamentalism which assumes that the fundamentals of the faith were delivered in Biblical times and can be understood today. Neither is it compatible with any variety of secular humanism that assumes we can know and hold sacred some sort of clear view of human nature.

Cultural relativists assume that it is possible for an individual to consistently adopt cultural relativism as a coherent ethical theory and as a coherent guide to practical living. I have said, I think, enough in the previous sections to indicate my reservations regarding cultural relativism as a coherent ethical theory. There are certainly formidable difficulties in adopting it. Sufficiently formidable difficulties, I think, such that the ethical absolutist or universalist need not cut and run at the first sneer from his relativist adversary.

What about adopting relativism as a coherent guide for life? I think here is where ethical relativism of any variety is least satisfactory. Doubtless the realization that "all proper ladies young and old must wear a girdle in public" is not an eternal absolute has had a tremendously liberating effect on at least one half of the population of the Western world. One wonders, however, if cultural relativism could have done it alone without the invention of control top panty hose. But what if I am considering whether I should have an abortion, go to war, be faithful to my spouse or choose between becoming a yuppie or giving my life in service to the poor. Whether it is possible to speak coherently of a single overarching Western culture is problematic from a social scientific point of view. It is certainly true that we have many subcultures, some that favor abortion, others that do not. Some subcultures believe in war, others are pacifist. Some subcultures preach fidelity in marriage, others proclaim free love (at least before the aids epidemic). Some subcultures reinforce yuppie values and others encourage love and sacrifice on behalf of one's fellow human beings. Which of these should the person seeking to decide on the meaning of life choose? Cultural relativism seems to be of little help.

Of course, despite the practical difficulties associated with the position, cultural relativism may be true and there just may not be any answers. The pragmatic consequences of adopting relativism, however, are certainly sufficiently negative that we should be disinclined to embrace it while there are so many intellectual difficulties in doing so. If cultural relativism does not cause cultural   conflict it seems to be little help in resolving it.

Some Positive Insights from Cultural Relativism

If cultural relativism has so many difficulties, why is it such an attractive perspective to so many? There are a number of answers to this question.   Doubtless one reason is that many people do not consistently think through the implications of any position. Many of us make convenient shifts from relativism to absolutism depending on the issue under consideration.   When my goal is to escape criticism for some behavior I am engaging in or to justify my liberty to engage in some practice which others condemn, I may espouse relativism. If on the other hand, I wish to condemn some behavior in which others may be engaged, then absolutism may be the more attractive theory. But there is more to the attractiveness of cultural relativism than the conscious and unconscious hypocrisy to which we are all so prone.

There are, as we shall see, genuine intellectual difficulties with the variety of universalist theories that are available.   Furthermore, it is certainly true that values are relative to the culture and to even specific situations within a culture *in their application.*   Fundamentalists and universalists of other types frequently are not sufficiently sensitive to this fact and therefore take specific applications at the case level (which are by definition relative to the particular case under consideration) and elevate those specific applications to universal rules or even more universal principles.   They then proceed to apply instructions appropriate to specific situations in ways which are totally inappropriate to a different cultural context.   Frequently, in the overemphasis on the details of their ethical system, adequate consideration of the basic rules, general principles and even basis of the ethical system is lost.   This appears to be what lay behind much of Jesus' criticism of the Pharisees when he summarized the whole law, including the ten commandments, in terms of loving God and loving one's fellow man with all one's being. Their interpretation of the law in the specific cultural context in which they lived was flawed in many respects but it was also inadequate because it would not suit the new age which was coming. Jesus was no relativist but he was very conscious of the fact that eternal values need to be applied in different ways in different historical contexts. Insofar as cultural relativism serves to remind absolutists, of all varieties, of this fact then it makes a positive contribution to ethical discourse.

There is another insight that is not unique to cultural relativism but is reinforced by our consideration of the arguments of the cultural relativist. It seems to be an empirical fact that values at various levels of generality are relative to subcultures in our society. One implication of this is that one should choose the subculture or cultures to which one becomes attached very carefully. Parents, of course, have known this long before they had cultural relativists, sociologists or anthropologists to tell them so. Thus, they attempt, insofar as is possible, to choose with care the friends, churches, clubs, schools and activities of their small children and respond with apprehension and even anxiety to the fact that they are not able to exercise as much control over their older children.

It takes little sophistication to realize that the subculture of the military officer is not compatible with the religious subculture of the Quaker. The stock market has its own subculture with its own values which would not fit well with the culture and values of an Amish community.

The young lady raised in the West with Western values and assumptions regarding the role of women in society who meets and becomes romantically attracted to a university student from a Near Eastern country should proceed with care. So much is obvious. But what if I am a young person trying to make a career decision not between working with the CIA. and the American Civil Liberties Union but between company X and company Y? It is fashionable these days in the literature on business management to speak of the "culture of a company". I think that this is appropriate. Different companies do have different cultures and different values, and living within a culture not only can but probably will shape the selfhood of those who participate in that culture. Therefore, young people (and those in mid-career as well) should look not only at the salary and the fringe benefits and the type of work associated with a company but also at its values. One should ask: "How do I fit with this career or company at twenty two or twenty five"? One should also ask: "If I fit well with this career or company at fifty what kind of person will I have to be and do I want to be that kind of person"? Of course people change careers, companies, geographical location, clubs, friends, churches, religious persuasions, and husbands and wives. But not always without trauma and profound changes in the cultural values to which they and their immediate families are exposed. It is not an easy thing to predict change with respect to either values or economics. This is equally true for the believer of absolute values and the relativist. All one can say is that even though the cultural relativist may be ultimately wrong that he does have a point. Values on the empirical level do vary relative to cultures and subcultures. This should serve to remind the absolutists that when they choose a subculture, they should be clear about those values they hold as absolute, examine the values of alternative possible subcultures with care, and choose accordingly.

Summary: Cultural Relativism, Secular Humanism, Fundamentalism, and Cultural Conflict

In summary, we may observe that although all fundamentalists are absolutists or universalists in some sense, that some secular humanists believe in absolute values as well. Humanism and cultural relativism are not synonyms, just as fundamentalism and Christianity are not synonyms. Furthermore, although fundamentalists hold certain ethical principles as absolute, they need to apply those supposed absolute principles *relative* to concrete situations. Though fundamentalists and humanists may disagree on the issue of the basis for ethical conduct, they may agree on the level of principles, rules, and applications. Rather than spending all of their time railing at one another, they might discover that they and the public in general would profit from a dialogue which assumed at least the possibility of agreement and common cause with respect to some issues. This is not a suggestion that either side should compromise or be insensitive to those areas where there is fundamental disagreement. It is simply a plea to not ignore those areas where there may be important agreement.

Furthermore, Christian fundamentalists, Christians who are not fundamentalists and humanists who hold to absolute moral principles need to appreciate both the weaknesses and strengths of cultural relativism. My own position with respect to cultural relativism should be clear from the preceding discussion. Nevertheless, cultural relativism has served to sensitize us to the fact that absolutists can be both rigid and intolerant, of those who disagree with them and of the very process of cultural change. After all, Jesus himself had to insist that his goal was not to undermine the law but to fulfill it. Socrates was put to death, in part, because he was identified with that group of relativists known as the Sophists. Jesus and Socrates both believed in absolute values. They were put to death by opponents who believed that they were undermining absolute values.

Finally, we need to remember the admonition given by J.S. Mill in his famous essay *On Liberty*[4]. An opinion that is never contested is likely to be held by its proponents with limited conviction, understanding and enthusiasm. From the point of view of the fundamentalist, as well as the secular humanist who holds to certain absolute values, it is far worse to have adherents to their viewpoint who have only weak conviction than to have honest critics. If your viewpoint is true, it will be strengthened rather than destroyed by honest and forceful challenge.

Notes

[1] Richard Brandt, "Ethical Relativism," pp. 76-7.

[2] See John Paul Sartre, *Being and Nothingness,* and "Existentialism," The essay "Existentialism" is a brief and widely anthologized summary of Sartre's philosophy. Although it indicates that Sartre is relativistic on the level of case application and of rules, his basic principle of freedom is clearly presented as an absolute by which he is willing to evaluate all other ethical systems and cultures.

[3] See Richard Rorty, *Philosophy and the Mirror of Nature.* Rorty's book offers a highly sophisticated defense of cultural relativism. The focus of his argument, however, is not to undermine the objectivity of moral values. This he appears to a large extent to take for granted. He develops a sustained argument against the fact/value distinction directed at showing that so called 'facts' do not *mirror* reality. They are merely interpretations of reality that are accepted as useful and hence true in given cultural contexts.

[4] J.S. Mill, *On Liberty,* pp. 989-90.

CHAPTER III

EMOTIVISM

The Primacy of Scientific Discourse

Emotivism is an ethical theory that in a curious way affirms the value of scientific discourse and the lack of value in ethical discourse. The fundamental reasoning is simple. Scientific discourse is the *only* type of cognitively meaningful discourse. Ethical discourse (along with religious and aesthetic discourse) is not scientific discourse. Therefore, ethical discourse is not cognitively meaningful. Scientific discourse is about what is factually true or false. Ethical discourse has to do with feelings. Ethical discourse, however, is not discourse *about* feelings. The science of psychology attempts to distinguish true and false statements about feelings. Ethical discourse is simply the *expression* of feelings. 'Expressions of feelings' are neither true or false. Scientific discourse excludes expression of feeling. Therefore, scientific discourse (which as we have said is according to the emotivist the only legitimate discourse) excludes ethical discourse. The rest of this chapter will constitute an explanation and evaluation of this simple straightforward premise.

The most basic assumption of the emotivist theory of ethics is that what we refer to as ethical propositions are not statements of fact that can be true or false but are expressions of emotion that, of course, cannot be shown to be true or false in any sense. For example: "Suzy has a red hat" is a statement that may be either true or false. "Wow!" expresses an emotion but does not tell us anything that we can either prove or disprove in any way. When most of us hear the words, "One ought not to engage in extra-marital sexual intercourse," we assume that we are hearing a statement that is either true or false. It is true if it is wrong to have extra-marital sex. It is false if it is morally okay to have extra-marital sex under some or all circumstances. The emotivist denies this. "One ought not to have extra-marital sexual intercourse" is more like "Wow!" than it is like the statement that "Suzy has a red hat." Nothing is being asserted, at least nothing that can be shown to be true or false. You cannot prove or disprove "Wow!" You cannot meaningfully argue about "Wow!" Likewise, you cannot prove or disprove or meaningfully argue about "One ought not to have extra-marital sexual intercourse." We all express emotions. They are, however, just not the sort of things that you prove or disprove. According to the emotivist there are other sorts of linguistic expressions that are merely expressions of emotion and not the sort of things concerning which meaningful argument is possible. "The sky is beautiful" or "God is love" are expressions of emotion but not statements strictly speaking.

The clearest expression of this position in English speaking countries, at least, was given by A.J. Ayer in his *Language, Truth and Logic.* Ayer at this point in his career was a representative of a philosophical movement known as logical positivism that took as its task the reformation of philosophy in a manner consistent with scientific method characteristic especially of the so called "hard" or natural sciences. To reform philosophy entailed adopting a particular view of the nature of language. Ayer observed that in scientific theories there seemed to be two kinds and only two kinds of linguistic utterances that are regarded as meaningful. These are statements that can be shown to be true or false by definition and statements that can be shown to be true or false by empirical investigation.

Statements that can be shown to be true or false by definition are referred to as analytic a priori statements. Examples of statements that can be shown to be true or false by definition are: "All circles are round," "All circles are square," "A unicorn is a one horned animal" and "A unicorn is a two horned animal." All of these statements are meaningful, even though "All circles are square" is not only obviously false, it is absurdly so. The statements about unicorns are also meaningful statements, one true and the other false, even though we believe that there is no such thing in the world as a unicorn..

These statements are referred to as analytic statements because their truth or falsehood is determined first of all by analysis of the content of the sentence. Empirical observation is not necessary. Secondly, the truth or falsehood is determined prior to examination of the subject matter to which we are referring. Hence, the term a priori. Analytic a priori statements give us absolutely certain knowledge but tell us not about the world but about how in the English language (assuming we are speaking English) we have decided to use terms. "A red hat is red" is another example of an analytic a priori statement. How shall we determine the truth or falsehood of this sentence? If we examine the subject 'red hat' we see that it already contains the predicate 'is red'. We do not need to examine ten thousand, ten or even one red hat to see if, in fact, it is red. We know with absolute certainty prior to and quite apart from any empirical examination of any red hats that all red hats are red. Even a color blind person knows that red hats are red. But what do we know about the world in itself. Nothing! All red hats are red is true, whether or not there are any red hats in the world, just as all unicorns are one horned animals is true, even though there are no unicorns.

"All red hats are red" is an obvious and trivial example of an analytic a priori statement. All analytic a priori statements and systems of analytic a priori statements are not so trivial. Many computer programs are examples of complex systems of analytic a priori statements. The inputs that we put into the program are usually purported statements of fact. The outputs, however, are (given certain inputs) *true by definition.* But what can computers tell us about the world? Nothing! They merely are able to show us various possible relationships of the inputs we have given them. Showing these relationships is frequently useful and even surprising but it is not strictly speaking new information about the world as it actually is constituted.

Statements that can be shown to be true or false by empirical investigation are referred to as synthetic a posteriori statements. They are synthetic because they *synthesize* or bring together information in the predicate and the subject that had not previously been related. They are called *a posteriori* because we can know that the subject and predicate are linked only after (post) empirical investigation. Let us take for example the statement, "Suzy has a red hat." We cannot tell whether or not this statement is true or false by analysis. There is nothing in the definition of "Suzyness" that either requires or precludes her owning a red hat. Furthermore, we can only have *probable* knowledge with regard to this statement. Suzy may tell us that she has a red hat but she may be lying. We may see Suzy with a red hat, but it may not be hers, or it may not be Suzy but her twin sister Mary, or we may be colorblind, etc., etc.

Thus, synthetic a posteriori statements give us knowledge about the world but it is only probable knowledge. Analytic a priori statements give us certain knowledge but it is not knowledge about the world but about the definition of terms and rules of syntax of the language in which we have chosen to communicate. Both sorts of statements, however, are testable. They can be shown to be true or false and are therefore meaningful. Statements that are neither analytic a priori nor synthetic a posteriori are not testable. They cannot be shown to be true or false. They are therefore meaningless.

What about the statement "You ought not to kill"? It is not a statement that is true by definition, hence it is not an analytic a priori statement. There is no empirical test that we can devise to prove the truth or falsehood of the statement. Hence, it is not a synthetic a posteriori statement. It is therefore meaningless as are all so called ethical statements.

The Relationship of Emotivism to Cultural Relativism

Are emotivists cultural relativists? Not necessarily! Does emotivism, if consistently held, have the same practical effects as cultural relativism? I think so!

Let us attempt to clarify this relationship. As we have observed earlier, the cultural relativist makes several different claims. Typically he makes a descriptive or empirical claim. He claims that all values are, in fact, derived from the culture. Since this is an empirical claim (a synthetic a posteriori statement) it would be regarded by the emotivist as a meaningful statement that could be tested scientifically.

Whether or not this claim, in addition to being meaningful, is also true is a problem that the philosopher who is an emotivist would leave to the social scientist. It is doubtless the case that many emotivists believe that this claim is true but the belief in the truth of the statement does not follow logically from the emotivist's position. For example, it is also possible to make the claim that all values or some values are genetically derived. This also would be a synthetic a posteriori statement. The emotivist could believe this statement to be true. In this case, he would be denying the descriptive claim of the cultural relativist without contradicting his own emotivism.

But cultural relativists also make other claims. The cultural relativist is generally concerned to assert that the claim of the absolutist, namely that "There are some absolute values" is false. On some interpretations of the cultural relativist position, the relativist is claiming that "We ought to obey the values of the culture in which we reside." The emotivist would regard both of these so called claims as meaningless. The cultural relativist says that the absolutist or universalist is wrong. The emotivist says that the absolutist or universalist is neither right nor wrong. Rather, the universalist is talking nonsense. Furthermore, when the relativist asserts that the absolutist or universalist is wrong, the relativist is also talking nonsense. Furthermore, if the cultural relativist asserts that we *ought* to obey the values of the culture in which we reside, then the cultural relativist is talking nonsense once again.

What about the practical consequences of emotivism? It seems clear to me that the impact of emotivism on everyday life is relativistic. The emotivist, like the relativist, has no intellectual resources by which to challenge the values of his culture or to choose between alternative courses of action when his culture is divided. Neither the cultural relativist nor the emotivist can consistently say that Hitler was right or wrong or that the position or work of Martin Luther King Jr. was good or bad. Relativists and emotivists, like everyone else, can an emotional reaction to King or the Ku Klux Klan. They both can also give expression to those emotions. They cannot, however, if they are to be consistent with their position, assert that the values of one position are morally superior to those of another. What then can the disciples of the emotivist do but acquiesce in the values of the culture? Thus, it would seem that many of the objections we would make to cultural relativism would also have to be made to emotivism. Emotivism offers no more support than cultural relativism as a coherent guide to practical living.

Emotivism and Subjectivism

There is another view with which emotivism is sometimes confused and from which emotivists take pains to distinguish themselves. This view is known as subjectivism. This view holds that so called normative statements are really statements *about the feelings* of the person making the assertions. Thus, on this view, if I say to you that "You ought not to kill me", this translates into "I have negative feelings about the prospect of your killing me." In other words, normative statements are *really statements*, not about an objective moral order but about the subjective feelings of the individuals making the statements. As such, they are meaningful and capable of being true or false. For example, if I do have negative feelings about the prospect of your killing me than the statement "You ought not to kill me" is true. If on the other hand, I have positive feelings about the prospect of your killing me then the statement "You ought not to kill me" is false.

The emotivist's claim, however, is that the assertion "You ought not to kill me" is not *a statement about my feelings but an expression of my feelings.* Statements *about* my feelings can be true or false, but *expressions* of those feelings can be neither true or false. Needless to say, neither emotivism nor subjectivism give any guidance in making moral decisions or in telling us how we ought to feel.

Critical Evaluation of Emotivism

"To be cognitively meaningful, a statement must be either an analytic a priori or a synthetic a posteriori statement," is a concise summary of the emotivist position. The case for asserting this definition of what it means to be meaningful rests on a high regard for the nature of science and an assumption about the nature of scientific language. Logical positivism, of which emotivism is the expression in the domain of ethical theory was an attempt to make philosophy conform to the canons of scientific inquiry.[1] Science, the positivists believed was clear and achieved results. Most of the history of philosophy was an example of murky and futile endeavor. Reform lay in the direction of cleaning up our language and addressing only those problems that are subject to scientific analysis. This entailed adopting

the language of science as the *only* appropriate form of discourse. We can engage in a useful critique of emotivism by examining closely this concise summary of the emotivist position. We will analyze carefully the status of the statement *"To be cognitively meaningful a statement must be either an analytic a priori or a synthetic a posteriori statement."*

The first thing we observe is that the statement itself does not appear to be an analytic a priori statement that we can regard as true. That is to say that *the definition of meaningful statements* in the English language does not exclude statements that are neither analytic a priori or synthetic a posteriori in the way that the definition of circle excludes things that are not round.

Secondly, the statement does not appear to be a true synthetic a posteriori statement. Certainly the emotivist view of language does not describe the way most competent users of the English language use the English language in their day to day discourse. Users of the English language function on a day to day basis as if non-analytic a priori statements and non-synthetic a posteriori statements are cognitively meaningful.

Is the formulation a statement about the way we ought to speak? Perhaps the emotivist is not describing how we do use the English language but making an assertion about how we *ought* to use it. But obviously this won't work, for if the emotivist is right about his view of language then any assertions claiming that we ought to speak in a certain way are meaningless. The emotivist would then be involved in a self-contradiction.

Could the emotivist be claiming that it is desirable *for us to define meaningful language according to emotivist criteria?* Certainly it may be desirable in some contexts to use only analytic a priori and synthetic a posteriori statements but we have already noted some of the negative consequences of restricting ourselves *exclusively* to this view of language.

Is it even possible to restrict ourselves to the emotivist formulation? The emotivist, of course, asserts that it is really impossible not to restrict ourselves to the use of analytic a priori and synthetic a posteriori statements. Whatever else we may think we are doing and what ever theory of language we may profess to espouse. Thus, emotivists may not deny that most competent users of the English language function on a day to day basis *as if they think* normative statements are cognitively meaningful. They merely assert that people are profoundly mistaken in supposing that their normative discourse is meaningful. How can we explain this confusion on the part of supposedly competent English language speakers? I would suggest that it is the emotivist who is confused and that it is really not possible to dispense with normative language if we are to provide cognitive meaning to a significant portion of our experience.

We can make this point by observing the obvious necessity of spatial and temporal categories and the equally obvious necessity of moral categories. In order to make sense out of our world we are required to use numerous categories: weight, mass, velocity, hot, cold, high, low, fast, slow, near, far, light, dark, etc. The categories listed above are not thought generally to be normative ones. When I say "Jones is near" I am making what Ayer would call a synthetic a posteriori statement which is capable of being true or false and is hence meaningful. Whether it is true or false is to be determined by the definition of near and my location relative to the location of Jones. Without these categories or their functional equivalents, it would be impossible for us to give any kind of cognitive meaning to my experience in the world. A person bereft of these categories would probably be judged insane.

There are, however, other categories that also seem necessary if we are to make sense out of a significant portion of our experience. Consider stealing, personhood, murder, justice, adultery, rape, prostitution, marriage, father, mother, daughter, son, a loving act, a hateful act, gossip, joy, ecstasy, etc.

Let us take, for example, the statement "John raped Suzy." What does this statement mean? To explain the meaning of this statement requires us to use physical and biological categories since rape obviously involves a particular type of physical activity. But we must also use social, psychological and legal categories to make sense out of the concept of rape. Defining prostitution requires the use of physical, social, psychological, legal and obviously economic categories as well. Without these categories the 'meaning' of the term 'prostitution' is lost. Can we make sense out of these terms without using moral categories as well? I don't think so.

What about the categories of marriage, daughter, friend, etc.? Marriage implies a relationship that has many ramifications, physical, social, legal, economic, historical, religious, etc. But surely a portion of what it means to say that "John is married to Suzy" is that John and Suzy have certain *rights* and *obligations* vis-à-vis one another. Rights and obligations are also part of the 'meaning' of the statement that "Harry is the son of John and Suzy." These are moral categories. They are certainly emotionally loaded categories. They are frequently categories concerning which we can and do debate extensively. Nevertheless, they are categories that we cannot do without if we are to make sense out of a significant portion of our experience. They carry an emotional load but they carry a heavy cognitive load as well. They are not meaningless concepts. They are on the contrary, concepts necessary to give cognitive meaning to our experience at the most rudimentary level. Neither we nor our emotivist friends (friend is a moral category as well) can do without them for any sustained length of time. Thus, it seems necessary that if we are to make sense of our experience, we must have at least three categories of statements that we regard as meaningful: analytic a priori, synthetic a posteriori *and* evaluative statements.

Thus, it seems that the emotivist theory of language is not just a theory of language that is not clearly desirable, it is an impossible theory of language. No human being could exclusively use it and remain functionally sane.

Cultural Conflict and The Pervasive Influence of Emotivism

How influential is emotivism in Western culture? In philosophical circles emotivism and its parent logical positivism are, to say the least, not dominant. The social sciences, business, the legal profession and popular culture are another matter. *In the fields of sociology, psychology and political science especially, there are schools of thought dominated by logical positivism.* People trained in these schools may not be positivists outside of the practice of the profession but they are committed to the view that to be truly scientific they must, when they are practicing their profession, (sociology, psychology or political science) avoid making any normative judgments. Value judgments are not scientific and therefore a 'good' social scientist qua social scientist will avoid making them. *Value statements for them, may be meaningful outside the parameters of the social sciences but within those parameters they are regarded as meaningless.*

The issues surrounding the possibility and desirability of a value free social science are too numerous to go into here in any great detail. One prominent view usually attributed to the sociologist Max Weber is that in the choice of the problems that are going to be studied, the social scientist must make value judgments. In the actual study and analysis of the problems, however, once they have been chosen, the social scientist is both able to be and is obligated to be value neutral. Weber's position seems to be that the social scientist has *no rational basis* for choosing to study one problem rather than another. This is a position which in its implications is close to that of the logical positivist. Furthermore, once the problem for study has been chosen, the social scientist qua social scientist cannot make value judgments and he must in his social science study avoid language which purports to make value judgments. This view has been roundly criticized by Marxists, social scientists influenced by the European philosophical movement known as phenomenology and by some attempting to do social science study from a Christian perspective.

I seriously question the possibility of a value free social science in the manner that Weber advocated. It seems to me that the case can be made that the concepts used in most social analysis are value laden in such a way that their use requires us to develop theories in which value assumptions are deeply embedded in the theory. If this is the case, then our social science theories and the concepts contained in them, (concepts like freedom, democracy, alienation, deviance, anomie, individualism, aggression, poverty, mental stability, criminal behavior, passivity, war, terrorism, normalcy, etc.) do not escape making implicit or explicit value commitments. But even supposing that Weber was right in his views, we still are forced to make value choices with respect to the problems we think worthy of study and those that we think can be legitimately ignored. Uncritical acceptance of positivism in the social sciences may involve us in making value choices in an unthinking way which we would never have made had we engaged in careful consideration of the issues involved.

A similar set of assumptions often prevail within business environments. 'Relevant assertions' are those which speak to the measurable dimension of 'profit.' Moral assertions are treated as if they are meaningless within the context of the business environment. Sometimes the positivistic assumptions within the business or corporation are quite explicit. At other times these assumptions are publicly repudiated. The claim is made that the corporation is very much concerned to think and act morally in all of its relationships. Nevertheless, despite public denials, within the corporation, the pervasive use of language makes clear that moral assertions are to be treated as meaningless. The use of obviously value loaded language is regarded with puzzlement, amused tolerance or even derision.

Similar observations can be made with respect to political activity. Here the relevant measuring stick is not profit but power. Statements that assert that action X will contribute to or diminish power are regarded as meaningful assertions worthy of debate and consideration. Statements about what most voters or interest groups are likely to regard as good are relevant, since they are measurable by the poll takers or at the voting booth. Statements about what is good in some absolute since are treated as not an appropriate part of the universe of discourse.

One can also see the effects of emotivist assumptions in less structured environments like; parties, bull sessions, TV talk shows, etc. How often in everyday discourse have we observed value assertions, our own or others, being treated as merely expressions of the feelings of the speaker. As a matter of fact, it has become fashionable in our society to respect the 'feelings' of others with respect to moral issues even when we have quite different feelings. "I understand how you feel about abortion or extra-marital sex, etc. but I have quite different feelings about these matters." It is, of course, easier to respect the different feelings that others have than different opinions. Different feelings do not entail that either of us is wrong. Different opinions require us to assume that either we or the other person is at least partially wrong.

In his *Culture Wars: The Struggle to Define America,* James Davison Hunter observes that technological and economic factors affecting the media encourage emotivist discourse and discourage sustained critical reflection. Television and direct mail are expensive.[2] Newspaper space is limited. Politicians, advertisers, and others trying to influence our behavior and thought processes including fundamentalists and secular humanists know that with limited time, space and money an appeal to the emotions is more likely to be effective than careful detailed reasoned discourse. Lengthy reasoned debates are out. Sound bites that go for the emotional jugular are in.

The Contributions of Emotivism to Moral Discourse

Despite the reservations expressed above, it is important to not overlook the positive contributions of emotivism to moral discourse. If the emotivist is wrong in asserting that *all* of our moral discourse is non-cognitive, it is nonetheless obvious that a great deal of it is non-cognitive.   Listen to any political speech, sermon, TV. or radio commercial which talks about 'the good life', ease drop on any conversation among your acquaintances, read any editorial in your newspaper, etc., and you will observe a tremendous amount of language directed at changing the emotional response of the hearer or reader to a particular matter.   The emotivist is certainly right in asserting that our beliefs about the facts in certain situations can change our attitudes.   Based on new information, things that we formerly found to be acceptable may come to be regarded as morally repugnant. Serious study of the ways in which these two dimensions of our discourse interact ought to be encouraged rather than disparaged.

Furthermore, it is obvious that various individuals and groups try to pass off as reasoned discourse on moral matters what is only or at least primarily an attempt to manipulate our emotions. The question is not whether *some* moral discourse is merely an attempt to manipulate our actions through manipulating our emotions. Some of it obviously is simply manipulation.   The question is whether *all* moral discourse reduces to manipulation. The emotivist says yes! The non-emotivist says no!

Theories which emphasize the cognitive dimension to moral discourse frequently need another corrective which can be indirectly, if not directly, provided by consideration of the emotivist perspective. Morality is probably as much concerned with right emotions as with right action. We are concerned that we and others *feel* guilt with respect to those actions or states of being which we *ought* to feel guilt about.   At the same time psychiatrists and psychologists work thousands of hours with people helping them to overcome feelings of guilt or shame regarding things that they and their patients have come to view as inappropriate under the circumstances. All of us have probably struggled with feelings of guilt that we regard on the cognitive level as absurd. We may even have feelings of shame due to our inappropriate feelings of guilt.   On the other hand, we would certainly regard it as a moral deficiency in persons if they feel pleasure when encountering the suffering of others and sorrow whenever they encounter the alleviation of suffering in others. The emotivist, of course, cannot consistently assert that we ought to have or not have certain emotions under certain circumstances. He can merely call our attention to the importance of emotions in the moral life. Calling attention to the importance of emotions in moral life is, however, an important contribution.

The Fundamentalist and Humanist Response to Emotivism

Are emotivists secular humanists? The term 'secular humanist' is a promiscuous one in the lexicon of the fundamentalist that can apply to any and everyone who does not agree with fundamentalism. In this very broad and imprecise use of the term the emotivist would qualify as a secular humanist. Consistent emotivists certainly are not a theists and adoption of the emotivist perspective would certainly have the effect of undermining the fundamentalist conception of morality. Of course, it would have the effect of undermining all Christian, Islamic, Hindu, and Buddhist morality as well.

If by 'secular humanist,' however, one means the view that humanity rather than God is the ultimate value in the universe, then the emotivist is certainly not a secular humanist. The emotivist would regard both the value assertions of the fundamentalist and the value assertions of the secular humanist as non-sense. Neither, on his view, is making any assertions at all. Neither can be said to be right or wrong. They may think that they are disagreeing with each other but in fact they are merely giving expression to different emotional responses. The fundamentalist and the secular humanist, of course, think that they have real disagreement on the cognitive level. Where they agree, as in "Murder is morally wrong," they think that they have genuine agreement on the cognitive level. However, much they both may use language regarding each other more designed to produce an emotional reaction than to promote reasoned discourse, they both believe that reasoned discourse between them is at least a theoretical possibility. Thus, in a curious way the fundamentalist and the humanist may have common cause against the view of language and morality of the emotivist. They also both have cause to be concerned about cultural influences that tend to make rational discourse impossible. Secular humanists are committed to the rational development and implementation of a moral view of life. Fundamentalists espouse a view of life that for its ultimate source, is dependent upon special revelation. Nevertheless, historic fundamentalism has been committed to a rational defense of its faith. Whatever others may think of them, generally speaking fundamentalists think that their viewpoint, especially with respect to moral precepts, should make rational sense to any fair minded critic. They believe that the Ten Commandments, The Sermon on the Mount and other moral teachings, although derived from special revelation, make sense to anyone who desires the good life. In short, neither secular humanists or fundamentalists believe that moral discourse is a non-rational enterprise.

Emotivism and Culture War

How should the person who rejects emotivism respond to the pervasive influence of emotivism in our culture? Obviously, carefully and critically!

A similar point can be made with respect to an uncritical acceptance of the definition of the situation in other contexts. Corporations, political parties, civic organizations, cultural organizations of various types and even churches are possible examples. The definition of the situation may contain implicit value assumptions antithetical to one's own. This fact may be masked by the claim of value neutrality.

Those who rejects emotivism should also beware when people attempt to subtly and automatically turn statements that make value assertions into expressions of feelings. Neither should they stand by silently when others attempt to pass off their own emotional expressions as carefully thought out opinions. One should also not, stand by silently when others assert that there can be no carefully reasoned opinions concerning moral matters and thus assert that all utterances regarding moral matters are simply the emotional expression of prejudices.

There are, however, some broader issues that need to be considered. It is one thing to use emotivist rhetoric against an opponent in a debate. Parties to disputes have always attempted to characterize the arguments of their opponents as based on emotion while insisting that their own arguments were based on reason. Each side to a dispute has always used emotion to persuade the undecided. This is not new.

The emotivist position affirms, however, that rational discourse about values is impossible for either side of a dispute. It is difficult to see how emotivism can have a positive impact in resolving cultural conflict at the *deepest level.*

The emotivist can engage in helpful dialogue in those case where the participants to a dispute have the same basic feelings with respect to basic concerns. The emotivist, in these cases, can help to show that when the 'facts' are carefully examined that agreement on certain issues will be forthcoming. This, however, is only because the parties to the dispute already agree on the most basic emotional level.

Even if emotivism is not true, however, it may be an epistemological perspective that is characteristic of our culture. This is what Alasdair MacIntyre Maintains in his *After Virtue.*[3] MacIntyre disagrees the with the emotivist theory of language and values. Thus, he rejects the epistemological claims of emotivism. He affirms, however, that we live in an emotivist culture in the sense that increasingly, in our culture, discourse about morality has become nearly impossible. In other words the term 'emotivism' provides an accurate description of the basic value assumptions of our culture. To the extent MacIntyre is correct the implications for cultural harmony are disastrous. If persuasion is impossible than that would seem to leave only the possibilities of manipulation and coercion. Rational persuasion is excluded. Once we reach the point, however, that everyone recognizes that rational persuasion is impossible, manipulation becomes more difficult. Successful manipulation is possible because at least one of the parties to a dispute believes that he or she is being persuaded. You cannot manipulate a person who knows that they are being manipulated. To the extent that we all become emotivists it would seem that the only way to resolve basic conflicts is through coercion.

Thus, it would seem that the resources for resolving cultural conflict provided by emotivism are very limited if not non-existent. An emotivist culture would seem to be doomed to some form of cultural war in any attempt to resolve basic cultural conflict. The potentially disastrous results of living in an emotivist culture will not become apparent as long as there is a congruence of feeling on major issues within the culture. As long as people feel the same way about an issue, the fact that none of them is able to give reasons for their beliefs does not emerge. When, however, they have conflicting feelings and try to resolve their conflict by rational persuasion, the lack of any foundation for rational persuasion becomes apparent. The causes for people having similar feelings about a given range of issues is a legitimate task of the discipline of social psychology. Shared beliefs systems and rational persuasion in the context of those shared belief systems are doubtless important factors in bringing about shared or conflicting feelings. There are doubtless other factors such as economic interest, personal desires, similar or differing life experiences, differences in social class, educational level, religious experiences, etc. The point being made here is not that a commitment to emotivism as a philosophical position is likely to be the principle cause of these different feelings regarding moral issues. The point rather is that when emotivists do differ regarding their feelings about a moral issue that they have limited resources within the emotivist perspective to solve these differences without resorting to manipulation or coercion. This is an argument that we will need to pursue further in subsequent chapters.

Notes

[1]For a fuller but still relatively brief treatment of the movement known as logical positivism see John Passmore, *A Hundred Years of Philosophy,* pp. 367-393.

[2] James Davison Hunter, *Culture Wars: The Struggle to Define America,* pp. 159-170, chapter 6, on "The Technology of Public Discourse." See also page 284 where Hunter observes that between the presidential elections of 1968-1988 the average radio and TV 'sound bite' decreased from 42.3 seconds to 9.8 seconds.   During this same period TV visual images without verbal commentary increased by 300%.

[3] Alasdair MacIntyre, *After Virtue,* pp. 1-37.

CHAPTER IV

EGOISM, HEDONISM AND UTILITARIANISM: THE HISTORICAL TRADITION

Reasons for Examining the Historical Tradition Linking Egoism, Hedonism and Utilitarianism

In analyzing the concepts of egoism, hedonism and utilitarianism it is useful to distinguish between the logical integration and the cultural integration of these concepts. These concepts are not necessarily logically related. It is possible to embrace any one of these positions and reject the others without being inconsistent. Nevertheless, in this chapter and the next, we will treat them together for a couple of reasons. In the first place, they are the primary ingredients that are interwoven into a world view that is one of the dominant cultural forces in the Western world. In a more or less self-conscious fashion and in a more or less consistent manner, millions of people in the West organize their lives around all three of the assumptions embodied in these philosophical positions. This fact makes them worthy of our consideration quite apart from their importance in the history of philosophical reflection or the degree of seriousness with which they are taken in academic departments of philosophy. This is especially relevant for the purposes of this book since we are concerned with the relationship of ethical theory to cultural conflict.

In the second place, in addition to being related in our contemporary culture, they have been historically related. It will be useful because of this historic relationship, to view how these various positions have been treated by four major thinkers in the history of thought. These thinkers are Aristippus, Epicurus, Bentham, and J.S. Mill. All four of these thinkers regarded themselves as hedonists. Aristippus, Epicurus and Bentham were also egoists. Bentham and Mill were utilitarians. Aristippus and Epicurus belong to the ancient world. Bentham and Mill were nineteenth century thinkers. For a variety of reasons, including their personalities, goals, and historical and cultural circumstances, these thinkers developed significantly different approaches to the meaning of life. This is true despite the commonalty of their assumptions.

We will begin this chapter by giving a brief sketch of the views and assumptions of these four thinkers. This will not be an attempt to give an adequate treatment of these thinkers for their own sake, even though the last three especially are certainly worthy of careful study and consideration. Our purpose in discussing these thinkers in particular is to clarify by flesh and blood illustrations the positions with which they have come to be associated. In Chapter V we will examine in a more detailed and systematic manner some of the assumptions which are made by adherents to these positions. We will also attempt to show there how a typical fundamentalist and a typical humanist might be inclined to respond to these assumptions.

Some Fundamental Conceptual Distinctions

Our exposition of the thinkers that we are considering will be enhanced if we first clarify some fundamental distinctions regarding egoism, hedonism, and utilitarianism.

The first distinction is between psychological and ethical egoism. Psychological egoism is, or at least purports to be, an empirical statement about human nature. It is the view that *all persons always do seek their own individual good.* It is to be contrasted with psychological *altruism. Altruism* is the view that human beings are at least capable of self-giving love and that therefore some persons, at least some of the time, *do* seek the good of others.

Ethical egoism, on the other hand, makes no assertions about how persons *do* act but about how they *ought* to act. The ethical egoist asserts that all persons *ought* always to seek only their own individual good. The ethical altruist asserts that all persons *ought* to, at least some of the time, seek the good of others.

Aristippus, Epicurus, and Bentham were all both psychological egoists and ethical egoists. John Stuart Mill denied ethical egoism, and asserted that human beings were capable of altruism and obligated to act on altruistic motives.

The second distinction is between psychological and ethical hedonism which parallels the distinction between psychological and ethical egoism. Psychological hedonism is the empirical theory that all persons *are* always one hundred percent motivated by the desire to get pleasure and avoid pain. As such, it *seems* to be cast in the form of a synthetic a posteriori proposition that emotivists would accept as meaningful.[1]

Ethical hedonism is the view that all persons *ought* always one hundred percent of the time to seek pleasure. If they are egoistic ethical hedonists, they should always seek their own pleasure. If they are altruistic ethical hedonists, they should sometimes seek the pleasure of others. Assertions regarding ethical hedonism would not, of course, be regarded by the emotivist as meaningful.

Aristippus, Epicurus, Bentham, and J.S. Mill were all both psychological and ethical hedonists.

We need to also distinguish between ethical egoism and ethical hedonism. Despite the ways in which they were united in Aristippus, Epicurus, and Bentham, ethical egoism and ethical hedonism are logically distinct (although not logically incompatible) positions. One could affirm that one ought always to seek one's own good without holding that the good is pleasure. For example, the good might be power, wisdom, knowledge, aesthetic development, athletic ability, etc. Furthermore, one can, as did John Stuart Mill, assert that one ought always to seek pleasure as the good, but also assert that sometimes the pleasure of others should be one's goal.

We need also to distinguish between hedonism and utilitarianism. Utilitarianism is the view that moral actions or moral rules are those that contribute to *the greatest good of the greatest number.* Obviously, one might be a utilitarian without being a hedonist. If, for instance, one believed that the good were wisdom, then seeking the greatest good for the greatest number would mean seeking the greatest wisdom for the greatest number.

One can also be a utilitarian without affirming that there is only one distinct thing in the world that we may call good. For example, if one held that wisdom and pleasure were distinct from each other and both good, then seeking the greatest good for the greatest number would mean seeking the greatest amount of wisdom *and* the greatest amount of pleasure for the greatest number. Having two or more goods could, of course, create problems for the utilitarian when it is necessary to choose between them. This problem we will discuss in more detail later.

There is also a distinction between quantitative hedonism and qualitative hedonism. If we affirm that there is only *one kind* of pleasure, as did Aristippus, Epicurus and Bentham, then we are quantitative hedonists. Quantitative hedonism implies the possibility of a mathematical treatment of units of pleasure. We can add "apples and apples." If we affirm that there are *different kinds* of pleasure, as did J.S. Mill, and that some kinds of pleasure are qualitatively *better* than other kinds of pleasure, we are qualitative hedonists. Qualitative hedonism disallows a mathematical treatment of units of pleasure. We cannot add "apples and oranges." The qualitative hedonist cannot simply talk about more or less pleasure or pain. but must also develop a criterion for determining which pleasures are qualitatively better than others.

None of these ethical positions are compatible with emotivism since they all make value claims that the emotivist would regard as meaningless. They all affirm that it is possible to make intelligible claims about what persons *ought* to do or about what is the *ultimate good in life.* These are just the sort of claims that the emotivist cannot allow as even meaningful.

We may also note that none of these positions is compatible with cultural relativism. They all seem to be affirming at least one absolute that transcends cultural values. "You ought always to love God and your neighbor" is one sort of absolute ethical assertion. "You ought always to love only yourself" is quite another, but they are both absolutes. Ethical hedonism affirms that pleasure is a universal good for all cultures. Utilitarianism offers a criterion for judging rules and actions that transcends cultural criteria for evaluating just action.

Aristippus

Aristippus is credited with being one of the first philosophical hedonists. Claiming to be a disciple of Socrates he emphasized that side of Socrates' personality that exhibited a zest for life. He argued that pleasure was the only good and *intensity* of pleasure was the criterion by which pleasure is to be measured. Since physical pleasures are generally the most intense pleasures, he deduced that the maximum amount of physical pleasure is the sole criterion for determining ethical behavior. Aristippus was a disciplined hedonist in that he also advocated control over one's desires and environment in the interest of maximizing intense physical pleasure.

Epicurus

The ontology and anthropology of Epicurus seem to clearly imply any lack of ultimate meaning in the universe or to human existence. Because of his personality or historical circumstances, or perhaps due to a combination of these and other factors, the approach of Epicurus to life was radically different from that of Aristippus. Epicurus adopted the ontology of the atomist philosophers Leucippus and Democritus. The world, he affirmed, was composed *solely* of material atoms falling in a void or empty space. Thus, Epicurus was a materialist in ontology. The atoms fell not in a straight line but swerved from time to time, thus accounting for a certain amount of indeterminism (which Epicurus believed made room for human freedom). The swerving of the atoms also caused them to come together in unique combinations and this explained the origin of all of the reality that we experience including human beings themselves. Human beings are composed of coarser *material* atoms that make up their bodies and finer *material* atoms that make up their souls. Thus, Epicurus was also a materialist with respect to his anthropology. The atoms themselves are indestructible. When we die, however, both the coarser atoms that comprise our bodies and the finer atoms that comprise our souls fly apart, and we ourselves as distinct personalities cease to exist. Thus, there is no personal immortality. The universe itself neither contains nor exhibits any transcendent meaning. All that comes into being does so by the chance clashing and coalescing of material atoms. All destruction comes about because of the chance flying apart of those same material atoms. Thus, it is not possible for us to find any meaning in life that transcends our own limited individual existence.

Epicurus' egoism, hedonism and his view that the universe is meaningless did not lead him to pessimism. To a broad spectrum of American thought, ranging from Jerry Falwell to Shirley MacLain, this would be regarded as a pessimistic view of life. Epicurus and his followers, however, did not think so. For him, and those who adhered to his views, this perspective was the source of profound relief and liberation.

Since there is no transcendent meaning in the universe the only possible good is the good of the individual. Hence, Epicurus was an egoist. The only good in individual experience that Epicurus found was individual pleasure. Hence, Epicurus agreed with Aristippus that pleasure is the good and espoused hedonism as an ethical philosophy. Thus he may be characterized as an egoistic hedonist. The hedonism of Epicurus however, was not the hedonism of the Schlitz beer commercial that admonishes us that "You only go around once. Therefore, you should get all the gusto you can." He argued that the real goal in life was to achieve the net amount of pleasure after one had subtracted for the amount of pain experienced. This seemingly sensible perspective opens up a choice between two possible strategies. One can develop a life style that maximizes pleasure or one can develop a life style that minimizes pain. Epicurus' view of existence and the human prospect was such that he believed that, clearly, the most prudent choice was the most conservative one. Therefore, for him, the good was not so much the maximum amount of pleasure but the achievement of the minimum amount of pain.

Epicurus, like Aristippus, was a quantitative hedonist. Unlike Aristippus, however, he affirmed that mental pleasure is better than physical pleasure. This was because mental activity produced more quantity of pleasure. Epicurus correctly observed that we could achieve pleasure either through physical activity or through mental activity. Neither means of achieving pleasure should be thought of as intrinsically superior to the other. There are no qualitative distinctions between pleasures, only quantitative ones. The differences in quantity, however, are significant. Physical pleasures tend to be more intense, of shorter duration and more likely to be accompanied by painful consequences. Mental pleasures tended to be less intense, of longer duration and less likely to be accompanied by painful consequences. The pleasure that comes from the activity of the mind is therefore better than the pleasure that comes from the activity of the body. This is not because the quality of mental pleasure is better than the quality of physical pleasure, but because mental pleasure leads to more quantity of pleasure, and more importantly, to less quantity of pain. Thus, the viewpoint of Epicurus may be described as that of an egoistic quantitative hedonist who emphasized the *duration* of pleasure. This is in contrast to Aristippus who was an egoistic quantitative hedonist who emphasized the *intensity* of pleasure.

Epicurus affirmed that the denial of the immortality of the soul relieved individuals of the burden of anxiety about the afterlife. Epicurus drew several consequences from this in regard to life style. One of his first priorities was to overcome the anxiety that comes through fear of the gods in this life and in the next. The study of philosophy is the answer here. Epicurus maintained that there were gods but that they would obviously be too wise to be interested in the affairs of human beings. Thus, neither God (whom Epicurus did not believe in) nor the gods were going to "get one" in this life. This relieved the individual from fear of the gods but also from the tremendous expense and burden of constantly trying to please them. Fear of the next life is also absurd since there isn't any next life. Death is nothing. There is obviously no point in fearing--nothing.

Disappointment caused by failing to receive the pleasure associated with achieving high aspirations can be avoided by avoiding high aspirations. The next problem that must be dealt with is disappointment and the fear of disappointment. This is easily handled. Do not expect much and you will not be disappointed when you do not get it. This perspective shows that Epicurus was typically un-American and alien to the contemporary Western spirit. Optimism and hope for the future, for him, was only a trap that a prudent person should avoid.

Self-conscious egoists do not believe in love and hence do not suffer the pain of love lost. What about love and the pain that is often associated with the loss of love? Well, in the first place, if egoism is correct, love is not a real possibility for human beings anyway. The pursuit of love is a delusion that will inevitably lead to frustration and pain. Thus, Epicurus advocated *friendship* that he believed to be possible for human beings but rejected love as a legitimate goal for humanity.

Epicurus renounced the pursuit of power and any pain that might be associated with active political or cultural conflict. The pursuit of power? Equally foolish! You would not pursue power for its own sake unless you thought power rather than pleasure was the good. If the world is uncertain and the pursuit of power is likely to fail, then you would not pursue power in order to maximize your pleasure. This could only lead to disappointment in the overwhelming majority of cases. If egoism is true, then it is also foolish to pursue power for the sake of helping others. Thus, political involvement of any type would only be engaged in if the individual had absolutely no other options. Clearly, the hedonism of Epicurus could be a cultural force if embraced by a sufficient number of adherents. It is not, however, an ethic that motivates its followers to engage in cultural or political conflict of any sort. Followers of Epicurus are not likely to participate in culture wars.

A summary of Epicurus' advice is "avoid pain by living a life of quiet contemplation." What then is the most appropriate life style? Epicurus advocated a life of quiet contemplation, withdrawal from the world, and philosophical discourse with a small circle of one's friends as the only sensible life for a wise person. This all seems strange and even amusing to those of us who have grown up with typical Western values. These values include a mixture of belief in material well being, technological progress, optimism about the future, the effectiveness of political power, and the joys of sex in this life and of heaven in the next. Epicurus' choice of life style is foolish for those who dwell in a world filled with meaning and hope. For those who dwell in fear of a capricious world and angry gods, however, this message would come with liberation if not hope.

Jeremy Bentham

Jeremy Bentham 1748-1832 was a man of a different age and different world. Epicurus advocated a life of withdrawal and philosophical contemplation. *Bentham was a social reformer.* Both were egoistic quantitative hedonists with respect to their view of human nature. *Bentham, however, had as his goal the welfare of humanity. For him the criterion for just rules and action is not one's own greatest good, as with Epicurus, but the greatest good of the greatest number.* This is what made Bentham a utilitarian. Every law is to be judged according to its utility or usefulness in advancing the general welfare.

Jeremy Bentham was a psychological egoist, a psychological hedonist and a quantitative hedonist. His quantitative hedonism made possible the development of the hedonic calculus. Bentham argued that both Aristippus and Epicurus were in part right. Both the *intensity* (Aristippus)and *duration* (Epicurus) of pleasure must be taken into account in determining the amount of pleasure or pain that a given action is likely to bring. In addition to *intensity* and *duration*, however, we need to consider *certainty* (the degree of probability that an action will produce a given amount of pleasure or pain), *propinquity* (how near or far away in time is the pleasure or pain produced), *fecundity* (how likely is the pleasure to produce additional pleasure), and *purity* (to what extent is a pleasure mixed with pain).

Let us illustrate how this system might work by comparing two possible actions. We will consider the spending of a sum of money on a vacation, or making an investment in our retirement fund. With the second plan we will assume that we will not spend the principle, but use the interest on the money to support ourselves in our retirement years.

The criterion of intensity seems clearly to favor the choice of the vacation since it will provide a great deal of *intense* pleasure. The investment, on the other hand, will provide only a modest increase in our yearly retirement income.

Duration, however, obviously favors the investment decision. The vacation will last only a short time. Of course the memory of the pleasure of the vacation will last longer but twenty or thirty years from now it will be very faint.

How about *certainty*? Certainty seems to favor the vacation. I may not live to retirement. The investment could be lost in a market crash, etc. Of course the pleasure of the vacation is not absolutely certain. I may not enjoy it. I may miss my plane. I may be killed or injured on the voyage, etc. Still, spending the money now on the vacation seems to be a safer if shorter investment.

Propinquity obviously favors the vacation. Retirement is a long way away. The vacation is now!

Fecundity favors the investment in my retirement. Money invested in a retirement fund will produce more money. The money spent on the vacation will be gone. Of course, we still have to take into account future memories of the vacation. Even with this consideration, however, the fecundity criterion seems to favor the retirement investment.

The criterion of *purity* seems to me to be a bit more complicated. I may eat too much on the vacation and have to suffer the pain related to being overweight. I may feel guilty about having possibly spent my money foolishly. It may rain the whole time and I will be frustrated. If we can assume that the weather holds, I can control my diet, and handle my guilt, the pleasure derived from the vacation seems relatively pure. How about the retirement investment? That too depends. How much pain will I suffer due to the regret over not having taken the vacation? Am I the type of person who watches his stock market investments with great anxiety?

Still, after taking into account both of these alternative actions, they both seem to rate quite high on the purity criterion as compared to an investment in narcotics for my personal use. The latter investment would be high on the intensity scale. It would be low on the duration scale. It would be high on certainty and propinquity. It would be low on fecundity. It would be very low on the purity scale, since it is likely to be a pleasure that will also tend to produce much pain.

Utilitarianism and the Criterion of Extent

The criterion of *extent* is the seventh and final criterion introduced by Bentham in his hedonic calculus. Bentham and Epicurus are alike at the base level. The criterion of extent, however, makes Bentham a utilitarian and constitutes a radical break with the viewpoint of Epicurus on the level of *principles.* It is also this criterion of extent that has been singled out as most problematic with respect to the consistency of his theory.

Bentham argues that before we make a moral decision we must consider not only the effect of a given action on our own experience of pleasure and pain but its effect on all other human beings. There seems, however, to be an obvious problem here. If Bentham is right in his egoistic view of human nature, why would anyone care about how actions influence the amount of pleasure or pain of others. To attempt to appreciate Bentham's answer to this question we need to consider several different distinctions and concepts. We need to distinguish between *the Person as Individual Decision Maker* and *the Person as Legislator*. We need also to consider the concepts of the *Marginal Cost of Charity, The Natural Identity of Interests,* and *The Artificial Identity of Interests.*

Sometimes Bentham in his discussion seems to be assuming the role of an individual as he or she makes personal decisions. Other times the role of the individual as citizen legislator is being assumed. In the example we have been using, we have been assuming the viewpoint of a particular individual making a particular decision between two possible courses of action. There is, of course, a great deal that is artificial about such a process. Most of the time most of us make hundreds, perhaps thousands of decisions in a week without taking the time or trouble to attempt to calculate in any systematic way the consequences of our actions. Much less do we use anything resembling Bentham's hedonic calculus. Sometimes, however, we do attempt to make moral decisions at least in part based on a systematic assessment of probable consequences. Should I buy stock in a company that invests in activities that I consider immoral? Should I be willing to pay more for goods made in America even though they may be of inferior quality to foreign made goods?

At other times, however, some of us in our role as citizens, and a much smaller group of us in the role as legislator, may be trying to decide whether a given law is beneficial or just. Here the standpoint of person as citizen *legislator* is being assumed. Bentham was very interested in legislation and the development of a criterion for determining just laws. His answer to the problem of a criterion for the development of just laws was to affirm that those laws that contributed to the greatest good of the greatest number were just. Those which failed this criterion were unjust. A law, by definition, is not designed to cover one particular case but to give direction with respect to thousands, perhaps millions of individual decisions. Sometimes, as we know, the enforcement of a particular law in a particular case will result in more evil than good. We defend the law, however, on the grounds that on the average, the greatest good of the greatest number will be realized by the enforcement of the law in question, even though in some particular instances this will not be the case. Ideally we try to arrange our political institutions so that our legislators have no "conflict of interest" with respect to a particular piece of legislation. We hope that they will be encouraged to pass laws that will benefit the public rather than their own private interest. *The standpoint of person as citizen legislator thus requires an impartial perspective on the totality of public experience.*

The 'marginal cost of charity' is related to another phenomenon with which we are all familiar. Normal human beings are able to derive a vicarious pleasure from observing the pleasure of others, especially if those others are relatives or friends. We also experience vicarious pain at observing the pain of others even if we are not acquainted with the sufferers. This latter phenomenon is perhaps nowhere more clearly exhibited than in those television adds for various charities that show pictures of starving and diseased little children with bellies bloated from the effects of malnutrition. Are these adds appealing to our unselfish love? It seems to me that Bentham or a disciple of Bentham could cogently argue that this does not necessarily count as evidence against egoism. Economists have long used the concept of 'marginal utility' that is based on the fact that each increase in the amount of a desired commodity decreases its value to the consumer. For example, if I have just finished eating one hot fudge sundae, then the marginal utility of a second sundae is considerably less than the first. If we can assume that I gain some pleasure from watching you enjoy eating a hot fudge sundae, the pleasure to be gained from giving the second sundae to you may outstrip the pleasure to be gained from eating the second one myself (especially when we subtract for the pain I would experience in the eating of that second sundae). Thus, the marginal cost of charity (as defined in terms of the sacrifice entailed by a so called charitable act) seems to decrease in direct proportion to the decline in the marginal utility of the commodity given. Indeed, if a person is sufficiently well off, the marginal   utility of the product given and therefore the marginal cost of the charitable act of giving that product may be at zero. A person might derive the pleasure of a charitable act (pleasure at seeing others happy, praise for his being a benefactor, tax write off, prospect of heavenly reward, etc.) at no cost since what is being donated are those things that have zero marginal utility to that particular individual. This view of the nature of charitable giving is entirely consistent with Bentham's egoistic perspective. Whether all so called charitable acts can be explained within this framework may be problematic. Can anyone deny that it does explain an enormous amount of what passes for charity in both secular and religious contexts, in our Christian churches both non-fundamentalist and fundamentalist?

The concept of the 'natural identity of interest' is also a very familiar one to all of us even though we may not have heard it described in this way. Sometimes our desires are such and the world is so constituted, that rather than there being a conflict of interest between two parties, there is an identity of interests. When this is the case, we do not need sacrificial love for two or more parties to get along. We merely need an enlightened selfishness. Perhaps the most familiar and widely discussed example of this is in the area of economic theory and policy. Under ideal conditions the capitalist is best able to make the largest profit while manufacturing and selling to the consumer a quality product at a fair price while providing good wages, benefits, and working conditions for the worker. The laborer is best able to make the highest wages while being hard working and efficient. The consumer is best able to satisfy his or her needs or desires while providing profit for the capitalist and good jobs for the laborer. Under these *ideal* conditions everyone can be 100% motivated by selfishness and the system will work well.

We get into problems with selfish motivation only if some conditions like those listed below occur. (1)The capitalist is able to make more profit by gouging the customer, making goods that are either unsafe or of poor quality, or polluting the environment. (2) The capitalist is able to increase his profits by exploiting the worker. (3) The laborer is able to make as much or more money by doing shoddy work, being inefficient or stealing from the employer. (4)The consumer is able to buy stolen goods at a cheaper price, etc.

Adam Smith's *The Wealth of Nations* was published in 1776. In this book he argued for a laissez faire economic theory chiefly on the thesis that with respect to the economy at least there was a *natural* identity of interests among capitalists laborers, consumers and governments. This meant that all that was needed was for the government to exercise minimal control over the economy in order for the individuals living in the nation and hence the wealth of nations to increase. Smith assumed in his economic theory (in contrast to his work on moral theory) that egoism not altruism was the driving force behind the economy. Furthermore, the best way to achieve the greatest good for the greatest number was to allow a rational egoism to run its course. Smith did not assume, nor is it necessary for the proponent of laissez faire economic theory to assume, that every thing is ideal. One can grant that there is a great deal of dislocation, exploitation, suffering and mismanagement of resources. What the proponent of laissez faire economic theory does assume is that things are as good as they can be, and that there is nothing that government interference can do to make them any better. Therefore, there is no possibility of making things any better by trying to do away with or interfere with egoism. If the proponents of laissez faire theory are optimists they will not only assume that things are as good as they can be. They will assume that if the natural forces of the market place are left to do their work that they will over time *naturally* get better. Bentham was influenced by Adam Smith and the economic assumptions made by Smith. In his legal theory, however, especially as applied to penal reform he made some different assumptions.[2]

The concept of the 'artificial identity of interests' is the complement of the concept of the 'natural identity of interest'. It is, of course, possible to assume that with respect to certain social phenomena there does not exist a *natural* identity of interests. We may nevertheless assume that it is possible to change the situation through legislation so that an identity of interests will be created. This would constitute not a belief in the *natural* identity of interests but a belief in the possibility of an *artificial* identity of interests. It is this belief in the possibility of creating an artificial identity of interests that Bentham applied to the problem of legislative reform.   If we can assume that both psychological egoism and psychological hedonism are true, then we can reduce the problem of human motivation to a simple formula.

If we can, in addition, assume that human beings are basically rational, we can exclude complicated theories of human nature.   We can, for instance, exclude the Christian view that talks about sin, guilt, a corrupt will, rebellion against God, grace, regeneration, the works of the flesh, the filling of the Holy Spirit, etc. We can also exclude views like that of Freud that talk about repression, suppression, ego, superego, id, neuroses, psychoses, the unconscious, the preconscious, etc. Bentham's human being is an uncomplicated pleasure seeker and pain avoider. The rationality of his human nature is purely selfish and calculating. It knows nothing of love, guilt, hate, or repressed anger.

Bentham's Vision and Contemporary Culture

Armed with this knowledge we can use the first six criteria of the hedonic calculus to *predict* what an informed person will choose in any given situation. If we change the laws to *control* the system of reward (pleasures) and punishments (pains), then we can *control* what an informed person will choose in any given situation. If we can control the educational system then we can *guarantee* that the subjects of our society will be *rationally informed persons.* If society is nothing more than the sum of the individuals that exist in it, then if we can control the behavior of individuals, we can control the behavior of the whole society.

But to what end? Hedonism professes to give us not only a theory of individual human motivation but a theory of the good for the individual. It professes to give us not only a theory about how society does operate but a theory of justice. We can create laws that will control human behavior in such a way that pleasure will be maximized and pain minimized in a given society. Since, pleasure is the good, this will be the greatest good for the greatest number. Where there is not a natural identity of interests, we can create an artificial identity of interests. If we define justice in terms of maximizing pleasure and minimizing pain, then a just law is one that achieves this goal for a given society. An unjust law is one that fails to achieve this goal. A legislator armed with Bentham's psychological and sociological theories is in a position to create Plato's dream of a just and ideal society, albeit using assumptions and goals of which Plato would not have approved.

It is worth noting that depending upon one's perspective on society, Bentham's theory could lead to either very conservative or very radical conclusions. If one assumes that there is a high degree of a *natural* identity of interests and/or that society has realized the maximum possible amount of identity of interest, then the implications for government intervention are conservative. This is also the case if we assume that we have already attained the highest possible amount of an artificial identity of interest. Even if there is a lot of conflict in society, if society is already good, or at least as good as it can be, then government intervention is either unnecessary, pointless, or probably destructive.

On the other hand, one could believe that it is possible to create through government intervention a significantly greater degree of identity of interests.   This belief in the possibility of creating an increased amount of artificial identity of interests could lead to a great deal of governmental intervention.   Much of the contemporary debate between the political right and the political left rests on different assumptions in this area. The debate over whether or not we need more or less governmental control rests, after all, on assumptions about how good or bad things are and whether government can make them any better.   This is, of course, for most of us a relative question.   As compared to Newt Gingrich, Ted Kennedy would argue for less laissez faire and more governmental intervention to create an artificial identity of interests. Marx, however, saw in capitalism an inescapable *conflict of interests* that would inevitably lead to the downfall of the entire capitalist system.   Gingrich might argue that it doesn't need fixing. Kennedy would argue that it does need fixing and can be fixed. Marx would argue that since it cannot be fixed it needs to be overthrown and replaced by an entirely different society that does manifest an identity of interests.

There is much to criticize about Bentham's theory and I will raise many of those criticisms somewhat later. First of all, however, I think it is important to appreciate the vision which Bentham and his followers embodied so clearly and forcefully. E*goism, hedonism and utilitarianism coupled with a social science theory (as articulated in the hedonic calculus) can create heaven on earth.* To the true believer this was (and is) heady stuff. It may be objected that neither Bentham's social science theories nor his ethical theories are popular today among trained social scientists and philosophers.   One can argue, however, that Bentham's vision has survived well into the 20th century. In can be argued that the exchange theory of the sociologist George Homans[3] and the behaviorism of the psychologist B.F. Skinner[4] are legitimate heirs of Bentham's social science. These thinkers popular in the fifties through the seventies are no longer in vogue. It is certainly the case, however, that the vision of using the social sciences to create an ideal world is alive and well and living in departments of psychology and sociology in our colleges and universities, chastened though it may be by much of the political, social and intellectual history of the twentieth century. Utilitarianism is certainly still considered to be a viable option among academic philosophers concerned with ethics and social philosophy.

Quite apart from what may take place in academic departments in our colleges and universities, however, this linkage between egoism, hedonism and utilitarianism is a powerful force. It exists on Madison Avenue, in Washington, in our soap operas, in our popular music, and even in our churches. Like cultural relativism and emotivism, utilitarianism of the egoistic, hedonistic variety is a powerful cultural force in American life and in the West in general. To many non-Westerners it is the philosophic perspective that is synonymous with capitalism. When they contrast the moral values of their own cultures with those of the capitalism of the "decadent" West, they have in mind, egoistic, hedonism. Ironically, the religious right tends to be politically committed to laissez faire economic theory. This is because they associate it with economic, political and religious freedom, not because they associate it with egoism and hedonism. To the extent that political conservatism in America is a coalition of believers in an economic system that is motivated by egoism and pleasure and believers in a cultural system founded on love and truth, there is likely to be great tension within the movement.

John Stuart Mill

John Stuart Mill was the intellectual heir of Bentham and of his father James Mill who was Bentham's friend and disciple. In many ways he was a more subtle thinker than Bentham who is certainly deserving of serious consideration as a philosopher. I will spend less time on Mill than on Bentham, however, for several reasons. In the first place, although Mill claimed to the last to be a hedonist and a true disciple of Bentham, he is thought by many to have really in principle rejected the hedonism of Bentham and his father James Mill. Thus, many of the criticisms leveled against Bentham by anti-hedonists were acknowledged or initiated by his disciple J.S. Mill. Secondly, our purpose here is not to discuss any of these thinkers for their own sake. I merely intend to illustrate the sorts of perspectives that will help the beginning student to grasp some of the basic issues in ethical theory. The thought of Bentham, however, it may compare with that of Mill in depth and subtlety, is more useful for that purpose.

Mill is instructive, however, when we look at the positions of Bentham that he felt forced to abandon and the implications of these changes. Whereas Bentham was a quantitative hedonist, Mill maintained that there were qualitative distinctions in pleasures such that some pleasures (the pleasures of the mind) were intrinsically better than other pleasures.

> It is better to be a human being dissatisfied than a pig satisfied; better to be Socrates dissatisfied than a fool satisfied. And if the fool, or the pig, is of a different opinion, it is because they only know their own side of the question. The other party to the comparison knows both sides.[5]

It is clear that this position presents a problem for the hedonic calculus. It also presents a problem for hedonism itself. The hedonic calculus is now impossible since we cannot mathematically compare entities of distinct qualities. But what of hedonism itself? Is not Mill saying in the above quoted passage that he would rather be a wise man who experiences more pain than a fool who experiences less? Mill tells us who will judge between the quality of pleasures and by what authority. The person who has experienced both the higher and lower pleasures is the competent judge. His competence stems from wider experience. But by what standard does the competent judge choose between lower and higher pleasures? In reading Mill, one gets the impression that the standard is realization of the higher faculties of the individual. Mill sounds, at times, very much like Aristotle and seems to be propounding a criterion of self-realization. Aristotle, however, is clear in affirming that man is superior to animals because of his rational capacity, and self-realization consists in the highest possible development of this rational capacity. For Aristotle, the achievement of this goal brings with it its own pleasure, but the goal is not the pleasure which comes with the attainment of wisdom but the attainment of wisdom itself. How can Mill choose between pleasures? Must he not use some criterion other than pleasure itself to do so?

Mill not only rejects Bentham's quantitative hedonism but also his psychological egoism. Human beings, according to Mill, are capable of a social feeling for humanity. Although Mill does not deny the importance of external sanctions derived from the natural and artificial identity of interests, he affirms that the ultimate sanction for morality is the internal sanction of this social feeling that causes us to want to contribute to the greatest good for the greatest number. Utilitarianism requires that we be as concerned with the happiness of others as we are of our own.

> I must repeat, what the assailants of utilitarianism seldom have the justice to acknowledge, that the happiness which forms the utilitarian standard of what is right in conduct, is not the agent's own happiness, but that of all concerned. As between his own happiness and that of others, utilitarianism requires him to be as strictly impartial as a disinterested and benevolent spectator. In the golden rule of Jesus of Nazareth, we read the complete spirit of the ethics of utility.[6]

Mill does continue to maintain that pleasure is the ultimate good and that the greatest good of the greatest number consists in the maximum amount of pleasure and minimum amount of pain. If I seek the good of others, it must be their pleasure that I seek. But here there seems to be some difficulty. Mill argues that the principle cause that makes life unsatisfactory is selfishness and next to that the lack of cultivation of the mind. He further advocates that the educational system encourage the impulse to promote the general welfare in every individual.

What can this mean? The best individual must be the most moral. The most moral individuals are the ones who care about the happiness of others equally with their own. Such persons are most likely to be happy themselves. But surely, love of others and treating their happiness as of equal worth to our own sometimes leads to pain, sacrifice and distress. Mill might answer that the quality of the pleasure we receive in loving, even when it leads to pain, is intrinsically superior to the quality of the pleasure we might receive by acting selfishly. Therefore, we receive greater happiness, not in greater quantity, but in greater quality. But once again, how can we judge quality? Is it not by some standard other than pleasure? Is Mill implicitly saying that something like agape love, not pleasure, is the good? If so, he is asserting something with which every Christian should agree, but it is not hedonism.

Hedonistic Utilitarianism and Culture War

Thus, the implications for cultural conflict may be significantly different depending on whether we are assessing the principles of Bentham or Mill.   Christians, Jews, Muslims and others both fundamentalistic and non-fundamentalistic would disagree with Mill at the base level. They all affirm the foundation of human personhood in a loving God, whereas Mill does not.   They all affirm that human beings are capable of love and to a significant degree our social order both is and ought to be founded on the expression of this capability. Mill would also affirm the possibility and importance of love. Bentham would deny it. None of the religions referred to above would assert that pleasure is the ultimate good.   They all would, however, assert that pleasure is a good and that some pleasures are morally superior to others. At the base level, therefore, there is disagreement. At the principle level, there is both agreement and disagreement. There seems, therefore, to be room for a very significant amount of agreement on the rule and case application level. Utilitarianism as the *ultimate and only principle* seems to be one that most of the worlds religions would deny.   Utilitarianism as one effective means of articulating and implementing basic moral principles some situations seems, however, to be quite consistent with Christian ethics and the ethics of the other world religions. Thus, Christians, Jews, Muslims, both fundamentalist and non-fundamentalist, may from time-to-time find themselves in conflict with a qualitative hedonistic utilitarian because of disagreement at the base level. There seems to be nothing intrinsic to the position that preclude cooperation in every situation. Even with respect to Bentham's philosophy, substantial agreement at the case application level will occur. Furthermore, the greatest threat to fundamentalists and other Christian constituted by Bentham's philosophy seems to be that they will uncritically adopt his egoism as the foundation of their social and economic principles.

Notes

[1] As will be made clear in chapter V, I do not think that the propositions affirming psychological egoism and psychological hedonism are really testable, at least as they are usually presented. They are, therefore, not genuine synthetic a posteriori propositions. See especially pp. 103-115.

[2] One of the best and most detailed treatments of Bentham and the movement he represented is Elie Halevy, *The Growth of Philosophic Radicalism.* For a treatment of the relationship of Bentham to Adam Smith see pages 88-120 of this work.

[3] See Lewis A. Coser, *The Masters of Sociological Thought* 2nd. ed., pp. 572-74.

[4] B. F. Skinner, *Beyond Freedom and Dignity* (New York: Bantam Books, 1971).

[5] John Stuart Mill, *Utilitarianism* in *The English Philosophers From Bacon To Mill,* p. 902.

[6] Ibid.

CHAPTER V

An Evaluation of Egoism, Hedonism and Utilitarianism: Some Essential Questions

As was noted in Chapter IV, egoism, hedonism and utilitarianism are related in the philosophy of Bentham in an interesting way. They also are the primary ingredients that are interwoven into a world view (what the Europeans called a Weltanschauung) which is one of the dominant cultural forces in the Western world. They are not, however, necessarily related either logically or historically. For this reason, they need to be treated as logically distinct positions that are often empirically related in our contemporary culture. Utilitarianism is an ethical perspective that especially deserves serious consideration as one of the contemporary options for defining the meaning of justice in the modern world. In the discussion that follows we will attempt to address separately several questions.

Is psychological egoism true? Is ethical egoism true? Is psychological hedonism true? Is ethical hedonism true? To what extent and in what contexts can we view the hypotheses of the natural and artificial identity of interests as adequately describing the social order? How shall we evaluate utilitarianism as a theory of justice?

The Empirical and Metaphysical Evidence for Psychological Egoism

Before we can adequately examine the question of whether psychological egoism true, we must first be clear about what is being affirmed by the psychological egoist. Secondly, we need to clarify the conditions under which psychological egoism could be proved or disproved. Thirdly, we must ask whether those conditions have been met. Finally, if we conclude that the conditions for conclusive proof have not been met, we need to assess who has the 'burden of proof.' Is the burden of proof on psychological egoists to prove that there thesis is the correct one? Or is the burden of proof on the psychological altruist to prove that psychological altruism is correct and that the psychological egoist is wrong?

Psychological egoists affirm that human beings are 100% selfish. The position of the psychological egoist is that *all* persons are *completely* selfish in their motivation *all* of the time. This is a very strong claim. It is not to be confused with the weaker claims that: (1) All persons are sometimes selfish, (2) That some persons are always selfish, or (3) That all persons in each particular act are always somewhat selfish in motivation. The weaker claims of (1), (2) and (3) are fairly non-controversial and would be agreed to by most persons and most religions. Christians, of course, would exclude Christ from the claim of selfishness. Buddhists would probably exclude the Buddha, etc., but all would agree that all adherents to their various faiths are at least partially selfish.

Psychological egoists also affirm that all human beings are *necessarily* 100% selfish. Psychological egoism, is not just a claim about how persons are motivated. It is not just an empirical claim, falling in the domain of the science of psychology, about the way persons *do* act. It is also a claim about all *possible* motivation for persons. As such, it is a claim falling within the domain of philosophical anthropology and has metaphysical implications. In this respect, it is a clear alternative to Christianity and most if not all of the world's great religions which assume that persons are both capable of love and find their highest fulfillment in expressing love.

We may put this distinction in the context of the emotivist perspective by making the following observations. Insofar as psychological egoists are making a claim about the way persons do act, they are making (on the face of it, at least) a synthetic a posteriori proposition that is testable and therefore meaningful. Insofar as the psychological egoists are making a claim about the ultimate nature of persons, they are making a metaphysical claim that the emotivist would consider meaningless.

If psychological egoism is to be treated as an empirical and therefore a testable claim, there are certain conditions that it must fulfill. We need to specify these conditions and then attempt to determine whether or not some typical arguments brought forth in defense of psychological egoism meet these conditions.

In the first place, we would need to specify the conditions under which we would identify the motive of an action as selfish and the conditions under which we would identify the motive of an action as unselfish. In other words we must define egoism or selfishness.

Secondly, we would need to specify some way of measuring or assessing the motives of our actions and those of others. For these first two conditions to be met the concepts of egoistic behavior and motivation and altruistic behavior and motivation must be defined with sufficient clarity so that they can be distinguished from one another within the framework of an empirical theory.

Thirdly, we would need to conduct an experiment or set of experiments to determine whether in all or in most cases that are investigated scientifically, selfish motivation is the exclusive motivation or is at least a sufficient motivation to explain the action involved. Presumably we would need to conduct tests involving a variety of persons, external circumstances and types of actions.

If our empirical investigation demonstrated in all, or at least in the overwhelming preponderance of cases that the motives of our actions were selfish then we would have evidence for the proposition that psychological egoism is probably true, at least as a descriptive account of the way persons do act.

The evidence for psychological egoism as a descriptive account of the way people do act would then doubtless be taken as constituting evidence for the metaphysical claim that all person are incapable of anything but egoistic motivation.

Let us now turn to the examination of two typical arguments for psychological egoism and attempt to determine whether or not they meet the test of empirical testability. In other words, we will ask whether or not they contain genuine synthetic a posteriori propositions. The first argument we will call 'the argument from self-realization'. The second will be referred to as 'the hidden motives argument'. A genuine synthetic a posteriori proposition is one that can be shown to be true or false by observation. Everything hinges on defining the propositions affirming psychological egoism so that they can be shown to be true or false by empirical investigation. To qualify as a scientific statement a proposition has to be falsifiable. Suppose, however, that we are given an argument such as the following which we will identify as the argument from self-realization.

(1) Even though self concepts differ, everyone has a concept of "self." (2) Different self concepts may include: "being rich," "being athletic," "being sexy," "being tough," or even "being kind and loving," (3) All persons (however confused they may sometimes be) are 100% motivated by a desire to enhance their sense of self. (4) Thus, when Mother Teresa, and other so called loving people, whose sense of self includes being kind and loving are motivated to act in a kind and loving way, they are 100% motivated by a desire to enhance their sense of self. (5) An act motivated by a desire to enhance one's sense of self is selfish. (6) Therefore all persons are 100% motivated by selfishness and psychological egoism is true.

Thus, when Mother Theresa devotes her life to caring for the lepers of Calcutta, she is fulfilling her own conception of her self and deriving satisfaction from this fulfillment. Her motives, therefore are just as egoistic and selfish as the yuppies who are seeking to fulfill their conception of themselves and are finding satisfaction in so doing.

There are two propositions that appear problematic in this argument. The first one is proposition number (3) that asserts that we always act out of a motivation to enhance our sense of self. This seems to preclude self-hate or a motive to self-destruction. It does not, of course, preclude self-destructive behavior. It merely precludes a motivation to self-destructive behavior. A theory that excludes the possibility of self-destructive motivation seems to go against such diverse perspectives as Freudian psychoanalysis and Christian theology.

Let us, for the sake of the argument however, treat proposition number (3) as unproblematic. We are still left with proposition number (5) that treats the concepts "selfishness" and "self-enhancement" or "self-realization" as synonyms. Treating these concepts a synonyms leads to some strange consequences. For example, orthodox Christian theology would claim that the self- concept of Christ at the time of the crucifixion included dying on the cross for the sins of humankind. His death on the cross was, therefore, a direct fulfillment and enhancement of this self-concept. Therefore Christ willingly died on the cross to achieve self-realization as the savior of the world and in so doing was acting out of selfish motives.

Of course, it is not only orthodox Christians that will have difficulties with this perspective. Psychological egoism seems to reduce all possible motivation to selfishness or self destruction and then rejects the possibility of self-destructive motivation. Only egoistic motivation is left. We are then left with no possibility of distinguishing between the motivation of Christ, Ghandi, the secular humanist philosopher Sidney Hook, and Jack the Ripper.

If we grant the egoist the definitions affirmed in proposition number (5) then his case seems to be established. One suspects, however, that we have been subjected to some logical "sleight of hand" here and in fact this is the case. What the proponent of egoism has done is to define egoistic motivation, selfhood, self satisfaction and selfishness in such a way that the propositions affirming egoism are in principle not falsifiable. All motivations are *by definition* egoistic ones. The propositions affirming egoism turn out to be not synthetic a posteriori propositions which are capable of being shown to be true or false by empirical investigation. Given certain assumptions about the impossibility of deliberately self-destructive behavior, the egoist has made egoism *true by definition*. If egoistic motivation is the only possible motivation then, "All motivation is egoistic." is an analytic a priori proposition. The egoist has substituted a set of analytic a priori propositions which masquerade as synthetic a posteriori propositions. But, of course, defining egoism in this way does not prove a thing unless we are prepared to accept this unusual definition.

Psychological egoists might at this point admit that they have not empirically proved egoism to be true but that this concept of egoism is an essential part of a more comprehensive psychological theory which has useful scientific, moral or political purposes. This may be so but I think that it would come as somewhat of a surprise if a concept which *by definition* prevents us from distinguishing between yuppies and Mother Theresa proved to be of moral, political or scientific value. In any case, what we have here is not scientific proof that psychological egoism is true but a recommendation that we define the terms "self-realization" and "selfishness" in an unusual way. In any case, the conditions of empirical testability have not been met.

We will now turn to a second argument that we will identify as the *hidden motives argument.* This argument draws heavily on both common experience and Freudian analysis. In the first place, people often self-consciously lie about their motives. It is certainly often the case that people claim to be interested in the welfare of others when they are quite self consciously merely interested in their own welfare. Many a young man has used the claim of undying love in order to persuade his girl friend to engage in activity which satisfies his short term desires. To be completely fair, many a young woman has talked herself into believing her boy friend's protestations of undying love in order to justify satisfying both his and her short term desires.

This example leads to consideration of another phenomenon with which we are all familiar. Sometimes we even lie to ourselves about our motives. Sometimes we all, young and old, with respect to sex and a variety of other things we want, sincerely believe that we are acting out of love for other human beings. Upon subsequent reflection, however, we conclude that what we thought were unselfish motives were really quite selfish. Our true motives had been hidden, not only from others but from ourselves. What the egoist asserts, of course, is that whenever we or others sincerely believe ourselves to be acting unselfishly that we have 'repressed' our true motives and are quite mistaken. We are really acting from a selfish motivation hidden even from ourselves.

It seems clear that sometimes we are mistaken about our altruistic motivation. The question is, are we always mistaken? The egoist, sometimes drawing upon Freud's elaborate theories of repression and defense, affirms that this is the case. What would it take to settle this dispute between psychological egoism and psychological altruism once the hidden motives argument is introduced?

We can come to a clearer understanding here by looking at the problem posed by the variety of interpretative frameworks within which we sometimes examine human motivation. Let us try to get at this problem by introducing an example from another perspective. Some Christians, fundamentalists and those who would not identify themselves as fundamentalist have claimed that the knowledge of God is pervasive such that even the atheist "knows in his heart" that there is a God. What is meant by such a claim and how could it be shown to be true or false? I doubt that what is intended is that all atheists are self-conscious liars.   More probably what the fundamentalist intends (despite his presumed rejection of Freud) is that atheists are *subconsciously* lying. The Freudian for his part, affirms that the belief in God is the projection of man's superego and that the theist is *subconsciously* lying.   Insofar as the Freudian affirms that man's behavior is *determined* by instinctual drives, the atheistic existentialist Sartre would assert that the Christians are trying to escape responsibility for their behavior by blaming God and that Freudians are trying to evade responsibility for their behavior by blaming biological instincts.   In other words, Sartre would assert, they are both lying in order to escape responsibility for their human freedom.   It would seem that the man who said that there were only three kinds of lies, lies, damned lies, and statistics, underestimated the variety of possible experience in this area.   How might we settle the dispute between Christians, Freudians and Sartrians?   Not, I think, by a simple clearly articulated scientific experiment.

We are dealing here not simply with a dispute about the 'facts' but with three very different interpretive frameworks within which the data is evaluated quite differently.   There is, I believe, ample room for debate between these perspectives, in terms of consistency, coherence, adequacy to deal with the totality of our experience, etc.   I doubt very much, however, if *empirical* discoveries about 'hidden motives' are likely to weigh heavily in the debate although rhetorical charges about hidden motives will doubtless abound.   This is because the very definition of what counts as a hidden motive is determined to a large extent by the interpretive framework within which one is operating, and by the presuppositions about the nature of reality to which one is committed.

How does this relate to the hidden motives argument when it is used in defense of psychological egoism? I think that it is clear that the very concept of hidden motives is a slippery one. This does not mean that it is not a useful concept that may help us come to a deeper understanding of human reality. It does mean, however, that it should not be introduced in an *ad hoc* and careless manner whenever one's perspective on reality encounters difficulties.

It seems that the burden of proof is on the psychological egoists to prove their case. Most people believe that they and their fellows are subject to both egoistic and altruistic motivation. This is the judgment of the common man quite apart from religious or philosophical presuppositions. It is also the judgment of the great religions of the world. It is the judgment of most philosophical perspectives in the history of Western thought. Of course, common perceptions, and religious and philosophical perspectives can be overthrown by reason and evidence. They can be challenged by alternative faith assumptions.

Nevertheless most persons, most religions, and most philosophical perspectives assume that altruistic motivation is possible for human beings. In the face of this fact, it seems that the burden of proof is on the egoist to show otherwise. If egoists claim that psychological egoism is founded on empirical evidence then they should be prepared to demonstrate this by scientific data. If they use the concept of hidden motives then they need to define their experiments with sufficient clarity and care so that the evidence here can be measured. Otherwise, we may suspect that the belief in psychological egoism is like the Christian's belief that human beings are made in the image of God, an article of faith rather than a scientifically validated assertion. Of course, egoists have as much right to make faith affirmations as Christians, but affirmations of faith whoever they are made by should not be passed off as science.

The two arguments examined above are doubtless not the only arguments that can be advanced to demonstrate the truth of psychological egoism. They are, however, two very common ones. Thus, it seems that at the very least, it is difficult to show that the arguments from self-realization and hidden motives meet the test of empirical testability. It is up to the psychological egoist to reformulate these arguments in a more rigorous form or to introduce new ones. In the mean time, the case for psychological egoism will have to be considered not to have been made.

The Case for Ethical Egoism

There are two arguments for ethical egoism that we need to consider. The first is the argument from psychological egoism which we have been considering. The second is the argument from utilitarianism. We will take these both up in the following paragraphs. First, let us consider the argument from psychological egoism that is stated immediately below.

(1) All persons always act only from exclusively selfish motives. (2) The fact that all persons act only from exclusively selfish motives proves that all persons are capable of acting only from exclusively selfish motives. (3) Since, people cannot be morally required to act in ways that are impossible for them, this proves that all moral theories that claim that persons ought to act from a motivation of love are false. (4) The only remaining alternative is to claim that all persons ought to act from selfish motivation. (5) Therefore, ethical egoism is true.

We may critique the argument stated above by examining each of the premises cited. As I have argued above, the basis of premise one seems to be weak. Many people, seem to act from motives that are at least partially altruistic. Secondly, it might also be argued that even if (1) were true that (2) does not follow. Premise number (2) is a metaphysical statement about the ultimate nature of personhood. Human selfishness might be explained by pervasive ignorance, deep-seated prejudice, or the 'fall' into sin. For example, if it were shown that all southerners before the Civil War were racists, that would not prove that Southerners were incapable of rejecting their racism. It would still be possible that under the right social historical circumstances, Southerners could overcome racism. Proposition number (3) claims that it is not possible to attribute moral blame to individuals for failing to love if they fail to be capable of love. This seems intuitively obvious. I think that even it is problematic but will not take the time to consider counter arguments here. Proposition number (4), however, does not seem to follow from number (3). We might recognize that humans are incapable of love but regard this state as deplorable or even disgusting. For example, we might recognize that an individual is mentally ill and incapable of refraining from raping infants when given the opportunity. It would not follow that the individual ought to act in this way. We may not blame persons for actions that they cannot control.   We still do not claim that they are under a moral obligation to act out their uncontrollable passions. Secondly, if it could be shown that all persons are completely selfish as is claimed in number (2). The move from (2) to (4) would have to deal with the emotivist argument that ethical propositions are untestable.

A second argument for ethical egoism is the *argument from utilitarianism.* This is summarized below.

> (1) actions, rules, policies, and laws that attempt to implement altruistic motivation do more harm than good. (2) actions, rules, policies, and laws that attempt to implement egoistic motivation lead to the greatest good for the greatest number. (3) Therefore, every one ought to act from selfish motives so that the greatest good for the greatest number may be achieved.

This argument for ethical egoism based on utilitarianism is more cogent than the argument from psychological egoism. It is also, as we shall see, a more popular one. For example, let us suppose that I am capable of acting from motives and in accord with rules that focus on my own good and ignore the good of others. Let us also suppose that I am capable of acting from motives and in accord with rules that take the good of others into account as well as my own good. In other words, I am capable of acting from both selfish and unselfish motives. These assumptions reject psychological egoism.

Let us further suppose that I conclude that every time I act from unselfish motives and in accord with rules, policies, and laws that regard the good of others that just the opposite of my intentions occur. Rather than being helped, others are hurt. Let us further suppose that every time I act from self-regarding motives and in accord with laws that ignore the good of others, that rather than being hurt, others are helped. Let us further suppose that what is true for me is true for everyone else.   Love injures.   Selfishness helps.   Under these circumstances, it would seem, paradoxically, that out of love for my fellow human beings I should attempt always to act from selfish motives and encourage everyone else to do the same.

If this is a paradox, however, it is no greater a paradox than the argument that comes from numerous religious leaders of all faiths. "If you wish to achieve self-realization and happiness live a life characterized by sacrificial love."

Are the twin assumptions that love injures and selfishness helps empirically true? Are they always true? Are they usually true? Are they sometimes true? Are they true in some social domains (like business) and false in others (like family, church, health care, education, and personal friendships)? What about government? What about government's role in domestic relationships? What about government's role in foreign relationships?

I will not take time to attempt to answer the questions raised above. I raise them to observe that the argument for ethical egoism based on utilitarianism is complex. Most of us would reject very quickly the thesis that egoism in all domains and relationships always or usually leads to the greatest good of the greatest number. It is an assumption that is common (if controversial) in business. Laissez faire capitalism is based on the assumption of a natural identity of interests that requires egoism as a primary motivation. Our legal system assumes that its attorneys (for a fee) are free, even obligated, to represent clients without regard to their guilt or innocence. The legal system guarantees the greatest justice for the greatest number. The judge is only obligated to see that the rules of the system are obeyed. Defense attorneys are equally obligated to defend to the best of their ability a guilty or innocent client. The prosecuting attorney need only consider whether or not there is sufficient evidence to bring the individual to trial. Only the jury need be directly concerned with guilt or innocence in any particular case.

The descriptions given above of a free market economy and a legal system that assumes that the participants are concerned with due process and not with truth may be over drawn. These are, however, common assumptions about the way these systems do or should work. They rest on the assumptions that Bentham made that in the case of business we have a natural identity of interests and that in the case of the judicial system we have created an artificial identity of interests. A more detailed exploration whether or to what degree they are true will have to await our examination of the assumptions concerning natural and artificial identity of interests.

The Case for Psychological Hedonism

The arguments for psychological and ethical hedonism parallel those of psychological and ethical egoism. Whether psychological hedonism is true depends a great deal on our definition of pleasure. Can we take terms like pleasure, happiness, joy and satisfaction to be synonyms in every context or are there contexts in which this is inappropriate. This is a dispute involving words but it is not just a dispute *about* words. It is, after all, appropriate to treat words as synonyms if they refer to the same type of phenomena, but not otherwise. The argument for psychological hedonism frequently rests on the assumption that the terms 'satisfaction' and 'pleasure' can be taken as synonyms.

> (1) Whenever we achieve a goal which we have been striving for we experience satisfaction. (2) Satisfaction is a synonym for pleasure. (3) Therefore, whenever we achieve a goal we have been striving for, we experience pleasure. (4) Our real goal is the pleasure associated with the achievement of the various goals we set for ourselves. (5) Therefore, psychological hedonism is true.

This argument contains two assumptions that are problematic. Is satisfaction a synonym for pleasure? Is pleasure the goal of all of our activities or is it the by-product of achieving goals that we have set for ourselves on other grounds? We will consider these questions one at a time.

It seems clear that pleasure is not a synonym for satisfaction. J.S. Mill, of course, recognized the distinctions among various forms of pleasure when he insisted that there are different kinds of pleasure and that some kinds were qualitatively better than other kinds. Is it useful to go beyond Mill and recognize not only different kinds of pleasure but also different kinds of satisfaction? It is useful to distinguish among different kinds of satisfaction if it helps us more effectively to get at the reality that we experience. Our vocabulary should fit reality rather than the other way around.

We could, of course, agree to call every type of satisfaction pleasure. We could also agree to call every color blue. We could agree to designate poetry, drama, novels, painting and sounds having rhythm and melody as "music". The latter is a usage similar to Plato's use of the term music. The question is whether such usage helps us to better describe reality or whether such usage blurs important distinctions in the world of our experience. It seems to me that treating the satisfaction that a Mother Theresa gets in caring for the lepers of India as identical with the satisfaction that comes from eating a hot fudge sundae is like calling every color blue or having only one word like music instead of several to describe the arts. It may emphasize important similarities but it also blurs important differences.

One way to test the use of our language is to ask ourselves questions that can be evaluated in terms of our own experience. Do I think the satisfaction that comes through winning a football game, the satisfaction from prayer, the satisfaction from falling in love, the satisfaction from helping others, and the satisfaction from eating a hot fudge sundae are sufficiently alike to identify them as all at bottom the same? Or do I regard these satisfactions as sufficiently different so that a richer vocabulary is needed to describe them?

It also seems to be case that pleasure is not always the goal of our actions. What about the argument that our real goal is always the pleasure that comes from achieving some designated goal rather than achieving the goal itself? This assertion also seems to me to distort our perception of reality. If I don't first have winning as a goal, then there is no pleasure in winning. If I don't perceive feeding the hungry as a desirable thing, then I will derive no pleasure from feeding them even if I should happen to do so. The pleasure of achievement, at least with respect to most of our activities, seems to be inextricably bound with our initial perception of the desirability of the goal in the first place. Thus, Mother Theresa would probably derive limited pleasure from a significant rise in her own personal material standard of living. The yuppie would doubtless derive limited pleasure from an increase in his wealth if all of that increase in wealth had to be devoted to the alleviation of the suffering of the poor.

Once again, J.S. Mill was perceptive. He recognized something that he called the hedonic paradox. This was the strange phenomena that one was more likely to gain pleasure if one pursued something else. I will gain the pleasure of wisdom more effectively if I pursue not the pleasure of wisdom but wisdom. I will be more likely to gain the pleasure of wealth if I pursue not the pleasure of wealth but wealth itself. Mill didn't quite know how to deal with this paradox. It seems best dealt with by abandoning psychological hedonism altogether. We don't all always seek only pleasure. We seek other things and pleasure is simply the by-product of achieving those other things that are the primary object of our desire.

The Case for Ethical Hedonism

The strongest argument for ethical hedonism is the argument from psychological hedonism. If all persons can seek only pleasure there is a strong presumption that, for humans at least, pleasure is the only good thing. If psychological hedonism turns out to be false or at least unsubstantiated, then this strong presumption for ethical hedonism is undermined.

It is, of course, logically possible that human beings do seek other things than pleasure but that pleasure is still the only good thing among those things that they do seek. It is difficult to imagine, however, a credible defense of ethical hedonism that is not founded on the presumption of the truth of psychological hedonism

Cultural Conflict and the Assumption of a Natural and Artificial Identity of Interests

There are many situations in which we regard the assumption of the identity of interests as unproblematic. Our discussion below, however, will demonstrate that although the concept appears to be unproblematic that this is frequently far from the case.

In many situations we all assume that a natural identity of interests exists. Therefore, in many situations we adopt in good conscience a self-regarding rather than a self consciously altruistic perspective because we assume that an identity of interests exists.

For example, for a great deal of our behavior in the market place, the only rational course of action seems to be to assume an egoistic posture confident that as we pursue our own self interest that the interest of others will be helped or at least not harmed by our actions. When I choose to buy brand X rather than brand Y, I normally think only of my own preferences and economic situation and not of the greatest good of the greatest number or of the good of some particular group with whom I have no direct contact. There are exceptions to this, of course. I may choose not to buy from companies which are heavily invested in companies that encourage the poor in underdeveloped countries to forsake breast feeding in order to buy their baby formula, even though I regard the price or quality of their product as superior to my other options. I may boycott a product that is advertised on a television program that I consider immoral. But these are specific exceptions for a specific moral purpose. The norm for most people, including both fundamentalists and secular humanists, when they go to the grocery store or to make most purchases in our economy, is to assume that because of a natural identity of interest, egoistic motivation is an acceptable moral posture in the specific context under consideration. In other specific contexts, different assumptions are made. When the humanist responds to pleas from charitable organizations it is assumed that the appropriate moral posture is an altruistic one. The fundamentalist makes similar assumptions when responding to pleas to contribute a tithe to spread the gospel or to feed the poor.

There is no necessary logical connection between Christian theological conservatism and secular political conservatism and the natural identity of interests. There is, however, a sociological connection such that many fundamentalists tend also to be political conservatives. The assumptions being made here are related, I believe, to what Max Weber has identified as the "Protestant ethic"[1] I will not take the time here to give a full exposition of Weber's thesis but a portion of that thesis asserted that in the minds of Protestant Christians it came to be assumed that there was an association between Christian faith, hard work and material blessing such that material blessing came to be regarded as a sign of spiritual and ethical virtue. What I wish to point out here is that someone who consciously or unconsciously makes this assumption is really also assuming that in our society, at least, *among the spiritually and ethically virtuous*, there is a natural identity of interests. It would seem to follow that a natural conflict of interests exists only among those who are not spiritually and ethically virtuous. If one makes these sorts of assumptions, then there is little motivation to change the structure of society in order to insure an artificial identity of interests. If identity of interests already exists for the virtuous then the only proper and loving thing to do is to convert, educate, change or transform in some way the non-virtuous individuals into virtuous ones. This means, for many fundamentalists, that altruism is the proper moral stance when it comes to evangelism while egoism is the rational and moral stance with respect to one's activity in the market place. If we add to this the assumption that God wants his children to enjoy the pleasures that come from material blessing, then we can assume that egoistic hedonism is the proper moral stance with respect to one's activity in the market place.

Fundamentalist espousal of a natural identity of interest is probably, in part, a reaction to secular humanist espousal of the possibility of an artificial identity of interest. Insofar as fundamentalists (and other Christians) consciously or unconsciously adopt these assumptions, they are in danger of espousing in a curious and selective way a position which is similar to Bentham's in many respects. Bentham's perspective of course is clearly a non-Christian one which fundamentalists would identify as a variety of secular humanism. Their espousal of a position similar to his may come about because of a preoccupation with avoiding what they regard as a worse variety of secular humanism. This variety of secular humanism assumes that human nature is basically good and that evil is a product not of a sinful nature but of a badly arranged social structure. A secular humanist argument for the possibility of an artificial identity of interests can be articulated in terms of these assumptions in the manner that I have depicted below.

(1)Human beings are basically good (by which is meant that they are both rational and not inherently self-destructive or destructive of fellow human beings. (2) If this true, then the source of evil must be our social reality. In other words, the human condition suffers from social alienation rather than alienation from God. (3) Although there is not a natural identity of interests with respect to our present social reality, it is possible to create a new social reality which will solve the problem of evil both individual and social. In other words, the creation of an identity of interests is possible. (4) The creation of this identity of interests will not only transform social reality but also human character. (5) Therefore, humanity can be transformed (the fundamentalist would say redeemed) through social reform.

My intent here is not to critique in detail these assumptions but to lay them bare in order to make possible further analysis. I will, however, make a few observations. In the first place, not all positions which the fundamentalist would identify as secular humanist assume that the problem of evil is exclusively a social one. Freudianism comes to mind most readily in this regard. Secondly, the fundamentalist or other Christians need not assume that it is only individuals which have fallen into sin and that therefore individuals but not social structures are in need of redemption. It is perfectly consistent with a quite conservative Christian theology to assume that the problem of evil is both an individual and a social one. As a matter of fact, this is what the fundamentalist does assume when condemning communism, becoming politically active by joining groups such as the Christian Coalition, seeking to stamp out pornography in the community, regulate the sale of alcohol and drugs, etc. It is also what is assumed when fundamentalists take the gospel to a culture which practices magic, polygamy, cannibalism, etc.

Thus, there is nothing in the logic of either the secular humanist position or the fundamentalist position that necessarily requires that either one be politically conservative or liberal. There are, however, historical and sociological forces that have shaped both movements in opposite directions on political and economic issues as well as metaphysical ones. Were the division only metaphysical and not also political and economic, we doubtless would be talking about cultural conflict but not about a 'culture war.'

The Ambiguity of the Term 'Interests' and the Non-Testability of the Concepts of Natural and Artificial Identity of Interests

Careful reading of the previous sections will indicate the difficulty in determining whether there is an identity of interests without examining basic metaphysical assumptions about the nature of persons and the cosmos. We do not seem to be able to articulate simple straight forward synthetic a posteriori propositions on this topic. Some careful analysis of language will indicate why this is so.

The first difficulty is that the term 'interests' is an ambiguous one. My 'interests' can mean simply that which I am interested in possessing or consuming. It can also mean that which is in my 'best interest'. Whether or not you think that what I am interested in is in my best interest depends upon assumptions about the nature of the world, the nature of personhood and the nature of the good. There is obviously an identity of interests (in one sense of identity of interests) between the illegal drug dealer and the consumer of illegal drugs. One wants to sell and the other wants to buy.

Our society has concluded, however, that it is not in the 'real interests' of either society or the drug consumer to obtain and use various sorts of drugs. But we also have legal drugs. Both alcohol and tobacco are physically and psychologically addictive drugs. Each year the manufacturers of these drugs spend millions attempting to convince us that if we truly want the "good life" then we ought to be interested in the purchase and consumption of these drugs. In other words, it is in our interest to be interested in them. Other segments of society in the form of counter advertising from voluntary organizations, denunciations by religious groups and governmental restrictions on the advertising, sale and distribution of these drugs have challenged this definition of 'the good life'.

This was a problem, that given his assumptions, Bentham did not have. His assumption of psychological and ethical egoistic hedonism made it possible for him to assume that the *psychological* interests of individuals were in their best *moral* interest provided that individuals were armed with a reliable social science methodology. If, however, two parties to a dispute come to their disagreement with fundamentally different conceptions of the good, then solution to the problem may become impossible. The determination of whether or not there exists a natural identity of interests or the possibility of the creation of an artificial identity of interests at an acceptable price (in terms of what other values must be compromised or sacrificed) cannot be treated as simply an empirical question.

Solution to the problem of identity of interests is, however, not necessarily insolvable in all cases. Should we assume from the above that since fundamentalists and secular humanists disagree on their conceptions of the good that there is no possibility of there ever agreeing on the existence or the possibility of an identity of interests in society? We can assume this only if we also assume that their conceptions of the good are so totally different that they do not overlap at any point. As a matter of fact, as we have observed earlier, two ethical theories may differ on the base level while agreeing on the level of principles, rules or cases. The converse is also true. There may be agreement on the level of bases and disagreement on the level of principles, rules or cases. There are doubtless situations where individuals agree on the base, principle and rule level while disagreeing at the case level. On the other hand, we may find agreement on the case level where there is disagreement on everything else. The thrust of our previous analysis is to show that the basis of agreement between fundamentalists and secular humanists along with those of us who do not identify with either camp, may be complicated but that it is not in principle impossible. This suggests that culture wars, however likely, are not a logical necessity.

Utilitarianism and Justice: Some Conceptual Distinctions

Does utilitarianism provide us with an adequate definition of what we mean by justice? If utilitarianism does not define justice, does it provide a criterion for the creation of a legal and ethical system which would always or usually lead to a just social order? I think the answer to both of these questions is no, at least not without the introduction of some additional principles. Before we proceed to the criticism of utilitarianism it will be helpful to make some further distinctions which we have not introduced up to this point. These are the concepts of teleological and deontological ethics and the distinction between act and rule utilitarianism.

The term 'teleological' comes from the Greek words 'telos' which means end and the word 'logos' which as we have come to see means 'theory of'. *A teleological ethic is one which determines what is right in terms of the production of good consequences or ends.* It requires us to first determine what is *good*. Only then, can we determine what is *right*. An action is morally right if it produces good consequences. It is held to be morally bad if it produces bad consequences. If we are choosing between two acts both of which produce some good and some bad consequences then, the morally preferable act is the one which produces the most good and the least amount of bad consequences. utilitarianism is a species of teleological ethic since it affirms that acts are moral or immoral depending on their consequences. Utilitarianism, however, adds a distributional requirement. It is the greatest good *for the greatest number* which is the criterion for a good act. We will examine the implications of this more fully below, after we have discussed the meaning of a deontological ethic.

The term 'deontological' comes from the Greek words 'logos' and 'deon' which means of necessity or binding. *Deontological theories assert that certain acts are right or wrong regardless of their good or evil consequences. For them the right is not dependent on the good but the other way around.* For example, one might affirm that murder is wrong not because the consequences of refraining from murder are the maximizing of good and the minimizing of evil (defined as pleasure, wisdom, wealth, power, etc.) but because God has commanded that we not murder or that we have some direct moral intuition that murder is wrong, etc.

The terms 'teleological' and 'deontological' are roughly synonymous with the terms 'consequentialism' (for ethical theories that determine what is right based on consequences and 'non-consequentialism' (for ethical theories that determine what is right without referring to consequences). All utilitarian theories are consequentialist theories. A theory may be consequentialist, however, without being utilitarian. For example, if my ethical theory affirms that I should do that which is for my greatest good, regardless of what is good for the greatest number, then I am a consequentialist but not a utilitarian.

Most of us are what William Frankena has described as 'mixed deontologists'.[2] That is to say, that we appeal to teleological (or consequentialist) principles when making some moral decisions but deontological (or non-consequentialist) principles when making others. For example, suppose that we had excellent reason to believe that if the state were to put to death certain individuals for crimes that they had not committed that this would lead to a dramatic reduction in the murder rate which would save more innocent lives than would be forfeited by the state's action. A pure teleologist would have to judge the action of the state in this instance as morally right. A deontologist might well argue that it is morally wrong for the state to knowingly take innocent lives regardless of the good which would be achieved. This same mixed deontologist, however, might argue that the allies were morally justified in going to war against Hitler even though this inevitably resulted in the allies being responsible for the taking of innocent lives. Some deontologists, however, are pacifists who would be prepared to argue that war is always a moral evil and that going to war in "a good cause" even if it maximizes the good does not ever make war morally right.

Rule utilitarianism affirms that we should always devise and obey rules which, if implemented in society, would result in the realization of the greatest good for the greatest number. Act utilitarianism affirms that we should always act in every situation (even if it means breaking some rules) in a manner that contributes to the greatest good of the greatest number. In certain situations there may be a possible conflict between act and rule utilitarianism. This conflict has been turned into popular drama in the form of the "Dirty Harry" films starring Clint Eastwood. It is also at issue in the controversy over euthanasia.

Whatever other reasons we may have for being against unlawful taking of human life most of us would agree that the implementation of rules prohibiting the taking of human life work for the greatest good of the greatest number. We doubtless also would be inclined to agree that in certain situations the greatest good of the greatest number would be achieved if those rules were broken.

We sometimes try to alleviate this conflict between act and rule utilitarianism by developing *rules* for determining when there should be exceptions to the rules. At times, however, there is no way to resolve the conflict and one must choose between affirming act or rule utilitarianism, at least in a particular situation. Despite the possible conflict, it is obvious that if we are trying to make just laws for society we must choose the standpoint of rule utilitarianism however much we may be attracted to act utilitarianism in particular situations.

Utilitarianism and Justice: Problems Associated with the Implementation of Rule Utilitarianism

The three most basic problems associated with the implementation of a rule utilitarian ethic are the problem of being able to predict the future, the problem of defining the good and the problem of equality. We will deal with these in the order they have been mentioned but will spend the bulk of our time on the last problem since it is the most serious one.

The problem of predicting the future is a problem which rule utilitarianism shares with act utilitarianism and, indeed, with all consequentialist theories. Whenever we choose to act based on the consequences of our actions we are always attempting to predict the future, since before we make our choice the consequences are always in the future and therefore uncertain. If we predict wrongly, the results of our action may be disastrous. Nowhere is this problem more evident than in our attempts to deal with the unintended consequences of legislation passed by our governments. We are constantly passing laws to correct the results of previous legislation which in turn was passed to correct the unintended results of other laws.

The non-consequentialist does not have this problem or at least not to the same degree. Non-consequentialists act, obey or formulate rules because they are *right* not because of predictions that these actions or rules will have good consequences. Although prediction is a serious problem, it seems to me to not be fatal for consequentialist theories as long as we are dealing with situations where we can predict the consequences of our actions or rules with a high degree of probability. Of course, when we reach the point where predictability comes close to randomness, then consequentialist theories become useless.

I might add parenthetically here, that the lack of predictability is an argument that is often used by political conservatives in defense of a laissez faire economic theory and against social welfare programs. Political conservatives need not argue that every thing is well and getting better. They may simply argue that government is incapable of either predicting or controlling social forces to a sufficient degree to make things better.

The problem of defining the good is the second major problem with consequentialist theories. This second problem with rule utilitarianism is also one that it shares with other teleological theories. How shall we define the good? Bentham attempted to solve this problem by identifying one single thing as good, namely pleasure. But what if there is more than one thing which is good? What if pleasure, wisdom, athletic excellence, aesthetic creativity and aesthetic enjoyment, scientific progress, ecological balance, the preservation of life, the minimization of pain, creative work, creative leisure, security, adventure, etc. are all good? As individuals and as societies our resources are finite such that we must sometimes choose between these goods. We can and do, of course, make choices among these goods randomly, by political conflict, by letting the market place decide, etc. But use of these methods does not presuppose any *moral* criteria for our choices.

The development of a set of moral criteria for choosing among these goods would seem to entail commitment to one or more ends which stand outside the teleological chain of ends. For example, I may balance my choices among goods on the principle that the *ultimate* good is the will of God, the glorification of the state, the development of the human race, the preservation of the species, the achievement of ecological balance, the realization of individualism among the citizens of society, etc. Whichever of these principles, one chooses will have to be defined since people differ in their views concerning what it means to do the will of God, achieve the glorification of the state, etc.

But even once we have spelled out what we mean by these concepts, it would seem to be the case that we must justify our choice of ultimate ends by criteria which in themselves are not consequentialist but non-consequentialist in character. The person who claims that "one ought to serve the will of God" does not usually add a reason like "because it will bring you pleasure". Conversely, if I hold pleasure to be the ultimate good, then I do not affirm that I ought to seek pleasure because it is God's will for me to do so.

If we are to choose among the many things we call good, then we must have at least one thing which we *ought* to choose above others not because it leads to some other good thing but simply because it is a good which *we ought to seek above all others*. Thus, it seems that all consequentialist systems of ethics must rest upon at least one non-consequentialist judgment.

The most serious objection to utilitarianism as a theory of justice is the problem of equality. For example, let us suppose that we have solved the problems associated with predicting the consequences of our legislative and social structure, and we have arrived at agreement on criteria for making societal choices among the various things which we call good. Let us imagine three societies with one hundred members each. The first two each have a total of one thousand U's (utiles) for an average of ten U's per person. The third society has two thousand U's for an average of twenty U's per person. Let us further suppose that the distribution of these U's is as follows:

1. *Society #1: Total 1000 U's. Each member has 10 U's. Average 10 U's per member.*
2. *Society #2: Total 1000 U's. 80 members have 12 U's each. 20 members have 2 U's each. Average 10 U's per member.*
3. *Society #3: Total 2000 U's. 80 members have 24.75 U's each. 20 members have 1 U each. Average, 20 U's per member.*

If we are trying to distinguish between societies #1 and #2 by using the utilitarian criteria for justice, we receive no help at all. By utilitarian criteria, they seem to be equally just. Furthermore, society #3 seems to be the most just of the three because the *average* utility is greatest in society #3. But society #3 has the greatest amount of inequality of the three societies. Critics of utilitarianism have consistently regarded the failure of utilitarianism to take adequate account of the problem of equality as a serious deficiency in the theory.

What is the utilitarian answer to these objections? Utilitarians respond that, of course equality is important but that it is already taken account of in the utilitarian system. In the first place, the principle of equality is built into the system in that the good of everyone is taken into account equally in the initial calculation. For example, for Bentham, the pleasure of the poorest and least gifted in society is calculated equally with the pleasure of the richest and wisest. Since presumably, in any given society there are more people of average or below wealth and ability than the other way around, there is a built in tendency in the system to treat all equally. Secondly, equality itself is viewed by the utilitarians not as a separate principle distinct from other things which we call good. Equality itself is a good (although not the only good) which must be figured in our calculus of the greatest good. Therefore equality is not in principle ignored in the utilitarian calculus as its critics suppose. Thirdly, the utilitarian would object that the social order is so arranged that the models which have been introduced above don't occur in the empirical world. In short, it is empirically the case that productivity and equality vary proportionately. Thus, the society with the greatest amount of liberty and equality is empirically likely to be the society that is most productive of utiles. The most productive society will be the society with the greatest average utility which is what we mean by the greatest good of the greatest number.

These and other objections will be taken up more fully when we come to our consideration of the theory of justice of John Rawls. I would note here that this third defense made by utilitarians rests on the familiar assumption of a *natural identity of interests*. Utilitarians argue that there is a natural identity of interests such that there can be no real conflict between an increase in equality and a rise in productivity which results in the rise of average utility. I think that it is perhaps not too much of an over simplification to say that a chief difference between utilitarianism and its critics is that utilitarians believe in this natural identity of interests and its critics do not believe in it or at least view this assumption with deep suspicion.

Summary: Cultural Conflict and Egoism, Hedonism, and Utilitarianism

It seems on the face of it that neither fundamentalists nor secular humanists can consistently be either egoists or hedonists.

Fundamentalists cannot be an egoists since their viewpoint requires them to affirm both that Jesus Christ in his death on the cross offers us the prime example of agape or sacrificial love and that all persons are both capable of and enjoined to exhibit this love. They cannot be hedonists since presumably the highest good is not the pleasure of the individual but the glory of God.

What about secular humanists? I think it safe to say that most thinkers who would self-consciously embrace the banner of secular humanism would be inclined to reject both egoism and hedonism. Humanism as a social ethic affirms humanity as giving expression to the ultimate value in the universe. As such, it calls upon its adherents to work on behalf of and even to sacrifice in order to help other human beings and to enhance the existence of human values in the universe. Whatever else this is, it is not egoism. Humanists also, it seems to me, should be inclined to reject hedonism. They certainly would be inclined to reject quantitative hedonism. Humanists view persons as having rich and varied possibilities. They object to theism, including fundamentalism not primarily because they think theism inhibits human pleasure but because it inhibits the development of human potential in all areas. For them, persons have moral and spiritual capabilities which far transcend the mere ability to experience pleasure and pain.

This comparison has some interesting implications for cultural conflict. Fundamentalism and secular humanism are assumed to be polar opposites, at least in many respects. They seem to agree, however, in their rejection of both egoism and hedonism as ultimate values in the universe. This agreement does not, of course, guarantee that adherents to these positions will agree on all or even many concrete issues. It does suggest, however, that on some issues their may be a basis for dialogue about culture rather than cultural war.

What about utilitarianism? Here there seems to be both incompatibility and compatibility. Utilitarianism is a species of consequentialist ethic. The right is defined in terms of the maximization of the good. Fundamentalism, on the other hand, seems clearly to be associated with a species of deontological or non-consequentialist ethic. The good is defined in terms of the right. Still this is a matter of degree. I have suggested above that utilitarians must make at least one non-teleological judgment. "You ought always to maximize the good and minimize evil" appears to be a deontological judgment. So it is with "You ought always to maximize the greatest good for the greatest number". The fundamentalist, on the other hand, doubtless would defend the morality of obeying traffic laws, refraining from consumption of alcohol, drugs, etc., because of the good consequences of doing so.

One of the characteristics of fundamentalist ethical theories, however, is the significant number of deontological judgments which they contain, relative to non-fundamentalist theories. Furthermore, when pushed in a debate in the defense of ethical principles, the fundamentalist is inclined to more quickly appeal to deontological principles than thinkers arguing from other premises. For example, the fundamentalist may defend the rule "Thou shalt not commit adultery" on the basis of the good consequences of the individual or everybody refraining from this activity. When pushed, however, the real reason is that the fundamentalist believes that God in his Word has *commanded* us to refrain from adultery. If this is indeed the case, then showing that good consequences sometimes or usually or always follow from committing adultery would not persuade the fundamentalist.

Not all attempts to develop an ethical theory within the framework of a Christian perspective affirm the existence of numerous deontological principles or rules. An extreme case of the opposite type is Joseph Fletcher's defense of situation ethics.[3] Fletcher asserts that there is one and only one fundamental principle that Christian ethics need take into account. Christians have a responsibility to maximize agape love in every situation. Fletcher would apparently be willing to grant that the ten commandments if followed tend to maximize agape love. Since this is true, they are useful 'rules of thumb' which it would be wise to follow most of the time. But all they are, are 'rules of thumb' which ought to be ignored in any situation where adherence to them fails to maximize the good, namely agape love.

Fletcher, of course, is no fundamentalist.[4] Many Christians, however, other than fundamentalists, and many who would consider themselves secular humanists would tend to think that Fletcher goes too far. Nevertheless, many Christians who would reject Fletcher's viewpoint as an over simplified and distorted attempt to develop a Christian ethic would be willing to admit a significant consequentialist dimension into their ethics. Fundamentalists, since they tend to be non-consequentialists rather than consequentialists have trouble introducing utilitarian principles into their ethics. For utilitarianism is, of course, one variety of consequentialists ethic.

I think it is important to mention one major exception to the immediately previous remarks. Fundamentalists tend to be non-consequentialists with respect to their development of personal ethics. With respect to social ethics, many fundamentalists have been inclined to embrace a politically conservative ideology which justifies laissez faire economic policy on utilitarian (and egoistic) assumptions which go back to Adam Smith. This seems to me to entail a fundamental inconsistency with respect to the development of fundamentalist ethics.

Utilitarians, do, however, argue that the ultimate criteria for ethical decision making must go beyond egoism and take into consideration the greatest good of the greatest number. This altruistic dimension to utilitarianism would tend to make it compatible with Christian ethics of various types, including fundamentalist varieties.

With respect to utilitarianism, I think humanists would be divided. There seems to me to be nothing in the humanist's premises that would necessarily preclude or require utilitarianism. Secular humanists would be concerned about all persons being treated with respect and dignity. The charge against utilitarianism that it allows a minority to be used for the benefit of the majority would be a matter of concern for them given their basic moral commitments.

Egoism, Hedonism, Utilitarianism, and Cultural Conflict

I think that there is no question that egoism and hedonism are two of the significant cultural forces in our time. Fundamentalism and secular humanism are commonly thought to be polar opposites in the culture wars that are currently taking place. It is also clear, however, that neither fundamentalists nor secular humanists (insofar as they are consistent with their basic assumptions) are likely to be attracted to or comfortable with these cultural forces. Thus, here there is at least one point where they are potential allies in the present cultural conflict.

Increasing cultural pluralism, especially ethical pluralism makes the efficacy of utilitarianism in solving cultural conflict more problematic. Utilitarianism calls those laws just that contribute to the greatest good of the greatest number. This gives useful guidance, however, only if we can determine and agree on that which is good. Thus, a society that cannot agree on at least a working definition of the good will not find utilitarianism a useful criteria for defining justice. Fundamentalism and secular humanism agree that exclusive concern with the individual self is not the good. They probably can agree that an exclusive preoccupation with pleasure is not the good. They disagree, however, on a great many things. Where they overlap in their definition of the good they may be allies against egoistic hedonism despite their very different foundations and methodological approaches. This, of course, assumes that they could become capable of avoiding the demonization of each other's positions sufficiently to recognize those issues where they do hold certain values in common.

Notes

[1] The relationship of conservative political thought and conservative Protestant belief has deep roots. There is also an extensive literature on the subject that bears careful reading by anyone who wants to go beyond the superfical treatment found in the contemporary media and political dialogue. See Max Weber, *The Protestant Ethic and the Spirit of Capitalism*. For a critique of the so called Weber Thesis see the classic by R.H. Tawney, *Religion and The Rise of Capitalism*. An interesting series of essays on both the historical roots and application of the Weber thesis to the problem of modernization can be found in *The Protestant Ethic and Modernization*, ed. by S.N. Eisenstadt.

[2] William K. Frankena, *Ethics*, pp. 43-45.

[3] Se Joseph Fletcher, *Situation Ethics: The New Morality*.

[4] As a matter of fact, although he is a Christian theologian, he also endorses the principles of secular humanism. See *Secular Humanist Declaration, p.26.*

CHAPTER VI

IMMANUAL KANT: REASON, SCIENCE, FREEDOM AND MORAL OBLIGATION

Why Study Kant?

Immanual Kant (1724-1804) is one of the most important figures in the history of philosophy and in the intellectual history of the West in general. We study him here, however, because he illumines many of the fundamental problems that anyone trying to think in a critical and systematic way about ethics must face.

In the first place, his ethical theory forms a sharp contrast to all of the ethical positions that we have studied thus far. Kant affirms the possibility of rational universal ethical norms that enable individuals to exercise control over there desires and determine morally right action *independently of any consequences*.

Secondly, one interpretation of the contemporary ethical theorist John Rawls, who will be considered in the next chapter, sees Rawls as affirming a Kantian view over against utilitarianism. Increasingly, on the contemporary scene, the debate about a theory of social justice is viewed as a choice between Rawls' revival of social contract theory which is heavily indebted to Kant and some form of utilitarianism.

Thirdly, Kant is one of the most important representatives of an ethic which stresses moral obligation to rules as contrasted with an ethic which emphasizes the development of virtuous individuals. This latter 'ethics of virtue' looks back to Aristotle for inspiration and sees Kant's emphasis on an 'ethics of rules' as representing a bad turn in the thinking about ethics in the Western world. Both Rawls and the ethics of virtue will be considered in later chapters.

Finally, this is a book about cultural conflict and ethical theory. Perhaps the single most significant source of cultural conflict in the West since the 16th century is the problem of dealing with the relationship of science and values. All of the other positions that we have considered thus far reflect this conflict clearly.   Perhaps no thinker explored this problem with greater clarity and depth, however, than Kant. It may be said that, for Kant, the problem of ethics is the problem of reconciling scientific method with human freedom and moral responsibility. Until we understand and come to some resolution of this problem we cannot begin to deal with all of the other conflicts of our age.

Without pretending in this chapter to do justice to the richness of Kant's writings on epistemology and ethics I will attempt to summarize here Kant's theory, particularly as it relates to the thinkers and theories we have studied thus far.   In doing so I will expand briefly on the following:

1. Kant's epistemology is directed, among other things, to the end of showing the limitations of a deterministic model of reality characteristic of the natural sciences.

2. Kant affirms at least two senses of the term 'rational'. The first sense is associated with determinism and what Kant refers to as hypothetical imperatives. The second sense is associated with freedom and what Kant refers to as the categorical imperative.

3. Kant rejects emotivism and asserts the meaningfulness of ethical discourse.

4.   Kant rejects cultural and individual relativism and affirms absolute moral principles based on reason.

5.   Kant rejects egoism and affirms our obligation to always recognize the worth of all rational beings.

6. Kant rejects hedonism and affirms that human beings must control their own lives by reason rather than being controlled by desire.

7. Kant rejects utilitarianism and affirms a deontological or non-consequentialist ethic over any variety of teleological or consequentialist ethics.

8. Kant affirms the rational autonomy of the human person. This affirmation is at the root of his rejection of the other positions which we have studied thus far and his rejection of any theonomous ethic characteristic of orthodox Judaism, Christianity and Islam. In this regard, he represents secular humanism, in the best sense, better than any other position studied thus far.

Kant's Epistemology, the Problem of Determinism and the Meaning of Rationality

The meaning of determinism. Whenever we seek an explanation of phenomena according to the methods of the natural sciences we assume that every event has a cause which is discernible by scientific method. This cause, is itself viewed as a phenomenon that has a cause which is discoverable by scientific method, and so on. To assume that there are or could be any uncaused events is to assume that the world is not fully rational. We may put this another way. The natural sciences function on the assumption that all events or happenings in the universe are *determined* by other events or happenings in the universe. Rocks don't fall, bombs don't explode, machines don't start or stop because they choose to fall, or feel like it or for just no reason at all. There always has to be a reason. The reason includes the notion that previous events made it *completely necessary* that the rock, bomb or machine acted in the way it did. Furthermore, the falling rock, exploding bomb, or starting or stopping machine become part of a chain of events that effect future events, all necessary, and all in principle predictable. Because natural events are in principle predictable, they are in principle controllable, provided we can effect a change in the prior events that make subsequent events necessary.

We are not, of course, necessarily able to predict the behavior of our physical world nor control it. We can predict the movement of the planets but not control them. We cannot *yet* predict and control the behavior of the aids virus. We assume, however, that one day we will be able to both predict and control the behavior of the aids virus because that behavior like every other physical phenomena is *determined* by rational physical laws that follow necessary and predictable patterns. If we assumed otherwise, we would be assuming that we lived in a universe that was not rational and a great deal of the meaning in our lives would be lost. Contemporary Westerners assume that all physical events are determined in the sense we have here described. There are some philosophers who assume that the entire behavior of human beings are determined in the same way that physical events are determined. This view, that every event, including all human behavior, is determined by prior events, is known as *determinism.* Determinists insist that the only alternative to determinism is the assumption that the universe, including human beings, is not fully rational.

Rationality, robots and persons. Fully rational in what sense? Let us suppose that you tell a friend that you are planning to finish college and medical school and become a medical missionary in India. Your friend, who is somewhat surprised, asks for reasons for your action. You answer in terms of your belief in God, that He has called us to serve others, that you believe that you have the ability to be a good physician in that setting, that God sometimes leads us through an "inner voice," etc. You answer, in other words, in terms of goals, purposes, the meaning of human existence, beliefs about the possibility of finding a particular meaning for one's life, and personal choices, etc. Are these reasons? The question is not are they good reasons. Your friend may think that you are very misguided in the assessment of your abilities, your view of the nature of the needs and possibility of serving in India, the nature of God's leading, etc. Your friend may be right. The question is not whether they are good reasons but whether they are reasons at all? Your friend may be a professing atheist who plans to work on Wall Street make an enormous amount of money and live the life of a yuppie. You may stay up all night arguing about the wisdom and morality of your respective choices and attempting to show why the reasons for your respective choices are good ones while the other person's reasons are bad ones.

If the methodology characteristic of the natural sciences provides the only adequate meaning of 'rational' then your all night debate with your friend is not truly a debate about the adequacy of reasons at all. Physical events are not interpreted in terms of purposes, choices and desires. We may say things like: "My car does not want to start."

Most of us don't take that as a serious explanation. Kicking vending machines in order to punish them is not considered rational, although doing so in order to punish their owners may be. Likewise it is not considered rational to think of an automobile as moral or immoral. A "good" car is one that runs well. It is not a machine that makes morally good choices. Machines don't make morally good or morally bad choices. If I take a gun and cause the death of an innocent person, a complete physiological analysis of my action from raising, pointing the gun, squeezing the trigger, etc., will not speak of purposes, choices or moral obligation.

If this complete physiological explanation is all that is rationally possible, then ethical discourse which speaks of rational purposes, moral responsibility, sin, guilt, shame and free choice will not really be meaningful. Robots can, of course, be programmed to respond to these words used as inputs. We can program a robot to hang its head when we use the word "shame." We will not, however, believe that the robot can or ought to be able to experience genuine shame. If complete physiological explanations of our behavior are fully adequate explanations, then human beings are no more moral beings than are robots. On this view of things, if the social sciences find it useful to use the language which we normally associate with moral discourse, this is simply because they have not yet attained a level of scientific sophistication which enables them to entirely dispense with this non-scientific vocabulary.

Robots are completely determined in their behavior. This is why their behavior can be completely explained in terms of chains of causal relationships. They are not free. They are not persons. We do not, therefore, attempt to explain their behavior in language appropriate to persons. We do not speak of them as morally good, obligated, sinners, saints, guilty, acting shamefully, being lazy or ambitious, having personal goals, purposes, choices, desires and personality conflicts. If explanation in terms of deterministic causal chains exhausts what we mean by rational, then we have two options. We may affirm that human beings are really like robots and are not persons in the sense that we commonly suppose This is the option affirmed by the behaviorism represented by B.F. Skinner.[1] We may, on the other hand, affirm that free choice transcends rationality and being a person implies being non-rational. This is the option affirmed by the existentialism represented by Jean Paul Sartre.[2]

Personhood and the limitation of the natural sciences. Kant denied that explanation in terms of deterministic causal chains exhausts what we mean by rational. There is another sense of rational; and using this other sense of rational we may intelligibly speak of rational choice. But this second sense of the term rational is possible only if there are limitations on the scope of the first sense, which we associate with the natural sciences (and to some degree with the social sciences). Thus, Kant, in his Preface to the Second Edition of his massive volume on epistemology *The Critique of Pure Reason* affirms "I have therefore found it necessary to deny *knowledge* in order to make room for *faith*." By knowledge, he meant scientific knowledge or rational explanation in terms of deterministic causal chains. By faith, he meant primarily the experience of the moral life.[3]

How did Kant limit knowledge? He did so by engaging in a critique of 'theoretical' reason (reason as used in the natural sciences). Here he attempted to show that what we experience as the reality of the physical world is really a combination of two factors. These two factors are inputs from the perceived world and an a priori structure which the mind imposes upon our experience of the world. Thus, we never perceive reality as it actually is. We only have experience of a world upon which the human mind has imposed its own structure. Whether the world which we experience corresponds to the real world we cannot know.

We can illustrate Kant's position with a little imagination and a device with which we are all familiar--a simple calculator. Suppose that we have a simple calculator with a metaphysical bent. The calculator asks about the nature of reality. It quickly concludes, based on its experience, that reality is the sort of thing which can be exhaustively known by adding, subtracting, multiplying and dividing. In short, reason is identical with mathematical reason. Reality, therefore, is identical with mathematical reality. This is precisely what we would expect. The calculator does not distinguish among such things as here and there, fast and slow, living and dead, pleasure and pain. It knows nothing about cultural development. Its only language is mathematical language. It does not have social intercourse with other calculators. It knows nothing about being rich or poor, being beautiful or ugly, legal or illegal. It neither loves nor hates, believes nor disbelieves in the existence of God. Its list of the sciences is very short. Mathematics! Since it has no concept of space, it does neither windows nor geometry. It knows nothing of physics, biology, psychology; of logic, except as it is related to mathematical reason; of language, other than the language of mathematics; of history, sociology, economics, the study of the arts, jurisprudence, ethics or theology. Indeed, if reality can be exhaustively known by mathematics it has no need of these other disciplines.

Let us suppose that our calculator, which is unusually precocious, begins to reflect on the nature of the knowing process. It begins to do epistemology. This reflection enables it to realize that its own experience is a combination of two factors--the inputs from the world "out there" (how the calculator derived this spatial metaphor, we will leave to another time) and the silicon chip which constitutes its mind. It would then perhaps realize as some sort of revelatory experience that reality might be far different and richer than the limited categories of its mind. It wouldn't know for sure that reality was other than and richer than the categories of its mind. It would only know that it couldn't know for sure that reality wasn't other than and richer than mathematics. It would have no certain (or probable) knowledge concerning the nature of reality as it actually is. It would have certain knowledge of the nature of reality as it must appear to any normally functioning calculator. It would know for certain that $7 + 5 = 12$. It would not know whether or not reality was composed of numbers.

For Kant the human mind is something like our calculator except a bit richer in terms of the categories which it has to bring to the shaping of the reality that we experience. We must, says Kant, organize our experience within space and time. Kant referred to space and time as 'forms of sensibility'. Furthermore, when we examine physical phenomena we must organize our experience in terms of deterministic causal chains. We must use the category of the mind known as causality. But has anyone ever had any direct experience of a cause? No! We have a visual, tactile or auditory sensation that we identify as phenomenon A. This is followed by a visual, tactile or auditory sensation that we identify as phenomenon B. When this happens over and over again, we take this repetition as evidence of the fact that A caused B. However, we never perceive A actually causing B. Sometimes we conclude upon reflection that something else is the cause of B, perhaps X. We never perceive X causing B either. We may doubt that A is the cause of B or that X is the cause of B or that some other phenomenon Z is the cause of B. We never doubt, however, that B has a cause that has determined its existence and behavior.

Whence this certainty that B has a cause even though we have never had any direct experience of a cause of anything? Whence this certainty that there is a rational explanation of phenomenon B, such that we can (if we have adequate knowledge and if we have adequate theories and if we search long enough) state the necessary and sufficient conditions for the occurrence of B in the context of a deterministic causal chain of prior events? The certainty comes from the same source that our precocious calculator derives its certainty that all inputs will have a numerical output. Causality is built into our minds in the same way that mathematical relationships are built into the mind of the calculator. To realize this is to have a revelatory experience similar to that of our precocious calculator. Maybe the truth about reality is completely exhausted by rational examination in terms of mathematics. Maybe not! Maybe it is completely exhausted by rational examination in terms of deterministic causal chains. Maybe not! Maybe persons are completely determined and it makes no sense to speak of them as a moral beings capable of making free, autonomous choices. Maybe not! Science cannot prove anything about this, either way.

Is there any evidence that can help us one way or the other, or are we left in complete doubt? Kant affirmed that our moral experience is just as authentic as our physical experience. If I am to make sense out of my reality I can no more dispense with moral categories than I can with physical categories. But moral categories make sense only if we assume that persons are free. It makes no sense to affirm that Jane ought to have refrained from murdering Jim, if Jane's behavior was completely determined. Only if Jane was free to have done other than she did, does analysis of Jane's behavior from a moral point of view make any sense. This then is our situation. If we try to rationally examine Jane's behavior from the point of view of the natural sciences, then we must assume she is determined. If we try to examine Jane's behavior from a moral point of view, then we must assume she is free and responsible. Science cannot prove that Jane is not free. Moral discourse demands that we assume that Jane is free. Since our moral experience is as authentic and as necessary to make sense out of our lives as our physical experience, we are not being unreasonable or anti-scientific in assuming that Jane and all other human beings are free.

Kant's Second Sense of 'Reason': Reason, Human Freedom, and the Categorical Imperative

The distinction between categorical and hypothetical imperatives. Kant makes a great deal in his discussion of the distinction between hypothetical imperatives and categorical imperatives. To affirm an imperative is to affirm a necessary relationship. If I say to you that "if you wish to learn French, it is imperative that you study," I am affirming a necessary relationship between study (at least in your case) and the learning of French. This is an example of a hypothetical imperative. Hypothetical imperatives are provisional. If you wish to learn French, then you must study. But one may always opt to not learn French. They are contrasted with categorical imperatives which are not provisional but absolute. "You ought to learn French," does not present the learning of French as a possibility related to a set of conditions but as a command. We can, of course, speak of other things than the learning of French in terms of both hypothetical and categorical imperatives. "If you wish to avoid jail, then you must not steal," is another example of a hypothetical imperative. "You ought not to steal", discusses the activity of stealing in the form of a categorical imperative. Kant argued that when we talk of science, we are dealing with hypothetical imperatives. Scientific language consists of networks of 'if/then' statements. The language of morality, however, is the language of categorical statements.

Categorical statements, rationality and freedom. Are categorical statements rational statements? As we have seen earlier, A.J. Ayer and those who affirm an emotivist theory of language hold that so called categorical statements are not rational statements at all but merely expressions of emotion. Kant affirmed, on the other hand, that categorical statements are indeed rational statements. Categorical imperatives, however, function differently than rational statements in scientific theories. Rational statements in scientific theories purport to be descriptive of the way things necessarily do relate to one another. Categorical imperatives in ethical theories purport to be rational statements which are descriptive of the way things necessarily ought to relate to one another. In the first case, we have an example of reason as descriptive of the way phenomena in the world are related. In the second case, we have an example of reason as descriptive of the way our choices in the world ought to be related.

In the Bible, in the case of the Ten Commandments, we have a list of categorical imperatives which purport to have originated from and been revealed by God.   It seems appropriate to interpret these categorical imperatives as a list of rules.   When Jesus summarized those commandments, he did so in terms of what we might call the fundamental principle of love.   We are enjoined to love God with all our hearts and our neighbors as ourselves (*Mark 12:29-31*). Kant is not interested in giving us a list of rules so much as a formula, or principle, for evaluating any and all possible rules by which we might consider governing our lives. The central principle appears to be the principle of rationality.

Why rationality? Because being rational is the key to being free. How is this so?   Because of the way in which Kant defines moral freedom. For Kant, moral freedom is defined in a way that is quite the opposite of the meaning that it has for Bentham. In Bentham's case, individuals are free when they are able to do what ever they wish to do. Kant, on the other hand, would assert that we are morally free when we are clear about and choose to do what we ought to do. What ought we to do? We ought to be true to our most fundamental human nature. What is that most fundamental human nature?   What are persons? Persons are rational animals.   Persons are true to their most fundamental nature when they act rationally, from a rational principle.

The categorical imperative is the expression of a rational principal. Kant gives several different expressions of what he regards as a single principle. He speaks as if there were three different articulations of the principle but as H.J. Paton observes, he really appears to give five different formulations.[4] It will be instructive to treat these separately.

Different Formulations of the Categorical Imperative

"Act only on that maxim through which you can at the same time will that it should become a universal law." The first formulation expresses what has come in the literature to be referred to as the universalizability principle.   The assumption here is that when we engage in ethical reflection on our behavior we do so in the context of rules or what Kant calls maxims.   We ask, what is the rule which is governing my behavior in this situation?   Secondly, we need to ask ourselves, would I be willing to make that rule into a universal law? Would I be willing to have everybody always act in accordance with

that rule? If the answer is yes, then the rule is rational and it is rational to act in accordance with that rule. If the answer is no, then the rule is irrational and it is irrational to act in accordance with that rule.

One example that Kant gives is that of borrowing money with the promise to repay it while intending to renege on that promise should it become convenient to do so. Is this rational? To answer this question we need to see if we could make the principle of borrowing money with no intention of paying it into a universal law. We need to ask, what if everyone did that? The answer here is obvious. If everyone borrowed money with no intention of repaying it, then no one would ever lend any money. The institution of promise keeping is possible because many people do keep their promises most of the time. To make breaking promises into a universal law involves us in a contradiction. It is therefore irrational and thus wrong.

Kant gives us some other examples that are not as obvious and convincing. He argues that suicide is irrational since the motive of suicide is to escape pain or misfortune, in other words, the motive of suicide is self-love. To destroy one's self as an expression of self-love seems contradictory. Therefore, it would be irrational and hence wrong to make into a universal law the principle that one should commit suicide in order to escape pain and misfortune.

More interesting and I think cogent is Kant's argument against egoism. We are all tempted in numerous situations to be selfish and to not go out of our way to help others. Can we rationally will that all persons, including ourselves, should always ignore the needs of others when it is convenient to do so? Kant argues that this would be irrational since life is uncertain and we never know when we ourselves may need the help of others. We may notice here, however, that Kant's attack on the irrationality of egoism depends on certain assumptions about the nature of the world. The first assumption is that the world does not universally exhibit a natural identity of interests. If it did then universal selfishness would be rational. Secondly, we must assume that the world is unpredictable. I may be well off and in no need of help today but I cannot be certain that the future will not find me in different circumstances.

Put another way, we may say that a selfish person cannot rationally will that everyone else in the world be selfish. An altruistic or loving person could rationally will that everyone else in the world be altruistic. Thus altruism as a motive passes the test of universalizability, in other words the rationality test.   Egoism as a motive does not.

Kant's fourth example is perhaps the most interesting and revealing of all. Is it rational for a person to fail to develop his or her talents and to instead adopt a life style that stresses ease and pleasure, in other words, a hedonistic perspective on life? Kant admits that this might work under the right environmental and social conditions, in the South Sea Islands for instance. Nevertheless, Kant dismisses this possibility almost out of hand when he asserts "For as a rational being, he necessarily wills that his faculties be developed, since they serve him, and have been given him, for all sorts of possible purposes."[5] Kant's argument appears weaker here than it might have been. Perhaps this is because to fail to develop one's talents in favor of a life devoted to hedonism appears unthinkable to him imbued, as he is, with the Protestant work ethic. Kant, however, has other arguments against hedonism that we will deal with in another section.

"Act as if the maxim of your action were to become through your will a UNIVERSAL LAW OF NATURE" This second formulation of the categorical imperative that Paton refers to as Ia[6] admonishes us to think of ourselves as a Creator who is constructing a utopian universe in which there is a harmony of purposes. Would the principle of your action be appropriate as a universal law of nature in such an ideal world? If so, it is rational and good. If not, then it is irrational and bad. It is important to distinguish Kant's advice here from that of Bentham. Bentham was interested in creating a harmonious world through the enactment of legislation. The greatest good of the greatest number represents his ideal of harmony. Kant is not saying that we should act in such a way that harmony is produced. Sometimes acting morally will have the effect of creating disharmony for ourselves and others. We are encouraged rather to imagine an ideal world in which there is a harmony of ends or purposes and to ask if the principle of our action would be appropriate to that ideal world. The principle is moral not because it necessarily or probably leads to harmony in the world in which we now live but because it would fit into this imagined ideal world.

"So act as to use humanity, both in your own person and in the person of every other, always at the same time as an end, never simply as a means." The statement given above is what Kant refers to as his second formulation of the categorical imperative. He also considers it

in accord with Christian morality since it is according to him a restatement of the golden rule, "Do unto others as you would have them do unto you." Several things may be noted about this formulation. It is humanistic. It is anti-egoistic. It is anti-utilitarian or at least sets severe limits on the application of a utilitarian formula. Finally, as is noted above, it affirms principles which certainly on the face of it, seem to be in accord with Christian principles.

The formulation enjoins us to respect humanity both in ourselves and others. There is something about human nature that demands respect such that it must be treated as an end in itself. We may never use human beings solely as a means. Persons and human personality are sacred and must always be treated with respect.

Secondly, the formulation is anti-egoistic. An egoistic person always sees others simply as means to get what he or she wants. This formulation demands that we treat others as something more than means to our own gratification. It also would seem to require that we never willingly allow others to treat us as simply means to their own egoistic gratification. Thus, it demands self-respect as well as respect for others.

Thirdly, the formulation sets limits to utilitarianism. One of the standard criticisms of utilitarianism is that the formula 'the greatest good for the greatest number' simply demands that we consider the impact of an act or law on the average utility to society taken as a whole. This allows for some people to be disadvantaged so long as the improvement for the lot of others outweighs this disadvantage. In other words some persons in society become simply means to the good of others and are not treated as ends in themselves.

Finally, the formulation seems to be in accord with the Biblical perspective, at least in terms of its ethical implications. It affirms that there is something sacred about human nature such that we should never use others or ourselves in a way that shows lack of respect for this human nature. This in itself does not settle the question of whether Kant's ethic is ultimately Biblical, at least in terms of the basis of that ethic. Christians, Jews and Muslims affirm that man is made in the image of God, and hence, that there is something sacred about human nature. Humanists while denying the existence of God and hence that man is made in the image of God, nevertheless, affirm the value of human nature. Indeed, for them human nature is the ultimate value in the universe. Thus, with respect to the value of humanity, there is at least substantial overlap regarding the beliefs of both Christians and secular humanists. Another way of putting this is to note that with respect to the value of human nature, theists and humanists may agree on the level of principle while disagreeing at the level of the basis of their ethics.

"So act that your will can regard itself at the same time as making universal law through its maxim." The above is what Kant refers to as his third formulation of the categorical imperative. The key thought here seems to be the instruction that the ethical persons regard themselves as making universal law. Paton refers to this as the formula of autonomy.[7] Autonomy comes from two Greek words 'autos' which means self and 'nomos' which means law. Thus, as an automobile is a self-moving vehicle (as opposed to, for instance, a horse drawn carriage), autonomous persons are persons who give laws to themselves. This is to be distinguished from heteronomy (from the Greek 'heteros' which means other) which is a person who obeys laws given by another. It is also to be distinguished from theonomy (from 'theos' which is Greek for God) or one who obeys laws which are given to by God. For Kant, the essential meaning of freedom is to be autonomous or one's own lawgiver.

There is here another central contrast with Bentham. Benthamite freedom consists in being free to follow one's own feelings or inclinations without outside interference. For Kant rational persons control their inclinations by means of rational laws which they have given to themselves. It is only thus that they are autonomous or free. We will discuss the relationship of Christianity and humanism in Kant's ethics more fully below. I will note here, however, that many have argued that Christianity assumes a theonomous ethic which on the face of it seems to be in conflict with Kant's autonomous ethic. This, despite the fact that Kant believes in and offers a proof for the existence of God.

"So act as if you were through your maxims a law-making member of a kingdom of ends." This formulation Paton refers to as formulation IIIa.[8] and he regards it as the most comprehensive of the formulations since it combines the features of the other formulations. What is emphasized here is the notion that one would always think of one's self as making universal law in a society in which one's self and all others are regarded as ends in themselves. This precludes acting as if one were making law for a society in which some persons were treated as

slaves or indeed a society in which some people were allowed to exploit others in any way.

Summary: The Meaning and Scope of the Categorical Imperative:

It is helpful in understanding Kant if we are reminded that Kant considered all of these formulations as formulations of one and the same categorical imperative. They are thus, according to him different ways of saying the same thing. Thus, it is part of the essence of being rational and hence free and moral to always think of one's self as a maker of universal law. Why might this be so? A plausible reconstruction of Kant's argument might be given along the following lines.

(1) Human beings in their very essence are rational animals.

(2) To be 'rational' entails that one govern one's life according to a consistent pattern and avoid being influenced by one's feelings to act in an inconsistent manner.

(3) The only way to live a consistent life and to avoid being controlled by one's own emotions is to obey a universal law.

(4) Thus, we equate consistent behavior, rational behavior, self-control and being true to the essence of one's being with universal law.

(5) Therefore I am most true to myself when I create universal law.

Were Kant alive today it is doubtful that he would go around singing the song, "I gotta be me." If he did, however, he would not mean that it was necessary for him to express his individual uniqueness but rather that it was necessary for him to be rational.

I have given these various formulations of the categorical imperative to at least suggest some of the richness of Kant's discussion. It is clearly an alternative to utilitarianism and to hedonism in a number of respects. For Bentham, the end of all persons is pleasure. For Kant a person's end is to be rational. For Bentham, a good law is one which contributes to the greatest good (pleasure) of the greatest number. For Kant, a good law is determined not by its consequences for the individual or the greatest number of individuals but by its rationality. For Bentham, a good act is one which leads to good consequences. For Kant, a good act is one which is willed for the right reason (respect for the universal law of reason) regardless of the consequences.

Thus, Kant is a deontologist or non-consequentialist, and not a teleologist or consequentialist. Thus, to be good, my action must not only be in accord with a rational principle but be willed because it is rational. What Kant purports to give us in his categorical imperative is not a list of commandments or rules but a test for any rule or action. Is the principle of my action capable of being made into a universal rational law which could be consistently embodied into an ideal social order in which every one is a rational autonomous being and in which all respect the rational autonomy of their own persons and the rational autonomy of the person of every other member of the society? If the answer is yes, then it is moral, otherwise not.

Kant and Emotivism

Kant and the affirmation of synthetic a priori propositions. Kant died in 1804. Emotivism as a clearly articulated ethical position is a twentieth century phenomenon. Ayer, however, clearly had Kant in mind when he wrote and was quite self-consciously rejecting Kant's position. It is equally clear that Kant would have rejected Ayer's analysis. Ayer and Kant would have agreed that all propositions were either analytic or synthetic. They would also have agreed that all propositions are either a priori or a posteriori. They disagree on the ways in which these categories can be combined. Ayer insisted that only two possible combinations are possible: analytic a priori and synthetic a posteriori. Kant affirmed a third possibility: synthetic a priori propositions.

Analytic a priori propositions give us certain knowledge about the way we have decided to define terms. They do not tell us about the world. Synthetic a posteriori propositions give us knowledge about the world but it is only probable knowledge. According to Kant, synthetic a priori propositions give us both certain knowledge and certain knowledge about the world. At least they give us certain knowledge about the world as it necessarily appears to human subjects.

As we indicated in the chapter on emotivism, Ayer asserted that only analytic propositions are a priori and that all synthetic propositions are a posteriori. Thus, we have two and only two kinds of propositions, *analytic a priori* and *synthetic a posteriori*. Since ethical assertions don't fit either category, they are cognitively meaningless and what are claimed to be ethical assertions are merely expressions of emotions which are neither true nor false.

But Kant clearly affirms that ethical assertions are rational and hence cognitively meaningful. The categorical imperative (in all its various formulations) is a rational assertion in that second sense of 'reason' that we have discussed above. How is this possible? It is possible only because Kant affirms the reality of a type of proposition the existence of which Ayer denies. This is a type of proposition which is both a priori and synthetic at the same time, hence a class of *synthetic a priori* propositions. Synthetic propositions contain new information in the predicate which is not already assumed in the subject. A priori propositions give us certain knowledge prior to and apart from sense experience. The categorical imperative is an example of a synthetic a priori proposition. Thus, the categorical imperative gives us certain knowledge not based on sense experience. This, Kant believes, is the only way to avoid relativism and ground absolute moral values.

Synthetic a priori propositions and the natural sciences. What are synthetic a priori propositions and how do they function? To illustrate Kant's position here, it is useful to consider his epistemology as set forth in his *Critique of Pure Reason.*[9] Let us return to the example of our simple calculator. Our calculator knows that $7+5=12$, not because it has counted seven objects and five objects separately many times and then counted them together and gotten twelve. Rather our calculator knows that $7+5=12$ because it is built into the structure of its mind that the inputs '7+5' will always give the result '=12'. This knowledge on the part of our calculator may be said to be known a priori and with certainty. Thus, the proposition 'Seven plus five equals twelve' is an a priori proposition. Is it also a synthetic proposition? Kant argues that it is a synthetic proposition because he asserts the predicate '12' *is not contained by definition* in the subject '7+5'. In this respect all mathematical propositions differ from propositions of the type 'A circle is round', where 'round' is contained by definition in the concept 'circle'. Therefore, mathematical propositions give us new information that is absolutely certain and not based on experience. What sort of information do mathematical propositions give us? Not necessarily information about the world as it actually is but information about the world as it necessarily must appear to anyone who chooses to think mathematically. One can (in certain contexts) refuse to think or apply mathematical concepts. It is really impossible, however, to organize one's life and make sense out of reality without using mathematical concepts. It is therefore, irrational to reject the use of mathematical concepts or to insist, for instance, that 7+5=13. To persistently attempt either one would tend to make chaos out of one's life and experience.

There are other propositions of this type. 'Every event has a cause', is for Kant a synthetic a priori proposition. It is obviously possible to disagree about the specific causes of specific events. It is not possible to rationally organize one's existence if we assume that we exist in a world full of uncaused events. I do not know a priori which specific cause accounts for which specific event, but I know a priori that every event has some cause.

A.J. Ayer, as we have indicated, denies the existence of synthetic a priori propositions. He maintains that mathematical propositions are analytic a priori. For Ayer mathematics does not tell us about the world but about how mankind has defined the structure of numerical systems. This is a debate about the philosophy of mathematics into which we will not venture further here. Kant, however, believed that he had established the truth of synthetic a apriori propositions in the natural sciences. This, he believed gave him grounds for moving on to assert the existence of synthetic a apriori propositions in ethics.

Synthetic a priori propositions and the categorical imperative. Kant appears to be making an argument with respect to our ethical experience similar to the argument he makes with regard to our physical experience. My moral experience is as real to me as my physical experience. I can no more make sense out of the totality of my experience in the world by denying moral experience than I can by denying my physical experience. We are, in our fundamental natures, creatures who have a sense of 'ought.' We are not only capable of feeling moral obligation and guilt when we fail to do what we believe we ought to do. We are creatures who are incapable of avoiding this sense of moral obligation. But how can we make sense out of our moral experience? The answer is by appealing to the fundamental organizing principles for all moral experience. In organizing our physical experience we do not have a priori knowledge about specific sense experiences. We do have a priori knowledge with respect to specific organizing principles. All events must appear in time and space, every event must have a cause, all physical phenomena are necessarily associated with some physical substance, mathematical relationships always necessarily hold true, etc.

In organizing our moral experience, we also appeal to basic rational categories. More specifically, we appeal to one rational principle that Kant identified as the categorical imperative. The categorical imperative, he affirmed, is a synthetic a priori proposition. To deny the categorical imperative results in rendering our moral experience fundamentally incoherent, just as to deny that every event has a cause would render our physical experience fundamentally incoherent.

This can readily be seen with a little reflection. It would be impossible to make sense out of an athletic contest in which half of the players were always allowed to ignore the rules while the other half were penalized for breaking them. Likewise, a social existence in which some or many participants are allowed to ignore the rules ceases to make sense. If I tell you that I should not be required to obey the same rules that you do, your first impulse is to demand a 'reason' why I should be the exception. Unless I can give you an adequate reason you feel that you are involved in a social situation which makes no sense.

The above should make clear Kant's differences with the emotivist position. Emotivists do claim that our moral experience is fundamentally incoherent. Moral claims are reduced to expressions of emotion which can neither be true or false. Rational discourse about moral disagreement becomes impossible. Kant and the emotivists agree that moral assertions are neither analytic a priori nor synthetic a posteriori propositions. But Kant asserts that they are a third type of proposition, namely synthetic a priori propositions. Ayer does not recognize the existence of this third type of proposition. Therefore, for him, moral assertions are meaningless.

Kant and Relativism

It should be clear from our previous discussion that Kant rejects all forms of relativism. The categorical imperative is an absolute moral principle. Strictly speaking, Kant is an absolutist on the level of base and principle and potentially rules but not on the level of cases. Kant's ethical system does not attempt to provide us a set of rules like the Ten Commandments or specific instruction with respect to cases as we find in the first five books of the Old Testament. The categorical imperative provides us with a criteria for testing any possible case which we may want to consider. Whenever we encounter a specific case we are to assume that the case potentially falls under some rule (which Kant calls a maxim). We are to figure out what that maxim or rule might be and then see if we are willing to make that rule into a universal law. If we can consistently make the rule into a universal law then it conforms with the categorical imperative which is our single absolute moral principle.

Kant's rejection of relativism is founded on his commitment to the Enlightenment. This commitment to a single moral principle which can be applied to all possible cases in all possible times and cultures clearly delineates Kant as a child of the Enlightenment. For him pure reason alone is sufficient to give us specific guidance in every situation. Thus, it is possible to rationally transcend all tradition and historical particularity. Reason is the foundation for all true community, morality and religion but it is not dependent upon any of these. Indeed, being moral is identified with being rational. Being rational implies independence from all empirical influence. True morality consists in the ability to make decisions which can be applied to any concrete particular historical situation but which is not influenced by the particular circumstances which surround the individual decision maker.

Kant's rejection of relativism is linked to a depreciation of historical experience. Kant is clear and consistent in his affirmation. Reason is absolute. It is the clarity and consistency of his rational absolutism which is both the strength of his theory and the source of much criticism. Kant appears at this point to be at odds with a number of ethical traditions which differ from each other in significant ways. He, of course, rejects cultural relativism which frequently defends its premises by pointing to the evidence that cultural norms seem to be the result of historical development. Christianity, however is an historical religion. Christian revelation is historical, progressive and concrete. It proclaims the 'Incarnate Word' not the abstract universal. In recent discussion by those advocating an ethics of virtue rather than an ethics of rules, Kant has been criticized from several directions for his failure to take into account the necessity for moral development within the context of concrete historical communities. Alasdair MacIntyre in his *After Virtue* advocates a return to a Christian Aristotelian perspective. Richard Taylor in his *Ethics, Faith and Reason* advocates a return to a humanistic Aristotelian perspective. They disagree on much but they agree that Kant's ethic is too formal and is not descriptive of the way our moral experience can work or ought to work.

Kant and Egoism

Kant and Bentham. Kant's rejection of egoism is as forthright as his rejection of relativism. The Kantian person, unlike the Benthamite person, is not fundamentally selfish. For Bentham the chief function of reason is to help individuals discern the most efficient way to satisfy their personal selfish desires. For Kant the chief function of reason is to enable individuals to transcend their personal desires and to govern their lives according to a universal rational principle which respects one's own rationality and the rationality of others equally. This is what Kant intends when he tells us that the categorical imperative demands that we always treat others as ends in themselves and never simply as means. According to Bentham, all of us always treat others simply as means to satisfying our own selfish desires. Even when we seek the greatest good of the greatest number our reason is not that we value the good of others but because we believe this to be the most effective means to achieving our own good.

Kant, egoism and never treating others exclusively as means. Kant does not forbid that we treat others as means. The check out person in the grocery store is a means to my getting groceries. The customer, on the other hand, is a means for the worker to receive wages, etc. We all use others as means to achieve our own self-interest. All social institutions: businesses, colleges, churches, hospitals, governmental agencies, etc., use persons as means to achieve their own purposes. This is an inescapable dimension of organized human interaction.

What Kant forbids is that we ever in any of our transactions treat each other simply or exclusively as means. The worker in the grocery store may be a means to my achieving my purposes. I must, however, remember that that worker is also a rational human being who is a person who has intrinsic and not just instrumental value. Likewise, I think it is clear that Kant would insist that institutions whether they be businesses, schools, hospitals, etc., must be so structured and so administered that they not treat persons as simply instruments to achieve their own institutional purposes. Customers are a means to the achievement of profit and survival of a business. They are also persons who have intrinsic value. Investors and laborers are a means to customers being able to purchase goods and services. They are also persons. Students, teachers, administrators and physical facilities are all means to each other and society. Physical facilities may be treated simply as means but students, teachers and administrators are also persons. They therefore must be treated differently from physical facilities. Patients are persons and not simply an economic resource for our hospitals, interesting case studies in specific diseases for our physicians, and a nuisance to our nurses. They may be all three of the above, of course, but they must always be treated as something more.

Kant, utilitarianism and treating others as means. This is why consistent Kantians have always objected to what they consider to be the implications of utilitarianism. Utilitarianism's goal to achieve the greatest good for the greatest number, allows for the possibility that the lesser number may be exploited (used simply as means and not treated as ends in themselves) in the process of achieving greater good for the majority. "What if, one of Bentham's critics is said to have argued, "in a society of thirty, twenty nine decided that it was for the greatest good of the greatest number to kill and eat the thirtieth?" The thirtieth, if he were a consistent utilitarian would have to agree that this action was moral. To put this in Kantian terms, the twenty nine would be treating the thirtieth simply as a means and not as an end in himself. If the thirtieth agreed with the others he would be treating himself simply as a means and thus violating the categorical imperative as well. I think that a good case can be made for asserting that it is the essence of egoism to treat others as means and not as creatures who are intrinsically worthwhile in themselves. If this is the case, then clearly Kant rejects egoism as either necessary or moral.

Kant and Institutionalized Individualism

It is useful to make some comparisons here between egoism, Kant's view and what has been referred to in the sociological literature as institutionalized individualism. Egoism is a type of individualism in that the assumption of egoistic theories of society is that the individual comes first and society exists only to meet the needs of individuals. Society is created by and for individuals and ought to be preserved in order to and only insofar as it meets the needs of individuals. Another way of putting this is to say that the social order has extrinsic value to the extent it serves individuals. It has no intrinsic value, however.

It is hard for Westerners to imagine how odd, not to say immoral, this position would sound to such diverse thinkers and groups as Plato, Confucius and the writers of the Old Testament. Plato affirmed that the good of the whole (the state) was of more importance than the good of the individual. The Confucian ethic is built on the assumption that the good of the family is more important than the good of the individuals who compose it. Confucius would never say that the family exists for the good of the family members. Rather, it is the other way around. For the writers of the Old Testament, the existence and well being of the people of God is primary. The covenant with God was with the nation of Israel not with a group of individuals who banded together to call themselves Jews so that they would be able to strike a better deal with Jehovah. Bentham might have so interpreted the Old Testament (I don't know that he did so interpret it, but it would have been consistent with his principles to do so). The writers of the Old Testament would have found such an interpretation incomprehensible.

Kant's individualism is of a different type. For Kant the ultimate value in the social universe is the rational autonomous individual. To say rational autonomous individual is somewhat redundant. To be rational is to be autonomous and to be autonomous is to be rational. Furthermore, one can preserve one's individuality only be being rational. Kant's autonomous person is not egoistic as we have observed above. Nevertheless, for Kant as for Bentham the individual is ontologically prior to society. In principle, the individual is the creator of society. This is part of what is meant when Kant instructs us to regard ourselves when we act as lawmakers in a kingdom of ends. We are to regard ourselves as creators of society. Kant's human beings might under some circumstances sacrifice themselves for the social order but if they did so, it would be because that was the only action consistent with the preservation of personal moral autonomy. Thus, both Kant and Bentham place the individual above society. In this sense they both are representative of Enlightenment ideals.

Talcott Parsons refers to this emphasis on the primacy of autonomy as it appears in modern Western society as institutionalized individualism.[10] He sees it as the pervasive cultural value of modern Western industrial society. Institutionalized individualism is encouraged by our society and its various institutional structures, education, economy, religion, etc. Furthermore, this ideal is functional for the survival of modern society. Modern industrial societies require a combination of cooperation and independent thinking on the part of their members if they are to survive and prosper. This means we must encourage the development of individuals who have personality structures which can tolerate ambiguity, make rational decisions on their own and work cooperatively with others with similar personalities and abilities.

But Parsons takes great pains to insist that this ethical ideal of autonomy is not egoistic hedonism. The autonomous person has more in common with the personality type described in Max Weber's *Protestant Ethic and the Spirit of Capitalism.*[11] Parsons' autonomous person is capable of hard work, deferred gratification, commitment to institutional goals which transcend personal desires, concern for others, and rational and cooperative behavior.

For the sociologist Parsons, however, this type of person is not a rational being which transcends and exists apart from society. He is the creation of the modern Western social order. Parsons is clearly committed to this ideal of autonomous persons and the social order which has created and encourages them. For him modern Western industrialized societies link technological progress, cooperative behavior, material abundance and the creation and encouragement of the rational free autonomous individual.

Is Parsons Kantian? Yes and no! He is Kantian in the sense that his ideal person is the rational autonomous individual and his ideal social order is a social order which requires and encourages such individuals. He further seems to think that the norms which govern such a social order are the natural working out of normative structures which are inherent in human nature and social structure. Accordingly, he refers to them as "evolutionary universals."[12] But unlike Parsons, Kant's rational autonomous individual is not a product of society. For Kant, to be autonomous is to have the ability through reason to transcend all empirical influences, including the influences of one's social structure.

We will return to this distinction later when we discuss in, chapter eight, MacIntyre's critique of ethical theorizing since the Enlightenment and his espousal of an ethics of virtue. Part of MacIntyre's critique of individualism of both the utilitarian and Kantian varieties consists in his insistence that the concept of modern individualism is not a universal feature of human nature but the creation of our modern Western social structure. For now, however, I wish to emphasize the similarities and differences between the Benthamite, and Kantian views of individualism and that of Parsons as representative of much of contemporary social theory. Bentham's individualism is egoistic. Kant's is no less committed to individualism but not to an egoistic variety.

Kant and Agape Love

If Kant's highest ethical ideal is not egoism, neither is it agape love. The test of a rule is not whether it is loving, but whether it is rational. Rational autonomy or freedom is the essence of human nature for Kant. This is not to say that Kant's ethic excludes or is incompatible with agape love in the same way that it is incompatible with egoism. Kant argues that the categorical imperative constitutes an explication of the golden rule, "Do unto others as you would have them do unto you". His most fundamental advice, however, is not "love thy neighbor as thyself" but rather to respect rationality in yourself and in others equally. Christians may make various responses to this. One possible response, of course, is to note the difference and to insist that Kantian and Christian ethics are fundamentally incompatible. Another possible response is to argue that Kant's ethical theory applies well to the development of laws for a just social order but that agape love is the standard for personal relationships. Thirdly, one might argue that Kant's categorical imperative is the standard for developing laws and for most of our interpersonal relationships but that Christians are encouraged (although not required) to go beyond justice and to practice charity. Whether these alternatives or others are chosen, however, it seems clear that the Kantian ideal and the Biblical one are not identical.

Kant and Hedonism

Control by Reason versus Control by the Passions. Kant's rejection of hedonism is clear cut and thorough going. Bentham writing after Kant but in a tradition with which Kant, was familiar wrote that "Reason is and ought to be the servant of the passions." Kant perceived the chief function of reason as keeping us from being controlled by the passions. If I am controlled by my passions, then I am controlled by my environment and am not free and autonomous.

Hedonism, by definition implies that individuals are controlled by feelings of pleasure and pain, and, hence are subject to their environment and unable to transcend it. This is true, since what will bring me the greatest pleasure and the least pain at any given time is contingent upon the possibilities present in my particular environment. Hedonists, of course, may be extremely rational in their approach to getting pleasure, as the examples of Epicurus and Bentham demonstrate. They may be committed to using any number of empirically verified hypothetical imperatives in the pursuit of their goal of maximizing pleasure and minimizing pain. They may be very much guided by reason but cannot be, in the Kantian sense, controlled by it.

'In accordance with duty' versus 'for the sake of duty'. Kant's rejection of hedonism is no where demonstrated more clearly then in his affirmation that an action to be moral must not only be done in accordance with duty but must also be done for the sake of duty. For Kant the only thing which is good in itself is a good will. Therefore, it is not enough to do the right thing. We must do the right thing for the right reason. It is not enough to act rationally. To be a moral act, an action must be done because it is rational. Let us take marriage as an example.

Let us suppose that Adam has been faithful to his wife Barbara all his life. This is in accord with his duty. But let us further suppose that he loves his wife and she loves him. She is beautiful, rich, loving, has a good sense of humor, etc. In addition to this she is a fine Christian woman who has a brother who is a hit man for the Mafia. His only virtue is that he loves his sister very much. Adam has acted according to duty in being faithful to Barbara, but has he acted for the sake of duty? Its difficult if not impossible to tell. Everything in the relationship is such that it would cause his inclinations to be to remain faithful. The possibility of losing the economic advantages of the relationship and even his life at the hands of Barbara's brother would tend to encourage even the most immoral of men to be faithful.

Now let us suppose that we have a second couple, Charles and Diane. Charles is also faithful to Diane, as Adam was to Barbara. Diane, however, although once beautiful, talented and possessed of a pleasant personality, has for some years been diagnosed as severely and persistently mentally ill. Her illness is not her fault but the result has been that she has become not a wife to Charles but a very serious burden. Charles could have committed her to a mental institution, divorced her and been free to marry again. His friends, his rabbi and even Diane's family, have all told him that they would not blame him if he ended the relationship. Charles, however, takes his marriage vows which included "in sickness and in health, for richer and poorer and for better and worse" seriously. He has made a promise and he intends to keep it. It is clear in that Charles has remained with Diane not only according to duty but for the sake of duty, since he has no other motivation but duty in this situation. We may think that Charles is either a saint or a fool, but he is no egoistic hedonist.

As far as Kant is concerned, we can be reasonably certain that Charles' action is a moral one but we cannot be sure with respect to Adam. Adam's action may be controlled by a desire to get pleasure and avoid pain. If this is his true motivation, then his action may be in accord with duty but it is not a moral action because it is not done for the right purpose. Moral actions are those which are done out of respect for the universal law of reason. Any other motivation renders an act immoral whether the consequences be good or bad.

Can There Be Any Saints in Heaven? There is a valuable insight in Kant's analysis of the nature of ethical action. It is true that people sometimes do very destructive things with the best of intentions. In such cases, we call their actions mistaken but not immoral. It is equally true that people sometimes commit acts that have very good consequences even though their intentions may have been to simply benefit themselves and not to help others. In some cases, people may even have intended to commit acts of destruction and have inadvertently done something very positive. But if Jones intends to murder Smith but by mistake kills Hardy, and thus prevents Hardy from murdering Smith, Smith may thank God but he will not thank Jones. Likewise, if Smith saves Jones' life only because Jones owes him money, Jones may be thankful to God for making him a poor man who has to borrow money, but he will not feel any need to express sincere gratitude to Smith. To be a moral action, an action must have a good motive.

Kant seems here to be affirming something which accords with our most basic moral intuitions, but does he go too far? Is an act moral only if I would have done it even though I didn't enjoy it and received no pleasure from it? To take this position is to be driven to some conclusions which are not only curious but counter-intuitive. A common Christian assumption about heaven is that it will be populated with persons who not only do the right thing but who are so constituted that they only *want* to do the right thing. The thoroughly good person is one who loves God and fellow humans. But could I possibly have a complete love for my fellow human beings and not take delight in doing good towards my neighbor? If Kant is right, then we will never be able to tell (apart from divine and miraculous insight) whether the inhabitants of heaven are operating for the sake of duty, since presumably their regenerate character, the political order and the complete social environment will all conspire to make them find satisfaction in acting according to duty.

The point I am making here does not, of course, rest upon assumptions about heaven. Whether we are fundamentalists or liberals, Christians or humanists, part of what we mean by good persons are those whose characters are such that they takes delight in seeing good come to others and experience pain at seeing harm come to others. A good person is one who does what is right even when it is unpleasant. But a good person is also one who takes pleasure in doing what is right. A good society is one which rewards behavior which is morally right and punishes or at least refuses to reward behavior that is morally wrong. In a perfect society where only moral behavior was encouraged, Kant would have extreme difficulty in determining who is moral.

All of this suggests that, in his effort to combat hedonism, Kant may have gone too far. The position of Aristotle, that although pleasure is not the goal of action, nevertheless, pleasure perfects an action may be closer to the truth.

Kant, Utilitarianism, and Teleology versus Deontology

I have already indicated in the previous discussion that Kant explicitly rejects utilitarianism. Kant is a deontologist in his ethical position and rejects utilitarianism and all other forms of teleological or consequentialist ethics. For him an action is right not because it leads to good consequences but because it is rational. This rejection of teleology is at the heart of his distinction between acting according to duty and acting for the sake of duty. I must do the right thing only because it is the right thing. If I do what is right because it would lead to good consequences then I am adopting (in my heart at least) a consequentialist ethic. This same point is brought out in Kant's discussion of the distinction between hypothetical and categorical imperatives. Hypothetical imperatives relate actions to consequences. Categorical imperatives say nothing about consequences.

Nevertheless, in his defense and articulation of the meaning of the categorical imperative Kant, has been accused of appealing to consequentialist considerations. We are told that it is irrational to borrow money while not intending to keep our promise to repay it because the consequences of everyone doing that would be that the institution of promise keeping would be destroyed. It would be irrational and hence against the categorical imperative to not help another person in need because we could not will a world in which everyone were selfish because we ourselves never know when we might need help. This sounds not only like utilitarianism but egoistic utilitarianism.

Despite this apparent appeal to consequences and even utilitarianism, I think it is a mistake to interpret Kant as affirming consequentialist considerations. He never asks what *will* be the actual consequences of a particular action or what will be the actual consequences of making a particular piece of legislation into law. His question is always what *would* be the consequences of everyone acting according to a particular principle or law. His concern is to test by more or less concrete illustrations the rationality of a particular principle. Thus, a social order in which everyone stole when they pleased would be an irrational social order. If everyone refused to respect the right of private property and stole when they pleased, then no one could have any property. If no one had any property then no one could steal. Thus, if everyone steals then no one steals. This illustration exposes the irrationality of theft in the Kantian sense of rationality. Of course, stealing often appears rational to the thief because he is confidant that most citizens will not steal and that therefore the consequences of his actions (assuming that he escapes detection) will be that he will have property that would not otherwise be in his possession. Stealing is sometimes 'rational' in the utilitarian sense of rational as applied in the concrete world in which we all are forced to live. But it is not 'rational' in the Kantian sense of rational as applied to the ideal world which Kant imagines. What Kant admonishes us to do is apply this principle derived from this ideal imagined world to the world in which we actually live regardless of the consequences of our action in this world. This is what makes him a consistent deontologist.

Kant and Rational Autonomy

Kant's consistent affirmation of autonomy. Kant's affirmation of the rational autonomy of the individual is what identifies him as humanist in the best sense. What is wrong with cultural relativism, hedonism, egoism and utilitarianism from his point of view is that they deny the autonomy of the human person. If cultural relativism is true, then individuals do not give laws to themselves but are at the mercy of their cultures. I do not define myself but am defined by my culture. If hedonism is true then I am controlled by my external environment in another sense; I am subject to my desires and am willy nilly controlled by pleasure. Utilitarianism in all its forms likewise robs me of self-control and makes me subject to the calculus of environmental concerns that happens to be characteristic of my particular situation. What is central for Kant is respect for free, autonomous personality. We show respect for our own personhood only when we are lawgivers unto ourselves. We show respect for the personhood of others when we respect their ability to be lawgivers unto themselves. To be a lawgiver unto one's self requires rationality of which the categorical imperative is the primary expression. Therefore respect for personhood becomes for Kant identified with respect for rationality.

Autonomy, and the nature and law of God. How does this all relate to theism? Although Kant is famous for his rejection of the traditional so-called theistic proofs, he in some sense believes in God and developed what has become known as the moral argument for the existence of God. His moral argument for the existence of God occurs in his ethical writings as one of the postulates of the practical reason-- God, freedom and immortality. As we have seen, human freedom cannot be strictly proven scientifically, but if the moral life is to make any sense then we must assume that man is free. Thus, we are justified in making and believing in the postulate of freedom. The belief in immortality is also justified by the demands of the moral life. The moral life demands a perfection which none of us reaches in this life. If there is no immortality then our drive for moral perfection ceases in failure at our death. It would then be irrational to strive for that which is impossible. But if there is immortality then we can continue in our striving and the demands of the moral life can make sense.

Kant believes in God because it is also necessary to postulate God if the moral life is to not be irrational. In rejecting utilitarianism, Kant rejects happiness as a legitimate goal of the moral life. We are to strive for virtue even if this negatively impacts upon our happiness, as it often does. But a moral order which allows that the most virtuous may be the least happy is itself unjust and hence irrational. We all know that frequently "the good die young" and we all think that this is unfair. So Kant reasons that we must postulate a God who reconciles virtue and happiness by rewarding the virtuous with happiness in the next life.

None of this, however, speaks of God as a lawgiver. Nor need it do so if Kant's perspective is correct. Reason gives us laws and God himself could not give us a law which would either contradict or be inaccessible to our reason. Were He to do so, then we would not be lawgivers unto ourselves. We would not be autonomous. We would not be free. We would not be ethical beings in the fullest sense of the term. Morality consists not in obeying the will of God but in obeying and having reverence for the reason which is within us. Not that God would or could disagree with any of this. God as a perfect being is perfectly rational and could not conceive of affirming that the irrational or non-rational is moral any more than can we. God's function is to guarantee man's autonomy and not to over rule it. This would be immoral. Neither does He serve to supplement that autonomy. This would be unnecessary.

The Humanist and Christian Response to Kant

The humanist response. As I have suggested in the preceding section the secular humanist would find much to applaud in Kant's analysis. It is true that Kant postulates the existence of God as necessary to make sense out of the moral life. A thoroughgoing humanist world find this postulate unnecessary. The humanist would, however, be in complete sympathy with Kant's affirmation of the autonomy of the individual and respect for the sacredness of human personality. Of course there are many varieties of secular humanists and many would disagree with Kant on matters that both would consider essential. Nonetheless, in affirming the primary value of the autonomous human personality, Kant is upholding a basic value of the humanist perspective.

Kant and Christian theological assumptions. How would the fundamentalist respond to Kant? Fundamentalists, like all Christians, must, if they are consistent, affirm the sacredness of human personality. Persons are made in the image of God and as such are sacred. But does this sacredness consist primarily in rational autonomy? Might it not consist rather in the ability to enter into loving relationships with God and one's fellow man? Can the meaning of *agape love* be reduced to or fully interpreted in terms of the category of rational autonomy? I think that such an assumption is one which would be questioned by a variety of Christians ranging from fundamentalists, to Joseph Fletcher, to Pope John Paul II. I think they would be right to question this assumption.

All Christians, it seems to me, if they are to be consistent must affirm some form of theonomous ethic which emphasizes the role of God as creator and lawgiver and not just as the guarantor of man's autonomy. Nevertheless, in addition to affirming the sacredness of human personality, Christians of all varieties should affirm, it seems to me, that an essential part of any moral order includes rational consistency and equal respect for human personality as such. For after all, Christians affirm that all men and women, and not just some, are made in the image of God. It might even be argued that Christians, if they are to be consistent, should be more committed to equality before the law than Kant. If 'rationality' is what is sacred, then it might be argued that some human beings have more of this than others. But if what is sacred about human beings is that they are made in God's image, then it would seem difficult to argue that some of us are made more in the image of God than others. Of course, it could be argued that some exhibit God's image more consistently than others but this observation leads us to a consideration of another problem.

How does Kant deal with the problem of evil, what Christians would call sin? For Kant the essence of personal evil is to choose to be motivated by irrational desire rather than by a respect for the universal law of reason. To sin is to be irrational. To live righteously is to live rationally. For Christians of all varieties, the essence of sin is rebellion against and rejection of a loving, obedient relationship with God. Neither Christians nor Kant, it seems to me, have a coherent 'rational' explanation of how humans comes to choose evil rather than good. In his *Religion Within the Limits of Reason Alone*, Kant deals with this question by distinguishing between two different concepts of will.[13] A rational will is naturally opposed to irrationality and causes us to choose to be motivated by reason rather than desire. But somehow, Kant recognizes, we are able to choose between rationality and irrationality. This choice to be irrational is obviously not a rational choice. That would be contradictory. But neither can the capacity to choose between rationality and irrationality stem from our irrational nature itself. For if it is a capacity to choose between rationality and irrationality, then it cannot be identified with either one of them. Kant identifies this capacity for choosing between rationality and irrationality with a second sense of will, concerning which he understandably has little to say. Thus, just as Christian theology has difficulty in explaining why a creature made in the image of God should choose to rebel against God, so Kant has difficulty in explaining why a basically rational creature should rebel against reason.

Whether the Kantian view of the problem of evil can be identified with the Christian view of the problem of evil depends on whether we can plausibly assume that the concept of rebellion against God can be identified with the concept of rebellion against reason. This seems to me to be a questionable assumption. But what about the cure for this evil? Fundamentalists share with a wide spectrum of non-fundamentalist Christians belief in salvation by grace through faith. This grace is mediated in a significant way by the Holy Spirit. There have been various attempts to demythologize and give a rational account of the meaning and work of the Holy Spirit, with that of Hegel being one of the foremost examples. Fundamentalists are hardly alone, however, among Christians in regarding the work of the Spirit as transcending reason and the possibility of human explanation. If the work of the Holy Spirit is not regarded as irrational, it is certainly thought of as non-rational.

Thus, in the final analysis, many Christians have regarded the fundamental nature of the moral life as beyond analysis. Kant would have regarded the understanding of the moral life as not reducible to explanation in terms of the natural sciences. It is doubtful, however, that the author of *A Critique of Practical Reason* and *Religion Within the Limits of Reason Alone* could accept the work of a Holy Spirit which transcends reason (in both the theoretical and practical sense of reason) as an essential factor in understanding the meaning of the moral life.

We have already noted that in the categorical imperative Kant does not provide us with a list of commandments but rather with a principle by which we can test any candidate for a morally binding commandment. This principle would presumably make the Ten Commandments, the Sermon on the Mount and much of the other specific teaching of the Bible unnecessary in the final analysis. Like so much of Christian, and especially fundamentalist ethics, Kant's ethics is deontological. Kant's ethics, however, is in no sense dependent upon an historic, progressive revelation embodied in either a Holy Scripture or a Holy Church. Kant is a child of the Enlightenment. Truth can be discovered by reason alone and is not dependent on history or a concrete community, religious or secular. The Kantian person does not need a Bible, a Pope or an historical community to guide in ethical decision-making. We shall have more to say about this latter possibility when we come to our discussion of the ethics of virtue.

Cultural Conflict and the Kantian Ethic

Kant's ethic is helpful in understanding the cultural conflict of our time because he lays bare all of the major themes that confront us in the contemporary scene. How shall we maintain personhood in the face of the overwhelming power of empirical science? Is there a universal reason that can enable us to transcend our particular cultures? Is a belief in the freedom and self-respect for individuals compatible with a belief in the Judeo-Christian God? Is a life devoted to pleasure the essence of freedom or is it the essence of slavery? Are human beings rational animals or are they fundamentally emotional beings? Is there a single rational standard for justice or is justice simply a set of power relationships? Are humans fundamentally selfish or are they capable of a devotion to duty? Can we know ultimate reality through reason? What, if any, are the limits of science?

Kant no only raises these questions, he gives answers. Whether these answers are ultimately satisfactory is another matter. Those who would seriously consider the questions in a systematic manner, however, must seriously consider Kant. Our next two chapters will deal with some contemporary responses to the Kantian perspective.

John Rawls, though he has significant reservations about Kant's development of a comprehensive theory, writes as a contemporary representative of the Kantian tradition. Alasdair MacIntyre believes that ethical theorizing in the West since the time of Kant has been based on a fundamental mistake. MacIntyre believes that we need, not to modify Kant with his emphasis on an ethic of rules, but to return to the development of an ethics of virtue as represented by the Aristotelian tradition. These two thinkers differ on their attitude toward the Enlightenment tradition. Rawls is attempting to preserve that tradition. MacIntyre sees Kant's affirmation of the Enlightenment as a fundamental mistake that has led inevitably to the emotivist culture in which we now find ourselves.

Notes

1
For a popular exposition of determinism see B.F Skinner, *Beyond Freedom and Dignity*. Skinner's *Walden Two* is a utopian novel that attempts to show how a society governed by behavioral psychologists could solve all of our social problems. It brings to life the free will/determinism issue for the beginning student in a readable and interesting fashion.

2 There are various forms of determinism with very important distinctions among them. Skinner and Bentham are both determinists. So also is Freud and in very different senses Marx and Calvin. Kant and Sartre both clearly reject determinism but Sartre would see Kant as falling into a rational determinism that denies human responsibility. His differences with Kant are clear despite his comparisons between himself and Kant in his essay *"Existentialism."*

3 Immanuel Kant, *The Critique of Pure Reason*, p. 29.

4 H.J. Paton, *The Categorical Imperative*. See especially pp. 129ff. for the various formulations of the categorical imperative.

5 Immanuel Kant, *Foundations of the Metaphysics of Morals*. p. 41.

6 Paton, 146-164.

7 Paton, 180.

8 Paton, 185.

9 See especially Kant, *Critique of Pure Reason*, pp. 52-55.

10 See Talcott Parsons, *Social Structure and Personality*, pp. 183-335. Chapter 8 of this work entitled "The Link Between character and Society," written with Winston White is a critique of David Riesman's *The Lonely Crowd*. Riesman in his work which first appeared in 1950 argued for the development of 'autonomous' persons and saw Western society fostering 'other directed' persons who had no center of self but were completely, in their personalities, the product of whatever peer group they happened to be associated with. Parsons is much more optimistic about the forces shaping personality development in the modern world. Both Resin and Parsons see 'autonomy' as the ideal type of personality. Neither would affirm egoism. In this sense they are both Kantians. They fit broadly into the tradition that embraces Piaget, Kohlberg and Rawls.

11 Max Weber, *The Protestant Ethic and the Spirit of Capitalism.*, pp. 47-78.

12 Talcott Parsons, *Societies: Evolutionary and Comparative Perspectives* and *The System of Modern Societies*. Parsons sees Western society as characterized by what he calls the value orientation of 'universalism' and 'achievement.' This value orientation promotes efficiency and autonomy. Thus, to the degree that societies are characterized by these values their survival will be promoted.

Parsons a sociologist is not in favor in sociological circles. It is interesting to note, however, that in the early seventies he was predicting that the Soviet Union would inevitably move in a democratic direction because the pressures of modernization would require more autonomous individuals who would clash with the authoritarian social structure of the Soviet Empire.   See *System*.....pp. 124-128.
13 Immanuel Kant, *Religion Within The Limits Of Reason Alone*, trans. Theodore M. Greene and Hoyt H. Hudson (New York: Harper and Brothers, 1960). See also in this edition the excellent essay by John R. Silber entitled, "The Ethical Significance of Kant's Religion."

CHAPTER VII

JOHN RAWLS: A THEORY OF JUSTICE

Rawls and the Western Liberal Enlightenment Tradition

There are many important differences between Kant and John Rawls (b.1921). One important difference, of course, is that whereas Kant died in 1804, Rawls is still a living and productive scholar. This is more than something that is of personal interest to Rawls. On one plausible interpretation of Rawls' work, he is offering a contemporary articulation and defense of a Kantian perspective over against various contemporary articulations of utilitarianism.

Rawls speaks to the contemporary scene but in the context of a debate rooted in the Western liberal Enlightenment tradition. The age of the 'Enlightenment' as an historical period, is strictly speaking, identified as roughly from 1688 to 1815. More broadly, commentators refer to the 18th century to the present as the Modern age (an extension of the Enlightenment) that we just now may be rejecting as an intellectual and cultural movement. Thus, we find commentators referring to this as the post-Modern or post-Enlightenment period.

The Enlightenment tradition upholds the value of scientific inquiry and is characterized by tremendous faith in the ability of science to solve our problems. It assumes that there is a rational universal perspective that transcends all particular cultural contexts. It emphasizes the ability of the autonomous individual to, through reason, grasp this universal truth. Through reason human beings have been enlightened and liberated from superstition and religious, cultural and political authority. The assumption of Western liberal democracies that assume the masses have the ability to govern themselves owes much to this tradition.

Thus, the Enlightenment is viewed as liberating the individual from both superstition and political absolutism. It is this tradition that still provides the framework for much of our discussion about social justice. This includes the debate about the nature of democracy, the value and defects of capitalism, civil rights, women's liberation, modernity versus traditionalism, etc. There is a sense in which all of the positions that we have studied so far in this text, including utilitarianism, are representatives of that tradition.

Cultural relativism and the Enlightenment. Cultural relativism might be seen as an exception to this statement. This is true for some cultural relativists and not others. Some cultural relativists are relativists with respect to ethical values but are firm believers in *truths* obtained from the social sciences. They even argue that it is on the basis of our *rational scientific analysis* of culture that we can conclude that there are no *ethical values* that are able to transcend any specific culture. The values that ground rational scientific inquiry itself, however, they hold to be true and transcendent of any particular culture. These cultural relativists are relativists with respect to ethics but not relativists with respect to science. Their faith in science justifies viewing them as representatives of the Enlightenment tradition. Other cultural relativists question even the values of rational scientific inquiry associated with the Enlightenment tradition. Persons taking this position are often identified with the so called postmodernists or deconstructionists. They are challenging the whole Western Enlightenment tradition and not just that part of it that assumes there are culturally transcendent ethical, political, or aesthetic truths.

Emotivism and the Enlightenment. Emotivism, of course, assumes that we can have scientific truth that transcends any particular cultural context. It, therefore, also represents the Enlightenment tradition. It limits, however, the rational scope of that tradition. It identifies reason with science and affirms that science can tell us nothing about ethics, beauty, or a just or good political order.

Kant and Rawls, and the Enlightenment. Kant and Rawls (at least the early Rawls) both assume that there are both natural scientific truths that transcend culture and also ethical truths that do so. This separates them from both the cultural relativists and the emotivists. These truths derive from reason and not revelation. This separates them from not only fundamentalists but most, if not all, varieties of Christians, Jews, and Muslims. In other words, from any group that believes that there is a source of truth that might either contradict or supplement human reason.[1] They have no place within the framework of their systems for any mystical truth that is anti-rational or non-rational. This separates them from Hinduism and Buddhism, as well as from mystical traditions within Christianity, Judaism and other religious traditions.

According to Kant and Rawls, these rational truths may come to us through a specific tradition but we are not dependent upon any particular tradition in determining their nature, reliability and proper implementation. Thus, Kant and Rawls represent the Western Enlightenment tradition in its full blown sense.

The importance of Rawls. It is doubtful that a hundred years from now philosophical circles will judge Rawls to be as important as Kant but it is safe to say, that in contemporary ethical discussion, Rawls is one of the most prominent philosophers on the Anglo-American scene. Furthermore, he is prominent not just among philosophers but in the fields of political science, jurisprudence, and the social sciences. Thus, all informed contemporary discussion of the nature of justice has to come to terms with Rawls.

In the context of our discussion of the relationship of culture wars and ethical theory Rawls and Alasdair McIntyre, to whom we will devote the next chapter, are certainly two of the most important philosophers on the contemporary scene. This is because they are among the foremost representatives, if not the foremost representatives, of liberalism and communitarianism respectively. The liberal tradition represented by Rawls is under attack from many quarters.[2] This attack includes deconstructionists who represent a radical relativism in their critique of all of Western culture, including our political institutions, and communitarians who argue against both liberals and deconstructionists in defense of communal relationships as the basis of all coherent thought and action. The debate between the traditions represented by Rawls and MacIntyre has yet to make the front page of *Time* magazine. Nonetheless, readers who would understand the basic issues at stake in our present cultural conflict need to be familiar with this debate.

Rawls' major work, *A Theory of Justice*[3] is a rich, complicated, carefully reasoned work of nearly six hundred pages and many digressions. Furthermore, there is a very considerable literature on the interpretation of Rawls. What is offered here is a relatively brief summary of Rawls' central thesis. I will interpret this thesis in the context of the philosophical positions that we have considered thus far. My treatment will doubtless disappoint Rawls scholars. My hope, however, is that the introductory student will achieve a basic understanding.

Consistent with the previous chapters in this book, I will organize my discussion of Rawls in terms of his relationship to the thinkers and positions that we have already studied. This is, of course, not the only way to approach Rawls' thought. Any discussion of Rawls' general theory, however, must take into account Rawls' relationship to Kant and utilitarianism since Rawls himself couches the development of his theory in terms his relationship to these two perspectives. Explaining Rawls' relationship to the other positions studied in this book, however, will enhance our understanding of his place in recent thought.

The Rawlsian Game of Life

As we shall see, Rawls defines justice in terms of three basic meanings of equality. These are: (1) equality with respect to civil liberty, (2) equal distribution of the goods of society (with one important qualification), and (3) equality of opportunity. To understand Rawls' basic assumption let us imagine that we are going to play a game. For lack of a better name we will call it the Rawlsian game of life. Before playing any game, however, it is important to agree upon the rules of the game. Deciding the rules of any game after it has already started is a procedure that will lead to trouble.

The game is a comprehensive 'political' one. As we have said this is to be a game about life. Like the game of monopoly, it is concerned about the ownership of property. It is more complicated than monopoly, however, in that it includes gaining access to civil liberties, political freedom, educational opportunity, professional advancement, status within the community, health care, leisure time, recreational facilities, cultural experiences, freedom of expression, etc. The game is intended to be a comprehensive political one but it is not intended to be a comprehensive moral theory. Neither is it intended to be a comprehensive world and life view that will include fundamental religious assumptions.

The players develop the rules themselves. The game will be unlike monopoly in some other respects. In the first place, the rules are not already set for us by somebody else. *We have to make up the rules of this game for ourselves before we start.* This includes setting the goals of the game and defining what it means to be a winner. In monopoly being a winner means that one gains so much control over the resources of society that everyone else is hopelessly in debt to you. One becomes a winner not just by scoring the most but by taking everything. The first question therefore, which must be faced is whether taking everything or getting more than anyone else is the point of the game. As we shall see, for Rawls, taking it all is not the point of the game. But if getting the most or getting everything isn't the point of the game, what can be the point?

Oh! There is something else. We all tend to like best those games that we are good at. Even those of us who don't always have to win don't like to always lose. We certainly don't like to lose badly, especially at games that we think are important. It's hard to be a gracious loser all the time, especially since the world seems to be full of people who are not very gracious winners. Because we like to be winners, we tend to choose those games that reward our particular talents. There may be a lot of short, fat, slow, out of shape, and uncoordinated people who like to watch basketball. There are not many such people who like to play it. Such people certainly do not want to play basketball with tall, fast, coordinated opponents who are in good physical condition.

The players develop the rules of the game prior to assuming any personal identity. Given this tendency to want to play those games we are good at, let us try to make this whole process more interesting. Let us imagine that before us, is a stack of cards laying face down. Each card contains a list with biographical information. All the cards contain different information. One card may describe a forty year old, male in good health. He has a Ph.D. in computer science and parents who own properties in the millions. Another card may describe a female minority living on welfare who has no high school diploma. Still another card may describe a person who has been disowned by his parents some years ago and has just discovered that he is HIV positive.

Another card describes an individual who for twenty years has been treated by the local mental health center for severe and persistent mental illness. Another is mentally retarded. Still another has the physical ability to be a successful professional athlete. Some are old. Some are young. Some are brilliant. Most are average in terms of physical and mental ability, educational level, likelihood of inheriting substantial wealth, etc.

Even personal religious or ultimate commitments are left undecided. Let us try to make the game more interesting still. In your present state, you are aware of whether or not you believe in God, are a skeptic or an atheist. You know whether you want to become a medical missionary or successful wall street broker. You are aware of whether you most value friendship or intellectual competence. You know whether you most like to party or whether your greatest joy is in helping others. You also know whether or not you are a member of a family, a church, or a professional or civic organization that you value highly.

In short, you have some conception of your own idea of 'the good life'. Let us assume that each of these cards also contains a brief definition of the good life affirmed by the individual who draws the card. It articulates the highest ethical values, commitments and social relationships of that person.

After you have helped decide the rules of the game you are going to draw a card and play the game as if you are the person with the basic values, abilities and situation described on the card. *In other words, after the rules of the game have been decided upon, and only then, will you discover who you are in the Rawlsian game of life. You will only then have a specific identity.* Before you draw and turn over the card, you will be in a 'veil of ignorance' with respect to your actual identity, preferences, abilities, general situation and ultimate commitments.

'Equality' as Rawls' Fundamental Principle of Justice

A summary of Rawls' two basic principles of justice. Let us assume that you and the other potential players in the game, (who are likewise in a veil of ignorance) are rational and have a general knowledge of the workings of society. Let us imagine that you and the other players have a general education that includes basic courses in the natural sciences, the social sciences, and the humanities as well as a general knowledge of the geography, politics and economics of the modern world. In short, you have a great deal of general knowledge but no particular knowledge with respect to your prospective self and situation. Under such circumstances it behooves you to choose carefully the rules by which you will have to live.

What sort of rules would a rational persons choose if they found themselves in this so called original position? Rawls' answer is fairly clear. There are two rules. Since the second rule has two parts, we have three separate considerations. *The fundamental principle common to all the considerations, however, is the principle of equality.* Rational persons will naturally want a system that guarantees them the greatest amount of primary goods possible. Since they do not know anything about their future abilities and powers relative to other persons, they will insist upon rules that guarantee equal treatment for all. They are willing to accept inequality, if and only if, assured that they will stand to benefit from this inequality. Rawls summarizes his theory as follows:

> First: Each person is to have an equal right to the most extensive basic liberty compatible with a similar liberty for others. Second: Social and economic inequalities are to be arranged so that they are both (a) reasonably expected to be to everyone's advantage, and (b) attached to positions and offices open to all.[4]

It can fairly be said that for Rawls everything else he writes is clarification of, commentary on and defense of the two principles quoted immediately above. The commentary and defense are indeed extensive. If, however, we understand these two principles, then we have understood Rawls' major project. Thus, for Rawls the fundamental moral consideration for political systems is equality. All else is commentary.

Equality as 'equality of civil liberties'. For Rawls, civil liberties takes priority over all other forms of equality. Civil liberties are what he refers to as basic liberties. What Rawls means by basic liberties is again fairly clear. It is also non-controversial, in a theoretical sense to those committed to Western democratic ideals. The actual implementation of civil liberty, of course, remains controversial even in American society.

> The basic liberties of citizens are roughly speaking, political liberty (the right to vote and to be eligible for public office) together with freedom of speech and assembly; liberty of conscience and freedom of thought; freedom of the person along with the right to hold (personal) property; and freedom from arbitrary arrest and seizure as defined by the concept of the rule of law.[5]

The first principle obviously excludes slavery or any kind of discrimination based on race, sex, religion, national origin, etc. This is just the kind of rule that rational persons (who are unsure what their race, sex, religion or national origin was going to be once the game starts) would choose. A rational person would want the maximum amount of liberty consistent with equal liberty.

Furthermore, Rawls argues that the first and second principles are to be taken in lexical order.[6] *By this he means that a rational person would not be willing to sacrifice basic liberties in order to be better off with respect to material goods and equality of opportunity.* Rational persons (assuming that their material situation places them at or above the subsistence level) would not accept slavery or less than equal civil liberties in order to achieve a higher material standard of living. Rawls presents two arguments for the priority of civil liberties. The first appears to be both clear and not controversial. The second is not as obvious, at least to this writer.

The first argument for the priority of liberty is that material wealth and freedom are a necessary means to achieving one's goals but wealth without civil liberty is useless. Rawls' first argument runs something like the following: I don't know in the original position what my final or ultimate end or ends in life will be. For instance, I don't know whether my ultimate goals in life are going to resemble more closely those of Mother Teresa or Donald Trump. Whatever those goals are going to be, however, I am going to want the maximum amount of goods that will give me the means to achieve those final ends. Thus, both Mother Teresa and Donald Trump want money, access to educational opportunity, ability to travel, freedom of speech and thought, etc.

A rational person would not, however, sacrifice liberty for material abundance. Once I have reached a basic level of material well being, what I will want most is the freedom to use my opportunities to pursue my chosen goals what ever they may be. A high level of material abundance may be far less relevant if I am not free to choose how to use it.

We can illustrate this in terms of our previous example. Increasing Mother Teresa's material wealth significantly would be of limited value if she had to live in Trump Towers and was not free to go to India. It would certainly be of little value to her if she was not free to speak out on behalf of the poor. Conversely, if Donald Trump was made richer on the condition that he must spend his life in India, he would not consider this a good trade off. Most of us, of course, never contemplate being either as rich as Donald Trump or as holy and self-giving as Mother Teresa. Nevertheless, material well being without the freedom to use those means as we choose would probably be of little value.

The second argument for the priority of civil liberty is that civil liberty is necessary for self-respect. The second basic argument which Rawls uses is somewhat more puzzling. Rawls argues that one of the most important primary goods, if not the most important primary good, is that of self respect.[7] He then proceeds to argue that to trade away equal liberty for increased material gain would be to sacrifice this basic self-respect. Why this seems puzzling, is that self-respect is treated as a primary good rather than as a final or ultimate good. Material wealth is obviously a *means* for doing various things. Freedom of movement, speech, conscience, political freedom, etc., are also *means* to doing various things from aiding the poor to attaining personal wealth. Defining these things and expressing a desire for them does not seem to require a commitment to some definition concerning the ultimate meaning of life, or the nature of ultimate values.

Self-respect, however, seems to be either an *end* in itself or closely associated with ultimate ends. It is certainly not commonly thought of as a *means* to achieving other goals. Can we know what we mean by self-respect, however, without first coming to some definition of what it means to be a human self? Can we come to some definition of what it means to be a human self without making assertions, at least implicitly, about the ultimate meaning of life and the nature of ultimate value? I think not. I will have more to say about this in the section entitled "Rawls and Neutrality Regarding the Ultimate Good." In this later section we will discuss Rawls' relationship to Christian values (fundamentalist and otherwise) and secular humanism. We will also consider Rawls' articulation of his theory in a later essay entitled "Kantian Constructivism in Moral Theory."

The second meaning of equality is 'equality with respect to distribution of wealth'. Rawls' second principle of justice deals with access to the material and social benefits of society and has two parts, equality of material wealth, and equality of opportunity. These two meanings of 'equality' are quite distinct. Therefore, although Rawls speaks of two principles, I will treat them here as three principles. The first part has to do with the equal distribution of wealth, which I will deal with in this section. The second part has to do with equality of opportunity, which will be dealt with in the next section.

Equal distribution of wealth is the most controversial equality. This is most directly related to his attack on utilitarianism. For this reason, among others, we will be dealing with the clarification and defense of the principle throughout our discussion. I will therefore give only a brief introduction to it here. Known as the *'difference principle',* this principle specifies that *inequality in the distribution of the goods of society can be justified only if that inequality benefits everyone in the society.* Rawls modifies this somewhat to specify that inequality is justified if it benefits the poorest or *least advantaged in society.*

We can illustrate this principle by imagining that we are capable of choosing among four different possible social economic orders. We will designate these as SEOl, SEO2, SEO3, and SEO4, where SEO stands for Social Economic Order. For the sake of simplicity we will assume that all four of these social economic orders have exactly thirty members. We will also assume that all of the societies are characterized by equal civil liberties and equality of opportunity. They thus meet Rawls' other criteria for equality.

SEO1 has thirty units of good that we will call Gs. (By G, I intend a shorthand for all of the good things, both material things and privileges that almost everyone values.) Furthermore, everyone in

SEO1 has exactly one G. Thus, SEO1 is a society characterized by complete equality. The average utility of SEO1 is thirty Gs divided by thirty (the number of its citizens) or exactly 1.

SEO2: The move from SEO1 creates more winners than losers but does create losers. SEO2 has 60gs or twice as much wealth as SEO1. It, therefore, has an average utility of 2 (60gs divided by the thirty members of the society). Let us suppose, however, that the increased wealth is not divided equally. There are three groups of ten each. The most well off group has 35gs for an average of 3.5gs per person. The second most well off group has 20gs for an average of 2gs per person. The least well off group has 5gs for an average of .5gs per person. This society is more wealthy than the first but it is unequal.

If someone in the original position in a veil of ignorance were to choose SEO2 over SEO1, he or she would have a chance of being 2 times as well off or 3.5 times as well off as in SEO1. This individual would also have a chance of being .5 as well off in the move from SEO1 to SEO2. There are more winners than losers but there are definitely losers. Rawls argues that a rational person in the original position would not make this choice. It does not benefit the least advantaged. It does not satisfy the conditions of the 'difference principle'. Therefore, it is not as just as SEO1.

This clearly illustrates the difference between Rawls' theory of justice and utilitarianism. SEO2 has twice the average utility of SEO1. The utilitarian would therefore choose SEO2 over SEO1. Rawls' rational individual in the original position would still not choose SE02. Relative to SEO1, it does not benefit the least advantaged.

SEO3: No losers but the move from SEO1 does not benefit the least advantaged. SEO3 also has 60gs for an average utility of 2. It is also has three unequal groups. The first group has 30gs. The second has 20gs, and the third has 10g's. If our hypothetical rational individual were to choose SEO3 over SEO1 there would be no losers. Some would be better off than they would be in the first group but everyone would be at least as well off as they would be in the first group. This is because the lowest group still has 10gs for an average of one G per person. Despite this fact, however, Rawls would reject this option.

Why? The difference principle requires that we may compromise with the norm of equality *only if it benefits the least advantaged in society.* There is no benefit to the lowest group in SEO3 as compared

Culture War and Ethical Theory

to SEO1. Therefore, the compromise with equality isn't worth it. According to Rawls, a rational individual in the original position would not choose it over SEO1.

SEO4: The move from SEO1 does benefit the least advantaged. SEO4 like SEO2 and SEO3 also has 60gs and an average utility of 2. There is, however, a different distribution of wealth in SEO4. The first group has 25gs for an average of 2.5gs. The second has 20gs for an average of 2gs. The third has 15gs for an average of 1.5gs. Rawls argues that rational individuals in the original position would choose SEO4 over SEO1. Even though it is an unequal society, the choice would benefit the least advantaged. SEO4 would also be preferred to the other two societies since it benefits the least advantage relative to these other two societies.

The different choices that we have outlined are depicted in the chart below. Rawls would favor SEO4 over the other three, since it increases wealth but also benefits the least advantaged. He would favor SEO1 over SEO2 and SEO3, because although they increase the wealth of society, they do not benefit the least advantaged. He would favor SEO3 over SEO2 (if those were his only choices) since SEO3 (compared only to SEO2) benefits the least advantaged.

	SEO1	SEO2	SEO3	SEO4
Group 1	10gs	35gs	30gs	25gs
Group 2	10gs	20gs	20gs	20gs
Group 3	10gs	5gs	10gs	15gs
Total	30gs	60gs	60gs	60gs
Ave. Utility	1g	2gs	2gs	2gs
Least Advantaged	1g	5gs	1g	1.5gs

Even first time readers of Rawls with limited backgrounds in social philosophy are frequently puzzled by Rawls' insistence that a 'rational individual' would not make a choice similar to that of choosing SEO2 or SEO3, over SEO1. SEO2 presents us with the possibility of losing. Still, the odds are two thirds in favor of a significant benefit. The choice between SEO3 and SEO1 seems to contain no risk at all. The gambler has a two third's chance of winning but no chance of losing. Why would it be irrational to make either of these two choices, especially the second?

Rawls gives the impression that first he is committed to rationality and that secondarily he is committed to equality *because* rationality necessarily leads to equality. Therefore, anyone who is committed to rationality as a fundamental principle will also necessarily be committed to equality. On this view, to reject equality is to be irrational.

The equation of rationality and equality is presumably demonstrated by reflection on what individuals in the original position would choose. Equality protects the individual from unacceptable loss. It avoids the gamble with unacceptable risk. Rawls' gambling man or women in the original position can only win. He or she can never lose.

What shall we make of the assumption underlying this claim that rationality excludes any risk of inequality? It is true that, all other things being equal, it is more rational to take a gamble with the possibility of some gain and a zero risk of loss than a gamble that includes the possibility of loss. People do, however, invest everyday in activities that imply considerable risk. Consider, for instance, business ventures, the stock market, political activity, interpersonal relationships (like marriage and the decision to become adoptive or biological parents), recreational activities, job changes, profound religious commitments, etc. Sometimes these investments are forced. Individuals must make some decision and every decision requires some risk. Sometimes, however, the risks are avoidable or individuals deliberately choose higher risk options in order to get higher gain. Whether or not these risks are considered rational rests on several factors.

What is the probability of achieving the goal? What are the consequences of failing to achieve the goal? Failure could mean a modest reduction in standard of living. It could, in some circumstances, mean abject poverty or even death. Is the risk being undertaken for a trivial or unworthy goal or for an important and noble one? To risk one's life for a few minutes of pleasure appears to be irrational because the goal is trivial relative to the potential loss. To risk one's life for the goal of gaining power over others for its own sake seems irrational because the goal (even though it may be our ultimate goal in life) is unworthy. It may, however, be rational to risk one's life for one's most deeply held conviction. Socrates' arguments in *Plato's Dialogues*, the *Apology* and the *Crito* are examples here. Socrates argues that an agreement to give up the privilege of free inquiry would result in a denial of his most fundamental self. For him, the risk of death and ultimately the certainty of death are not sufficient reason for him to cease his critique of life's ultimate meaning.

My point in raising these considerations is certainly not to argue against the moral importance of the principle of equality. It is not even to argue that 'equality' properly understood is not grounded in 'rationality' properly understood. Rawls' argument for the relationship of rationality and equality, however, seems to rest on the *prudential considerations of a very conservative gambler*. For 'rationality' to bear the weight he wishes to place upon it, would seem to require the meaning of rationality that we find in Kant. For Kant, rationality is the essential principle of human nature that demands our ultimate respect. For Kant rationality is sacred and not simply prudential. We will consider these issues in more detail later on in our discussion.

Equality as 'Equality of Opportunity'. The second part of the second principle is less controversial in Western democratic societies. It is one that we are probably all committed to in principle, however, much our society may fail to achieve it in practice. It is simply the principle that everyone regardless of race, creed, religion, sex or national origin should have an equal opportunity to gain access to wealth, professional and social status and any other goods of society. Rawls argues that rational persons in the original position would insist on this principle being basic since they would not know into what state of affairs they would be born.

The criterion of equality of opportunity excludes a number of possible social arrangements that would otherwise be consistent with the liberty principle and the difference principle. For example, there might be economic and social circumstances which would make a society rigidly divided along class lines to the material benefit of the least advantaged in society. If this society also provided equal civil liberties, it would satisfy Rawls' first two criteria for a just social order. Failure to satisfy the criterion of equality of opportunity would still exclude the justification of such a society.

For example, there are many good arguments for a free public school system through high school and making college available to all citizens regardless of economic class or income. Utility is one such argument. Rawls' theory provides a different argument. Utilitarians argue that it increases the average utility to have an educated citizenry. Doubtless their argument is empirically correct. Rawls, however, need not argue for access to college or university training for all on the basis of utility or even that such access benefits everyone, including the least advantaged. Access to college or university training is necessary in our society to provide for equality of opportunity. It is justified, therefore, even if it could be shown that the resources spent on education do not increase the average utility or even benefit the least advantaged.

Equality of opportunity is a relatively uncontroversial principle (as distinguished from its implementation) in American society. Still we may raise some questions here about its relationship to the concept of rationality. Is it completely irrational to trade equality of opportunity for an increase in material wealth and comfort? Usually we associate equality of opportunity with equality of civil liberty. But this is not necessarily the case. The writer of this book, for instance, is a non-Lutheran teaching in a Lutheran school that requires that the president be Lutheran. Like approximately two thirds of the faculty, he does not have equality with Lutherans with respect to being president. I think, however, that a visitor to our campus would find it difficult to find any non-Lutheran faculty member who would prefer the right to be president to a significant raise. Are we all irrational on that account? I think not. If, however, non-Lutherans had less academic freedom than Lutherans, that would be a different matter. It would be regarded as intolerable. Whether 'equality of opportunity' is necessarily linked to 'rationality' appears therefore to depend on the answer to more specific questions. 'Equality of opportunity' with respect to what?

Rawls and Kant

The 'veil of ignorance' the 'categorical imperative' and the goal of impartiality. It seems that the veil of ignorance in Rawls serves the same function as the categorical imperative in Kant. This is to enable the individual to reason in an objective and impartial manner regarding just principles and action.

Because of the veil of ignorance, you do not know your ultimate commitments and wants, and what specific means and resources are likely to be available to you to achieve those commitments and wants. The veil of ignorance, therefore, protects you from the biases or prejudices that otherwise might tempt you. You will not be tempted to prefer rules that favor the rich over the poor, the young over the old, or one race over another. You will not want to prefer males over females, the religious over the non-religious, the person of above or below average intelligence, etc. Under these conditions you will presumably be disposed to make up and commit in advance to rules that everyone and anyone would be willing to live by.

This looks rather close to Kant's admonition to "act only on that maxim through which you can at the same time will that it should become a universal law." The focus is, of course, somewhat different. Kant is giving us a formula to check out any *particular* action that we are inclined to commit.

Kant assumes that the ethical problem is to place the right action under the right rule. For every contemplated action there is a possible rule that may be formulated to govern that action. Kantian individuals unlike, Rawlsian individuals, know a great deal about themselves and their situation. When confronted with a moral dilemma, the first task is to formulate an appropriate rule. "Everybody should cheat on exams if their grades are as bad as mine and they get as good a chance as I have." "Everybody should steal a car if they need one and want one as badly as I do." Then the individual must ask if he or she would be willing to make that rule into a universal law that anyone and everyone should live by. If the answer is no, then the act shouldn't be committed. If the answer is yes, then the act is permissible. It is according to duty. Thus, with Kant we start with the particular and reason back to the universal.

With Rawls, we are engaged in an analogous but somewhat different enterprise. We are starting not with a particular action, in a particular situation and a particular set of presumed motives and then moving to the higher ground of general principles. In what Rawls calls the original position --the position of the participants before the rules are formulated and before they have begun to play the game--the individual has no particular action, situation, or motives in mind. The individual in this situation is trying to formulate a general set of rules that can apply to any situation that may arise. Thus, with Rawls we start with the universal and avoid any particulars in our initial formulation.

Thus, Kant's strategy is to start with the particular and reason to the general. Rawls' strategy is to start with general rules that can be applied to any particular situation imaginable. In both cases, however, the goal is to transcend prejudice and bias which are impediments to objectivity and rationality. To the extent this is possible our rules will be rational and hence fair. To be rational and fair is equated with being good.

Kant and Rawls and the disembodied self. It is worth noting at this point, a standard criticism that is brought against both Kant and Rawls and the type of ethical thinking they represent. Both seem to be seeking a device that enables the individuals to mentally separate themselves from all concrete particular situations, goals and feelings-- except the goal to be rational. It is argued that this disembodied individual is a fiction. It not only never really exists or could exist, it cannot even be imagined in any meaningful sense. Real people inhabit real worlds full of particular goals, desires, possibilities and conceptions of the good life. Both Kant's and Rawls' ethics, these critics argue, are too abstract, formal and ethereal. When put to the test in real life situations, they give us no meaningful guidance. Kant and Rawls, of course, would reject this criticism. Rawls, particularly has in his *A Theory of Justice* offered a long (nearly six hundred pages) detailed treatment showing how his theory is to be applied to the development and articulation of law and social policy in a modern liberal democratic society. We will consider this criticism in more detail in the chapter on the ethics of virtue.

Kant and Rawls, and the ultimate good. There is one other comparison between Kant and Rawls that needs to be mentioned here, although we will need to return to it later. Kant is quite clear about the fundamental basis of his ethical theory. To use the categories we have used earlier, he is explicit about the nature of his ethical theory at the base level. It is the rational autonomous individual that is the foundation of all else. Nothing is good in itself but a 'good will'. A 'good will', however, is a will that has determined to not be controlled by any external (non-rational, heteronomous) factors. It is a rational autonomous will. If a rational autonomous will is the base for Kant's ethics, the categorical imperative is the fundamental principle of that ethical system. When we come to the rule level we find that moral rules are those rules or maxims that are consistent with the categorical imperative. At the case application level, we are instructed that those particular actions that would be allowed or mandated by rules that are consistent with the categorical imperative are moral actions. This much is clear in Kant's ethics.

Kant, therefore, appears to be quite clear about his conception of the ultimate good. It is a conception of ultimate good that rejects heteronomy (control from influences external to the individual). Thus, it rejects a personality controlled by hedonistic desire as immoral. It is also a conception of ultimate good that rejects what some thinkers have called theonomy (personality controlled by the will of God). Theonomy, like hedonism would be a variety of heteronomy. Kant, of course, makes room in his system for God. This, however, is only because the will of God is defined as a rational will which is consistent with the direction of the individual's own human rational will.

Rawls, on the other hand, wishes in his theory to avoid making any commitment to the ultimate good. He rejects the strategy of starting with what he calls a 'thick theory of the good'. He chooses rather to found his initial view of a theory of justice on a 'thin theory of the good'. The thin theory of the good does not propose to instruct us with respect to the nature of ultimate good. It merely assumes those good things that any rational being would want to the extent that he or she is rational at all.[8] Furthermore, Rawls (unlike Kant) does not intend to develop a complete ethical theory. He wishes to develop only a theory of political justice that can provide the basis of cooperation among individuals and groups that hold to quite different and incompatible positions with respect to what is the ultimate good. Thus, if Rawls does avoid making even an implicit commitment to the nature of ultimate good for all human beings, then he seems to differ from Kant in a very fundamental respect.[9]

Rawls, and the exercise of moral power. Rawls, however, in his essay "Kantian Constructivism in Moral Theory"[10] makes an explicit commitment to a clearly Kantian definition of individualism. This consists in the expression of the individual's two basic moral powers. The discussion of two basic 'moral powers' introduces a cluster of considerations.

> The first moral power is the capacity for a sense of justice, that is, the capacity to understand, to apply and to act from (and not merely in accordance with) the principles of justice. The second moral power is the capacity, to revise and rationally pursue a conception of the good[11]

Rawls links the expression of these two moral powers with the Kantian conception of autonomy. Moral personality consists in the ability to freely express these two moral powers. There are several things which are worth noting here. Individuals have the capacity to "revise and rationally pursue a conception of the good." Rawls also insists that individual conceptions of the good must be plural in number.[12]

There are several separate considerations here. (1) Rawls claims to be developing a theory of justice and not a complete moral theory. (2) Individuals must respect the sense of justice in herself and others. (3) Individuals posit conceptions of the *final* good in addition to political justice and the ideal of autonomy associated with political justice. (4) All individuals must be able and must think of themselves as able to *revise* their conception of the good. (5) They must be able to *rationally* pursue a conception of the good. (6) Rational individuals cannot have a single good or final end for their lives. We are all committed to a *plurality* of final ends which we seek to balance throughout our lives. (7) Different individuals will have *different sets of final ends and give different* weights or values to those ends.

Does this cluster of considerations adequately represent Kant's theory? Rawls' chief concern is neither to be a faithful interpreter or follower of Kant. If his theory departs from Kant in some major respects this is not necessarily an argument against it. Nonetheless, Rawls has chosen to elucidate his theory in the light of Kant's theory and to identify his own perspective with that of Kant in at least a general sense. Furthermore, Rawls asserts that Kant's theory offers the most adequate articulation of the Western liberal democratic tradition.[13] Therefore, significant distinctions between Rawls and Kant can illumine the thought of both thinkers.

Some Comparisons Between Rawls and Kant

Unlike Kant, Rawls claims to offer only a political morality. In the first place, Rawls is attempting to develop not a complete moral theory, which would include individual morality, but only a political morality or theory of justice. This distinction, of course, rests upon the ability to differentiate individual and political morality in a useful and meaningful sense. The ability to distinguish between political morality and individual morality is complicated by Rawls' recognition that for his political morality or theory of justice to be implemented requires a society in which individuals have a particular conception of self-hood. This is an issue to which we will return later.

Like Kant, Rawls affirms that we must respect the sense of justice in both ourselves and others. Secondly, it is clear from Rawls' discussion in the Kantian Constructivism essay that a significant part the ability to act for the *sake* of justice, not just in *accord* with justice, must include the ability to respect and encourage the ability of others to exercise *their* moral powers. This is similar, if not identical, to the formulations of the categorical imperative that instruct us "to treat others always as ends in themselves and never simply as means," and to act "as if we were law making members in a kingdom of ends." Applied to Rawls' principles for the formulation of the foundations of political philosophy, this would mean that we should not only seek to create laws which allow us to exercise our moral powers. It also requires that we seek to create laws which allow others to exercise their moral powers. We must treat both ourselves *and* others as ends and not just as means. Thus, a sense of justice requires that we respect the 'sense of justice' in ourselves and others. This emphasis strikes one as thoroughly Kantian.

Unlike Kant, Rawlsian individuals may legitimately posit final ends other than autonomy The point being made here is not explicitly made in Rawls writing but it seems to be a clear implication from his work. Kant seems to hold that the final end of a rational autonomous individual is just that--to be rationally autonomous. The ideal of rational autonomy serves to give guidance in the formulation of both political theory and individual morality. Furthermore, for Kant, rational autonomy is the litmus test for all moral behavior. A moral person neither has nor needs any other final end to his existence. Rawls, on the other hand, clearly seems to wish to allow for final ends other than rational autonomy--*although not for final ends which are contrary to rational autonomy (at least to the extent they have implications for the political realm).* Rawls would doubtless argue that he is simply intending to give some content to the Kantian notion of rational autonomy. Still, although Kant would certainly recognize that different individuals will have different ends depending on their abilities, inclinations, and life situation, it is doubtful that he would call these different ends *final ends.*

How shall we account for this seeming difference between the two thinkers? It rests, I believe, on Rawls desire to develop a political theory that provides for social harmony while allowing for genuine pluralism with respect to ultimate commitments. For Rawls, political justice does not entail either a complete moral theory, an all encompassing epistemology, or an ultimate metaphysical or religious commitment. Rawls would never write nor desire to write a book with the title which Kant gave his *Religion Within the Limits of Reason Alone.* To do so would lay him open to the charge of developing a theory of justice which places severe restrictions on the religious and philosophical liberties of its citizens. Political theory, or a theory of justice within the limits of reason alone, is all to which he aspires. This is because for Rawls, a just political order must leave open the choice of ultimate or final ends.

Unlike Kant, Rawls affirms that individuals must think of themselves as able to revise their final ends. We all revise our goals frequently throughout life. For example, I once had the goal of having wall to wall carpeting in my house. My goal is now to have oak flooring. In the grand sweep of a lifetime this is a trivial adjustment. People also revise what they or impartial observers would deem their ultimate goals. Saul of Tarsus the persecutor of Christians became the leading exponent of Christianity.   Less ambiguously but nonetheless dramatically, Oscar Schindler the Nazi became a life saver to over a thousand Jews. When we speak of the transformation of goals of this magnitude, we seem to be dealing not just with adjustment to changing circumstances but with a fundamental change of self identity.[14]

Describing rational autonomy in terms of the necessary ability to *revise* one's *final* ends sounds more like Sartrian existentialism than the rational Enlightenment perspective of Kant. Sartre insists that there is no essential human nature. Therefore, human beings are not defined by transcendent religious truth, physical nature or any universal law of reason. They are always free to choose their identity at every moment in a radical sense. Kant on the other hand, seems to assume a universal reason which, given the same circumstances, would cause every rational individual who correctly applies the categorical imperative to act in the same way.

Both affirm that the individual must be able to rationally pursue a final good, but Kant and Rawls appear to interpret rational pursuit of final goods differently. The ability to rationally pursue one's final good sounds Kantian enough.　But this depends upon what is meant by 'rational' in this context.　When speaking of the moral life, Kant means by 'rational' the ability to abide by the categorical imperative.　He defines the categorical imperative as a synthetic a priori proposition. When it comes to morality, Kant has no interest in synthetic a posteriori propositions or, in other words, in a definition of rationality that has to do with the rationally effective relating of means to ends. The rationally effective relating of means to ends is the essence of morality for Bentham, Mill, and the utilitarian tradition.　It has no place in Kant's ethics.　This, of course, is not to say that Kant thinks the relating of means to ends is unimportant.　He would never, however, place the rationally effective relationship of means and ends at the center of moral personality.

It is this non-Kantian sense of 'rational' that is associated with synthetic a posteriori propositions or relating means to ends to which Rawls seems to be referring.[15]　This is not to say that Rawls may not be more right than Kant here.　It is, however, an important difference between the two thinkers.

Unlike Kant, Rawls affirms a commitment to a plurality of final ends.　Kant tells us that the only thing which is good in itself is a "good will."　This is at the very center of his conception of moral personality. Many thinkers have been stuck by what seems to them to be the austere single-mindedness of Kant's ethical theory.　The categorical imperative in its various formulations is designed to insure rational autonomy. Autonomy entails the exclusion of all motivation based on satisfaction of personal desires, hedonistic or otherwise.　Satisfaction of personal desires is heteronomy and is the antithesis of morality.　Thus, a plurality of final or ultimate ends seems to be excluded from the Kantian ethic.

Rawls, on the other hand, takes an opposing viewpoint.　He seems to assume something like the following:　We all have not only a plurality of ends, but a plurality of ends which we consider final or ultimate.　There is not necessarily any single end which we take to be prior to all the others and which can unify our quest for the good life. His statements about this are very strong.　In a passage which occurs in the context of a discussion about such diverse viewpoints as St. Ignatius Loyola, Thomas Aquinas, and hedonism he equates all single-end theories with madness.

Human good is heterogeneous because the aims of the self are heterogeneous. Although to subordinate all our aims to one end does not strictly speaking violate the principles of rational choice (not the counting principles anyway), it still strikes us as irrational, or more likely as mad. The self is disfigured and put in the service of one of its ends for the sake of system.[16]

Rawls, of course, does not view himself as critiquing Kant with these remarks. On the contrary, he regards himself as consistent with Kant as well as with Aristotle.[17] I suspect that his viewpoint is not consistent with Aristotle but will not pursue that connection here. I will return to some of the matters discussed above with respect to Kant in the section which deals with Rawls' attempts to avoid ultimate metaphysical commitments.

Rawls and Cultural Relativism

Rawls clearly rejects cultural relativism in his *A Theory of Justice.* In some of his later writings, however, he appears not to be affirming a rational theory of justice that transcends all particular social contexts. He rather seems to be committed to the more modest goal of giving an articulation of the most basic assumptions that characterize Western liberal democracies. On this interpretation, the Western liberal democratic tradition is viewed as only one cultural tradition among others.[18]

Rawls' most recent view appears to be a political absolutism (political liberalism is superior to all other political systems) and metaphysical agnosticism (Rawls wants to avoid making assertions about comprehensive moral theory or the ultimate nature of reality).[19] If this interpretation is correct, then Rawls clearly rejects cultural relativism as a norm for contemporary society.

Rawls is not trying to develop a complete ethical theory that would cover both social justice and personal ethics. He merely intends to develop a theory of social justice that could provide the framework for a just political society. The presumption is that within the structure of these 'political absolutes,' which constitute a just political order, individuals and groups may espouse different and even incompatible absolutes regarding the good life, and the ultimate nature and meaning of the universe.

His theory of justice could even accommodate both absolutists and relativists. This assertion would appear to entail two qualifications. Relativism is restricted to the range of values which individuals and groups choose to hold within the framework of a political theory which holds to the absolute value of rational autonomy in political theory. Absolute values for individuals or groups, on the other hand, must be compatible with the absolute value of rational autonomy in political theory.

This is a position that is likely to be unsatisfactory to either absolutists or relativists. Rawls might well respond that his social theory although completely satisfactory to no one provides the basis for fairness, tolerance, and social harmony for a wide range of individuals, groups, religions, and philosophical positions. It excludes a Hitler, a Stalin, a Khoumani, and the KKK. It may be incompatible with a state where militant and thorough going cultural relativists are in complete control. It rejects anarchism. It does, Rawls would argue, allow for a Martin Luther King Jr., a Ghandi, a Mother Teresa, Muslims, Jews, Christians, and secular humanists of a wide variety of stripes. It won't enable us to avoid cultural conflict. It isn't designed to do that. Rawls would regard the avoidance of cultural conflict as impossible and probably undesirable. It will enable us to avoid a culture war. Where political liberalism is adopted, despite James Davison Hunter's catchy title--the shooting doesn't have to start.[20]

If Rawls is understood as an absolutist, then the restricted nature of his absolutism is critical to his project. What Rawls desires to do is to make it possible for persons holding to a wide variety of absolute goals in life to live in harmony. *The rules of the game must be absolute. The meaning of the game is not.* For example, Rawls wants to accommodate the person who believes that this game of life is all that there is to human existence. He also wants to accommodate the person who believes in an after life that is infinitely more important than this life. Furthermore, persons in both categories will be allowed to have enormous differences of opinion concerning the priorities that should be given to the various good things in life. Rawls wants a social order characterized by tolerance, pluralism, and social harmony. He believes that a just social order founded on rationality is the means to achieving this goal.

Rawls is not explicitly embracing relativistic assumptions here. He simply wishes to avoid making comprehensive absolutistic claims. The problem for Rawls is whether it is sufficient for his purposes to avoid making ultimate metaphysical commitments to culturally transcendent truths.

In the first place, we may ask whether there is such a thing as a *single* Western liberal democratic tradition? Optimists who view our society describe it as pluralistic. Pessimists view it as fragmented. Rawls hopes to develop an overlapping consensus which embraces the basic beliefs that all believers in liberal democracy have in common. For this to work there must be some tenets that we all do have in common. Whether there is a common core or not is a complex historical and sociological question which we cannot fully explore here. It is clear, however, that this is an assumption which cannot be taken for granted.

Secondly, if there are conflicting traditions that can make a legitimate historical and social claim to being a part of the Western liberal democratic tradition, when they conflict over important political issues (abortion, homosexuality, definition of family, fundamental values to be taught in public education, etc.) an agnostic Rawlsian perspective can give us no basis for choosing among them. The Judeo-Christian heritage and the Enlightenment are absolutist (comprehensive) and part of that tradition. The hedonistic utilitarianism of Bentham and Mill are also absolutist (comprehensive) perspectives which are part of that tradition. These seem on the face of it to contain elements that contradict each other in fundamental ways.

Thirdly, it might be argued that until fairly recently, at least, one of our shared assumptions was that Western liberal democracy is superior to all alternatives, including alternatives based on comprehensive moral theories and world and life views. Most Americans do not think that our political philosophy is simply different from Soviet Communism, Hitler's National Socialism, and Islamic fundamentalism. We think it is superior on moral grounds that we hold to be absolute. The Rawls of a *Theory of Justice* seemed to be providing a philosophical defense of this comprehensive absolutism that is part of our tradition. Kant, utilitarianism, the deism of many of the founding fathers of the nation and the Judeo-Christian tradition are all absolutist. It is difficult to see that a relativistic interpretation of our tradition is an accurate interpretation of the roots of our tradition or of what most Americans or Westerners believe today.

In the fourth place, it is problematic whether we can conduct either international trade or a foreign policy without assuming the moral superiority of our own liberal democratic tradition over clearly incompatible traditions, including political systems and traditions founded on comprehensive world views. Can we really be neutral with respect to the issue of the establishment of liberal democracies in formerly communist countries? Can we be neutral with respect to the role of women in Islamic or African cultures including the denial of basic civil liberties in Islamic cultures and the practice of female circumcision in African cultures?

If it is to be consistent, Rawls' political liberalism seems to have many of the problems associated with cultural relativism. If Rawls rejects his agnosticism with respect to comprehensive world views he inherits many of the problems associated with absolutism.

Rawls and Emotivism

The early Rawls obviously rejects emotivism. For him rational discourse about normative issues is meaningful and relevant. Whether or not Rawls, especially the later Rawls, entirely avoids the critique of the emotivist is, of course, another question with which we will have to deal.

Emotivists do not claim that we may not reason about the relationship of one moral idea to another or on the relationship of a moral idea to a particular action. They simply maintain that we cannot reason about the ultimate ground of our ethical principles. For example, an emotivist would agree that if we think persons should not be killed for the sake of the convenience of others and that the fetus is a person, than it is rational to maintain that the life of the fetus should not be taken for the convenience of others. The emotivist simply maintains that the original moral principle (in this case that persons should not be killed for the sake of the convenience of others) cannot be given a rational ground. It is grounded on emotion and not on reason.

We can give an emotivist account of how persons may be persuaded of the value of Western liberal democracy. For example, suppose that I happen to be raised in such a way that the ideal of autonomy elicits a positive emotional response. Let us further suppose that Rawls or some other philosopher can show me that there is strong correlation between autonomy and Western liberal democracy. Then the positive emotional response to one idea (autonomy) will be transferred to the other idea (Western liberal democracy.) I will have been "persuaded" that liberal democracy is a good thing.

Suppose, however, that due to my cultural upbringing or some other factor that my emotional life is differently constructed so that I do not respond positively to the idea of autonomy. Then the rational linking of autonomy and liberal democracy will not have the desired effect. Furthermore, no rational defense of autonomy is ultimately possible. I will not be persuaded of the value of liberal democracy unless it can be linked with some other phenomena to which I am emotionally drawn.

Suppose, for example, I have a positive emotional response to the idea of maximizing my pleasure. If it can be demonstrated that I am most likely to achieve this goal in a liberal democratic society, then I will develop a positive emotional (not a rational) response to liberal democracy.

Or suppose rather that I have come to develop a positive emotional response to the idea of converting the world to some particular religious viewpoint. If I can be persuaded by sound sociological arguments that this goal is most realizable in a liberal democratic society, then the positive emotional response regarding my religious views will be transferred to the idea of liberal democracy.

Rational persuasion *on this level* is possible on the emotivist position. What is the possibility of consensus on emotivist assumptions? If we have a culture in which the majority of individuals have similar emotional responses over a wide range of phenomena, the possibility of consensus is pretty high. If, however, we have not a pluralistic but a fragmented culture with little coherence regarding emotional responses to moral issues, then the possibility of rational discourse about moral issues, including political issues is low.

The degree to which our culture exhibits this coherence is a matter for sociologists to determine. Many observers claim that rational coherence is breaking down and emotional coherence with it. They claim that we live in an emotivist culture where the manipulation of feeling rather than rational persuasion is the primary mode of discourse. The Rawls of *A Theory of Justice* has a clear rational ground to which to appeal when consensus breaks down. The later Rawls has by no means completely abandoned that rational ground. He is willing to argue within a range of various comprehensive theories that political liberalism is the best articulation of a reasonable political order. When confronted with an individual with a comprehensive perspective incompatible with political liberalism, however, Rawls appears to have nothing more to say than the emotivst. Furthermore, what is being asserted by many is the sociological fact of the breakdown of comprehensive perspectives of all sorts. Dialogue, it is affirmed, is impossible because of the fragmentation of our social and intellectual life. Rawls' ability to assist us in the avoidance of culture wars seems to rest on intellectual and social foundations that are eroding away.

Rawls and Egoism

It seems clear that Rawls is not an egoist. In the first place, Rawls wants to make room in his social order for individuals and groups holding to a wide variety of views of the ultimate good. This may include egoism but it is not intended to exclude agape love.

Secondly, Rawls is clear that individuals in the original position may regard themselves as representative of communities or groups with strong moral and emotional ties. Individuals in the original position doe not know what if any groups they will be connected with but they know that they will want the maximum amount of equality for those groups vis-à-vis other groups.

Thirdly, the ideal of equality itself appears to be one that is contrary to egoism. Egoists want it all. They may agree to equality as a backup position because they know they can't get it all. Equality is not their first and highest commitment, however, as it appears to be with Rawls. Rawls wants a society which inculcates the virtue of fraternity. Fraternity, as a civic virtue, he defines as the desire to not possess more than other members of society, which he equates with commitment to the difference principle.[21] Fraternity is a virtue which is contrary to selfishness.

Fraternity, as Rawls defines it, is not love. At least it is not agape love. Rawls, however, is not attempting to define all the virtues or even the highest virtues. He defines the basic civic virtues as *liberty, equality and fraternity*, thus linking himself with the French Enlightenment. But these are only intended to be the highest civic virtues. Whether or not they are the highest virtues of all is an open question for Rawls. Thus, because Rawls says nothing about agape love, we may not infer a commitment to egoism on his part.

In the fourth place, the Rawlsian conception of individualism is not egoistic. There is a stain of individualism that is clearly based on egoism. We have encountered this already in our study of Bentham. The individualism in Adam Smith's *Wealth of Nations* is egoistic. Individuals in the social order are conceived of in an atomistic fashion. They pursue their own selfish ends. Because of a natural identity of interests, however, the greatest good for the greatest number is achieved and the economy thrives and coheres "as if controlled by an unseen hand."

There is, however, at least one other strain of individualism in the Enlightenment literature. We have already encountered it in Kant. Kant's rational individualism with its emphasis on autonomy is not egoistic. The sociologist Talcott Parsons analyzes what he calls "institutionalized individualism" which he traces from the "Protestant Ethic."[22] In the field of popular entertainment the Western film depicts heroes who are at the same time both highly individualistic and altruistic. This individualism has as strong sense of social responsibility. It may be a vice to ask for help but it is a virtue to give it to others in need.

Why then is Rawls sometimes accused of egoism? First there is the erroneous assumption that individualism is necessarily associated with egoism. Secondly, Rawls' limited project of providing a theory of social justice rather than a comprehensive ethical theory including a theory of the virtues prevents discussion of the nature of love and other associated virtues.

Thirdly, however, there seems, to be another reason why Rawls is sometimes interpreted as an egoist. Despite his protestations to the contrary, (at least in his *A Theory of Justice*) Rawls rational individual in the original position seems to argue for equality on the basis of rational prudence. Rawls' individual seems to be a very conservative gambler who opts for equality out of a concern to protect personal interests and not out of any concern for the interests of fellow players in the original position. The individual may have love, community and interpersonal commitments after entering the game of life. But individuals have none, and by definition can have none, in the original position. In the original position persons neither love nor hate. They have no specific desires or aversions. They have no long or short term goals. They seem, therefore, to choose equality with the exception of the difference principle on the basis of a 'rational cool calculation'.

This disembodied rational maker of choices seems, therefore, to epitomize the rational egoist who chooses a safe social order where there can never be anything other than a natural identity of interests. Rawls argues, however, that the parties in the original position are not choosing as rational egoists but as trustees who are acting as the faithful representatives of persons and interests that transcend their own selfish desires.[23]

Rawls and Hedonism

There seems to be no evidence that Rawls endorses hedonism. I deal with the question here only because we have specifically considered hedonism as one of the options in this book. In the first place, hedonism is a theory about the *single* ultimate good for all human beings. Rawls is interested in developing a theory of justice which allows for individuals to make numerous *different* choices regarding the ultimate good once they leave the original position. Secondly, Rawls seems to assume throughout his discussion that normal individuals use their reason to achieve a balance in their lives among a *number* of competing goods. The normal Rawlsian individual holds to no single ultimate good but to a number of goods. Thirdly, if there is a single ultimate good which could be distinguished in Rawls position it would not be pleasure but the ability to develop one's potentiality to the highest possible degree.

Rawls and Utilitarianism

Rawls rejects utilitarianism. In fact, utilitarianism is the chief object of attack in his theory. There is clearly a large place for teleological considerations in Rawls' theory. To this extent he has something in common with utilitarianism. Nevertheless, he defends the priority of equality on deontological grounds and criticizes utilitarianism for its failure to do so.

His chief criticism of utilitarianism is that it may under certain circumstances justify inequality and exploitation of the few by the many. The chief virtue of Rawls' theory, as he sees it, is that it only justifies unequal distribution of wealth. Furthermore, it only justifies unequal distribution of wealth under those conditions where exploitation of the few by the many is excluded.

Rawls seems to assume that the chief rival to his own theory is utilitarianism, at least in modern liberal democracies. He regards his theory as having all the virtues of utilitarianism. Like utilitarianism it allows for equal civil liberties, equality of opportunity, and unequal distribution of wealth under certain circumstances. Unlike utilitarianism, it does not start with what is useful and argue for equality because it contributes to the production of good and useful things. His theory starts with equality up front as an absolute good and does not defend it as a means.

Nevertheless, by making equality primary, his theory does not foreclose on the enhancement of productivity and the increase of the general wealth of society. It only prevents the enhancement of productivity and the increase of the general wealth of society in those situations where this would lead to exploitation. Rawls argues that rational individuals, at least as this is defined in Western liberal democracies would reject increased productivity of wealth under these conditions anyway.

The Importance of Neutrality Concerning the Ultimate Good

As we have emphasized previously, one of Rawls' important goals is to avoid metaphysical or ontological commitments (in his later writing he refers to the avoidance of comprehensive doctrines). He desires to develop a theory of justice that can serve as a basis for political community for persons holding a wide divergence of religious and ultimate commitments. His goal, therefore, would be to develop a theory to which both the fundamentalist and secular humanist, *insofar as they are rational*, could agree. Presumably, Donald Trump, Mother Teresa, Jerry Falwell and the secular humanist philosopher Sidney Hook should all be in essential agreement with Rawls' basic premises.

The main point is clear enough. Rawls is attempting to define a theory of justice for a culture characterized by pluralism with respect to the ultimate good. A theory of justice that makes a specific commitment to a single theory of the good would be necessarily oppressive with respect to those holding alternative views regarding ultimate good. An oppressive social order is in principle unjust.

A secondary consideration is that a theory of justice which required individuals to give up their ultimate commitments would not only be unjust. It would also be unstable. It simply couldn't win and maintain the allegiance of large segments of the population.

Thus, if Rawls' theory of justice does require its adherents to make commitments to the ultimate good, in other words, if it is at heart a metaphysical or comprehensive doctrine, then according to his own criteria, it is both unjust and unworkable. I believe that it can be shown that Rawls does not escape making commitments regarding the ultimate good. Furthermore, I think that this failure to escape ultimate commitments is fatal to his project. It must be noted, however, that Rawls both intends to avoid ultimate commitments and that he believes that he has succeeded in doing so.

Rawls theory of personality and the ultimate good. I believe that Rawls fails in his attempt to avoid making a commitment to an ultimate good at the basis of his theory and that this failure is clearly seen when we examine the view of personality which is central to his political theory. Specifically there are several assumptions which need to be examined here. (1) In the first place, Rawls theory requires the separation of the political self from the non-political self. (2) Secondly, Rawls' insistence on the necessity that a healthy individual have a plurality of ultimate ends seems to exclude adherents to a wide variety of religious perspectives. (3) Thirdly, the definition of a self committed to a plurality of ultimate ends imposes a peculiar definition of 'rationality' on adherents to his theory. In fact, it appears from another perspective to be by definition irrational. (4) Fourth,, Rawls' insistence that the persons in the original position regard themselves as capable of changing ultimate ends seems to both exclude a wide variety of religious perspectives and to be irrational from those perspectives. (5) Fifth, Rawls insists that free selves must regard themselves as a self-originating source of valid claims. This seems to preclude not only moral obligations being derived from society but from a transcendent deity or religious order. It may even preclude moral claims derived from natural law. We shall now proceed to examine these assumptions in order.

The separation of the political from the non political self requires the separation of metaphysics and the state, or as Rawls puts it the separation of the political self from the more comprehensive value system of the self. As we have observed previously, it is clear enough why Rawls would want to make this separation. In the first place, he affirms that pluralism regarding the ultimate good is a simple fact of life in Western liberal democracies. This assertion seems to be true. Secondly, if this pluralism regarding the ultimate good is reflected in the political behavior of a society it will be destructive of social and political harmony. This second assumption is not so obviously correct, at least to this commentator. In any case, Rawls is making an argument here that might be regarded as an extension of the argument for the separation of church and state. What Rawls is calling for, however, is the separation of metaphysics and the state. This is a stronger and more extensive separation than separation of church and state.

Not only is the separation of metaphysics and the state stronger and more extensive than the mere separation of church and state, it calls for a more complicated and less obvious set of assumptions. The separation of church and state although not uncontroversial is a relatively clear notion compared to the separation of the state and metaphysical assumptions. The state may not support any particular organized church or religious organization. But what does it mean to articulate and implement the separation of metaphysical assumptions and the state? What does it mean to articulate a conception of the self which is not metaphysical?

The non-metaphysical self must not be about ultimate personhood. A conception of the self which is not metaphysical would seem to have to satisfy several conditions. First, it must not be about the *ultimate nature of personhood.* There are several problems with satisfying this criteria. (1) It is a vague concept not only to the lay person but to professional philosophers. (2) More importantly, cultures, religious groups, and individual philosophers disagree regarding what constitutes 'ultimate personhood'. Is personhood defined in terms of rationality? Supra-rational freedom? Creaturehood of a loving God? An Atman which is one with the Brahman? A totally physical pleasure seeking animal?

How an we separate our ultimate personhood from our social and political reality? Secondly, satisfying the separation of ultimate personhood from political commitments requires a definition of ultimate personhood which is capable of being distinguished from our social and political reality. On the face of it this conception of personhood would seem to exclude the sense of self of a Ghandi, a Martin Luther King Jr., and Mother Teresa. It creates grave problems in interpreting Marcus Aurelius, Homer and Plato. It would require us to reject or interpret in some unusual ways: "Thy Kingdom come. Thy will be done, on earth as it is in heaven." It would also exclude Confucianism and Islam in its various branches. Sociologists from Irving Goffman to Robert Bellah would doubtless find it a difficult notion to either understand or accept. All of these individuals and traditions, not to speak of the various branches of Judaism, would seem to *define* self-hood in ways that make the separation of self-hood from political commitments highly problematic. In addition to all of this, it is a strange notion for a philosopher who has devoted his entire adult life to political philosophy.

Rawls insistence on a normal self having a plurality of ends excludes a wide variety of philosophical and religious positions and a considerable segment of the American and world population. We have referred above to Rawls' assertion that a single ultimate end seems to us not only to be irrational but almost mad. For Rawls this excludes the hedonist Bentham, Loyola and Thomas Aquinas. Alasdair MacIntyre observes that this would also exclude Aristotle.[24]. It would also exclude those who affirm the Westminster Confession of Faith when it asserts that "the chief end of man is to glorify God and enjoy Him forever." Indeed, it would seem to exclude not only all fundamentalists but Christians from a wide spectrum.

One of Rawls' goals is to develop a theory of justice which will be relatively stable over time. For this to be true, the theory of justice must not threaten or exclude the fundamental goals of its potential adherents. The conception of the self required by Rawls' theory seems to not meet his own criteria. It seems to exclude the ultimate commitments of a wide variety of possible positions and their adherents. It seems not only to fail to avoid ultimate metaphysical commitments. It seems on closer examination to not be able to tolerate a very diverse group of commitments which have had and continue to have millions, perhaps billions of adherents.

Rawls' position that rational individuals must have a plurality of ultimate ends seems to be less rational than the alternative of a single ultimate end. Contrary to Rawls' position, it would seem that the assertion of a single ultimate end by which to organize one's life is more rational than to have a plurality of ultimate ends. Why is this the case? Let us suppose that we have three individuals with different conceptions of the ultimate good. One claims that the ultimate good is to glorify God by expressing love to fellow human beings. The second believes that the ultimate good is to maximize one's own pleasure. Let us suppose that the third affirms intellectual development, physical pleasure, and aesthetic expression as equally ultimate. All three try to organize their lives according to a rational plan that realizes their goals.

All three may have a difficulty developing a rational plan for life but it seems to me that the first two will have an easier time of it. When conflict between subordinate goals and the means to attain them arises, the first two who have a single ultimate goal have a principle by which to resolve the conflict. The first can ask what maximizes love to one's fellow creatures. The rational course of action will be to choose that course of action which maximizes love. The second can ask what maximizes pleasure. The rational course of action will be to choose the strategy which maximizes pleasure. But what can the third do if it becomes necessary to choose among strategies which maximize one ultimate goal at the expense of one or both of the other two ultimate goals? There would seem to be no 'rational' way to resolve this conflict. Any choice at this level will be irrational.

These considerations cause me to affirm that it is self with a plurality of equally ultimate goals and not the self with one ultimate goal which is likely to be most irrational.

Critique of Rawls' position that individuals must be capable of changing their ultimate ends. Rawls has argued that the self in the original position must regard itself as capable of changing its ultimate ends. Rawls comments on this matter are confusing. He recognizes that persons often regard a change in their ultimate ends as constituting a change in their personal identity. It is not clear from his comments whether he agrees with these individuals that a change in ultimate ends does constitute a change in *personal* identity. He does seem to think that when an individual changes his or her ultimate ends that this does not constitute a change in the individual's *public* identity.[25] If this is so , then it appears to be possible to change my personal, (ultimate identity) without changing my public (non-ultimate identity).

To make sense out of Rawls' claims about the self we need to distinguish three different sorts of questions. Is it rational to desire a political order in which one is free over against the state to change one's personal identity if personal identity is defined in such a way as to include commitment to ultimate ends? If one lives in a pluralistic society (with respect to ultimate ends) the answer clearly seems to be yes. One may not want this freedom because one thinks that one is likely to change one's own ultimate ends but still want this freedom vis-à-vis the state for others. Missionaries, for example, both Christian and non-Christian attempt to convert adherents of other faiths to their own. People of all sorts of persuasion, who would not consider themselves missionaries, try to persuade others to change their views concerning matters which one or both parties regard as ultimate. They all would prefer to do this without interference from the state.

This first question must be distinguished from a second question. Is it rational to think of the human self as capable of changing its ultimate ends? The answer to this question is less obvious. Some human beings on some occasions do change their ultimate ends. This seems to clearly be an empirical fact. Whether they are 'rational' when making these changes is not so clear. Some people claim that they are making reasonable choices based on good reasons. Others observing their choices, regard them as unreasonable choices made for bad reasons. Still others claim that they are making reasonable choices, for example to accept Jesus Christ as Lord and Savior, but that the basis of this reasonable choice is the supra-rational working of the Holy Spirit in their hearts and lives. Buddhists think it reasonable to regard the self as transcending reason and even desire, which is normally associated with choosing. Thus, different philosophical and religious positions have held different views concerning the relationship of rationality and the changing of ultimate ends.

The two former questions need to be distinguished from a third question. Am I not a rational person if I do not *regard myself* as capable of changing my ultimate ends on rational grounds? The answer to this question seems unclear. Changing one's ultimate ends seems to involve changing one's very self concept. What 'reason' could I give for changing my very 'reason' for being? It seems likely that any reason I would give would assume the truth of the new set of ultimate ends which would be part of the definition of the new me.

Perhaps an example would help here. Mother Teresa is presumably politically free to reject her world wide ministry to the sick and poor and choose between opening a topless bar in Pittsburgh (assuming they are legal in Pittsburgh), an abortion clinic in Chicago, or an agency trading on the New York stock exchange. I question whether it is of the essence of rational choice for her to think of herself as capable of any of these alternatives. Furthermore, if she does regard herself as capable of any of these or similar alternatives, she doubtless does so because, in spiritual humility, she regards herself as capable of irrationally choosing to be in bondage to sin. In other words these choices would be regarded by her as against both reason and freedom. The first two would probably be regarded by her as sinful for anyone. The last alternative would be regarded as sinful for her (although not necessarily for others) because it would be contrary to her specific calling. Were she to make any of these choices, it would doubtless be possible only by changing her fundamental ideas on the nature of both reason and freedom.

Let us attempt to summarize the implications of these considerations for Rawls' theory. It is one thing for Rawls to claim that rational individuals should choose a political order which will not interfere with persons making changes in their ultimate goals or ends. It is another thing to claim that a rational individual in order to be rational must regard one's own selfhood as the kind of entity which may change its ultimate ends. It is still another claim that this change in selfhood must have a motivation which is primarily or exclusively rational. These latter two assertions seem to make implicitly or explicitly *metaphysical claims about selfhood.* Rawls' project rests upon the ability to *avoid* making such metaphysical claims. It may be that Rawls can interpret his theory in ways that avoid this difficulty but surely clarification is needed if this is be achieved.

Critique of Rawls' claim that freedom entails that persons regard themselves as self-originating sources of valid claims precludes a variety of philosophical and religious positions. Once again we need to make a distinction between possible interpretations of Rawls theory. Rawls uses the language of "self-originating."[26] This explicitly precludes the view that valid moral claims must be derived from the state, the culture or the political order. Does he also mean to reject various religious and philosophical perspectives, including Judaism, Christianity, Islam, Buddhism, or Natural Law? Reference to persons as free only if they regard themselves as self-originating sources of valid claims does seem to preclude these other perspectives. This being the case, it is hardly pluralistic or tolerant by any definition which could claim to be part of the Western liberal democratic tradition. Furthermore it does not appear to avoid making sweeping metaphysical assumptions concerning the nature of the self.

Summary: Rawls theory of personality and the ultimate good: The various things which Rawls has to say about 'self' have a number of implications. I have indicated throughout the discussion how important avoidance of metaphysical assumptions is for Rawls' whole project. It seems clear that, in his view of the self, he fails to avoid making these metaphysical assumptions. This is not because he hasn't tried. What is the explanation for this failure? It may be that Rawls has not thought through on this issue and will come up with satisfactory answers to the objections I have raised above at a later date. On the other hand, it may be that Rawls theory has a particular theory of personality *deeply* embedded in it. It may be so deeply embedded that the value neutrality that he seeks and that is essential to the success of his theory is not possible on the foundations that he proposes. If this is so, then the solution to the difficulty of achieving freedom, justice and social harmony in a pluralistic society requires a theory founded on radically different assumptions from the one that Rawls proposes. I happen to think that this is the case. Criticizing Rawls, however, is one thing. Working out that alternative theory, is another matter.

The Fundamentalist and Secular Humanist Response to Rawls

I have attempted to document Rawls seeming failure to develop a theory of justice which is both fully rational and neutral with regard to assumptions about the nature of ultimate good. If I am correct about this failure on Rawls part then it is clear that fundamentalists would not find Rawls' theory acceptable. The probable reaction can be summed up by quotations from two philosophers. The first, William Galston, is sympathetic to Rawls' project but thinks that Rawls fails to find a political consensus in Western democracy precisely because no such consensus exists. Though not personally sympathetic to fundamentalism, Galston sums up the fundamentalist response quite well.

> But I wonder whether, for example, religious fundamentalists would regard the capacity to form and revise a conception of the good as a good at all, let alone a highest order interest of human beings. They might well declare that the best human life requires the capacity to receive an external good (God's truth) rather than to form a conception of the good for oneself, and to hold fast to that truth once received rather than to revise it. Rawls' Kantian conception would strike them as a sophisticated, and therefore dangerous, brand of secular humanism. Nor would they be impressed with the suggestion that whatever may be true of their nonpublic identity, their public personality should be

understood in Rawls' fashion. From their perspective, the distinction between the public and nonpublic realms represents an injunction to set aside God's word, the only source of salvation, in determining the principles of our public order. I would argue, in short, that Rawls' conception of moral personality will appeal only to those individuals who have accepted a particular understanding of the liberal political community and that our public culture is at present characterized not by consensus but, rather, by acute conflict over the adequacy of that understanding.[27]

Galston's answer is to abandon both the notions of metaphysical neutrality and relativism. Liberal democratic principles need to be defended on rational grounds, although Galston does not offer such a defense in the above quoted article.

The second quotation from Alasdair MacIntyre does not mention Rawls but is directed at the whole tradition that Rawls represents. MacIntyre sees both the fundamentalists and the Western liberal Enlightenment tradition as founded on pre-rational faith commitments. In this regard they both are expressions of what he refers to as fideism. Fideism usually refers to a religious perspective which is founded on faith with no appeal to reason. MacIntyre regards the Western Enlightenment tradition as a secular fideism. The difference between the fundamentalists and a thinker like Rawls is that the fundamentalists are self aware and honest with regard to their fideism, whereas Rawls and the tradition he represents are not. MacIntyre sums this up in a passage which is both instructive and amusing.

> To the readership of the New York Times, or at least that part of it which shares the presuppositions of those who write that parish magazine of affluent and self-congratulatory liberal Enlightenment, the congregations of evangelical fundamentalism appear unfashionably unenlightened. But to the members of those congregations that readership appears to be just as much a community of pre-rational faith as they themselves are but one whose members, unlike themselves, fail to recognize themselves for what they are, and hence are in no position to level charges of irrationality at them or anyone else."[28]

I will discuss MacIntyre's own perspective which is neither fundamentalist nor Rawlsian in the next chapter. I will also have a few things to say about the definition of fideism and some possible alternatives to fideism and Enlightenment rationalism.

The Rawlsian Project and Cultural Conflict

Rawls project may be viewed as one grand effort to provide a framework to manage cultural conflict and avoid cultural war. This is the point of his whole effort to be neutral with respect to ultimate values. His ideal is one of value neutrality and rational tolerance in political life. I have attempted to document with some care the fact that he has failed and some of the reasons why I think that he did fail. This failure, however, does not prevent one from admiring the attempt. His motive was noble. His theory is both detailed and brilliant. His effort to articulate for our times the essence in political theory of the Enlightenment tradition is indeed impressive. His failure may have much more to do with the inherent weaknesses in the Enlightenment tradition than any lack of erudition, hard work and good will on the part of Rawls. For a critique, not of Rawls in particular but of the tradition he represents, we will turn in the next chapter to the work of Alasdair MacIntyre. Macintyre represents the important movement known as communitarianism. It has emerged in recent decades as the chief alternative to political liberalism. Like Rawls, one goal of the communitarian movement is to manage cultural conflict and avoid cultural war.

Notes

[1] As will become clear from our discussion of Rawls, he does not reject the possibility of rationally transcendent truth in all spheres of life but only with regard to political issues.

[2] Liberalism as it is used in this context is not defined precisely in terms of contemporary American politics. The Western liberal Enlightenment tradition is associated with a faith in rationality, individualism and the autonomy of persons, at least in their political activities. Both Ted Kennedy and Newt Ginrich are liberals in this sense. In fact, as the term is used in this context, a case can be made for affirming that Ginrich is more representative of liberalism and Kennedy more sympathetic to communitarianism. If this sounds confusing, it is confusing. It is hoped that it will be somewhat less so after a careful reading of this chapter and the next.

[3] John Rawls, *A Theory of Justice was published in 1971.* Rawls most recent work is *Political Liberalism (1973).* This book is a reworking of lectures and essays that he has been giving in defense of his theory since the 1980's. There is an extensive literature which comments on Rawls. *Ethics* Vol. 99 No. 4 July 1989 is devoted entirely to Rawls' work. *Ethics*, Volume 105 No. 1 October 1994 includes a symposium on Rawls containing three articles. One of the best treatments of Rawls' work that compares his theory to McIntyre among others is Stephen Mulhull and Adam Swift, *Liberals and Communitarians.*

[4] Rawls, *Theory*, p. 60.

[5] *Ibid., p. 61.*

[6] *Ibid.*, pp. 541-48.

[7] *Ibid.* pp. 174, 179, 253, 362,400, 544.

[8] *Ibid., 395-99.*

[9] This is a persistent theme throughout Rawls' work (even though he is not always consistent). See especially, Rawls, *Political Liberalism,* pp. *99-101.*

[10] John Rawls, "Kantian Constructivism in Moral Theory," *The Journal of Philosophy, Volume LXXVII*, NO. 9, September 1980, pp. 543-45.

[11] *Ibid.*, p. 525.

[12] *Theory*, pp. 554, 565-6.

[13] Rawls, "Kantian Constructivism....." p. 518.

[14] Rawls allows for a non-public or political stability with respect to final ends. "They may have attachments and loves that they believe they would not, or could not, stand apart from; and they might regard it as unthinkable for them to view themselves without certain religious and philosophical convictions and commitments. But none of this need affect the conception of the person connected with society's public conception of justice and its ideal of social

cooperation. Within different contexts we can assume diverse points of view toward our person without contradiction so long as these points of view cohere together when circumstances require." Rawls, "Kantian Constructivism......" p. 545. This is problematic for a number of reasons. First it requires a potential bifurcation of the self that may describe accurately the psychological condition of contemporary Westerners but one that we are still not prepared to declare as healthy. Secondly, even if defensible, it needs considerable unpacking for us to understand the implications of the Rawlsian 'political psychology.' Thirdly, Rawls later affirms the primacy of political values when they conflict with ultimate religious and philosophical values. "..the political values expressed by its principles and ideals normally have sufficient weight to override all other values that may come in conflict with them." Rawls, *Political Liberalism*, p. 138. Fourthly, one of the conditions of any stable political order is the creation of cultural structures--education, media, etc., that reinforce that political order. In other words, children must be socialized to support that political order. Rawls seems to be attempting to avoid political and cultural conflict or, if you prefer, culture wars by separating and insulating the political self from other possible selves. Not just fundamentalists, but adherents of various philosophical and religious persuasion are likely to view this move with some suspicion. Kant is much more consistent in his view of selfhood.

[15] Rawls, *Theory*, p. 143.

[16] *Ibid.*, p. 554.

[17] *Ibid.*, pp. 548ff.

[18] Rawls, "Kantian Constructivism....." p. 518. One of the problems in interpreting Rawls is that he is not only living but actively writing and revising his theory. Interpretation of Rawls, therefore, resembles trying to hit a moving target. In my view, however, Rawls is for the most part consistent with his basic presuppositions.

[19] "...no comprehensive doctrine is appropriate as a political conception for a constitutional regime." Rawls, Political Liberalism, p.135. The above is just one quote. The entire argument for political liberalism seems to hinge on the possibility of avoiding making commitments, for or against, any comprehensive world view. There is one important restriction on this agnosticism with respect to comprehensive doctrines. Only those comprehensive doctrines compatible with political liberalism are acceptable.

[20] I do not mean to suggest that Hunter is less concerned to avoid violent conflict in our society than is Rawls. He is simply less optimistic. One way to view his sociological studies is as empirical documentation of the breakdown of breakdown of political liberalism in American society.

[21] Rawls, *Theory*, p. 105ff.

[22] For an extensive treatment of Max Weber's thesis on the relationship of religion to economic life, including Weber's analysis of the relationship of

Protestantism, individualism and capitalism, see Talcott Parsons, *The Structure of Social Action,* pp. 500-577.

23 Rawls, *Political Liberalism,* pp. 105-106.

24 Alasdair MacIntyre, *Whose Justice Which Rationality,* p. 165.

25 John Rawls, "Justice as Fairness: Political not Metaphysical" *Philosophy and Public Affairs, Vol. 14, NO. 3,* 1985, pp..241-42.

26 *Ibid., p.42.*

27 William A. Galston, "Pluralism and Social Unity," *Ethics, Vol. 99, N0. 4,* July 1989 p. 714.

28 Alasdair MacIntyre, *Whose Justice....,* p. 5.

Chapter VIII

Alasdair MacIntyre and The Ethics of Virtue: Postmodernism and Culture War

The Enlightenment Under Attack

I discussed the fundamental assumptions of the Enlightenment in the previous chapter. The following characteristics are listed by way of review. The Enlightenment was characterized by: (1) the belief in universal laws of reason accessible to all intelligent and informed individuals, (2) the rejection of tradition as an authoritative source of knowledge or guidance regarding the nature of reality or the meaning of human existence, and (3) the rejection of religious faith as necessary or authoritative. Enlightenment thinkers did not necessarily reject religion. Religion in their view, however, contained no insight that could not be grasped independently by reason. Furthermore, in the case of conflict, reason not religion was held to be authoritative.

The Enlightenment has been the dominant perspective in Western culture for several centuries. It is true that its dominance has not been complete. There have been numerous limitations made with respect to the three affirmations cited above. Historians speak of the age of Romanticism (roughly identified with the 19th century) following the age of the Enlightenment (roughly identified with the 18th century). One of Kant's famous works is entitled *Religion Within the Limits of Reason Alone.* He was, however, also very much influenced by the great Romantic philosopher Jean-Jacques Rousseau. Various religious groups and movements have (following Kant) sought "to limit knowledge in order to make room for faith."[1] Protestant theologians and various Protestant denominations throughout the nineteenth century have argued that faith and reason are compatible provided they each stick to their appropriate spheres of authority.

Great thinkers who have influenced the 20th century have included Darwin, Freud, and existentialist thinkers like Kierkegaard, Nietzsche, and Sartre.   All of these thinkers profoundly challenged the fundamental assumptions of the Enlightenment.

Hitler's National Socialism and Mussolini's Fascism were powerful political movements founded on the repudiation of the adequacy of reason to provide meaning for either individuals or the social order. On the more positive side, the civil rights movements in Ghandi's India and Martin Luther King's America were informed and undergirded by strong religious faith that rejected the assumption of the ultimacy of reason while at the same time embracing Enlightenment ideals.

The counter-culture movement of the sixties, as symbolized by the "Woodstock Generation," represented in many respects a rejection of faith in reason to provide insight into the nature of the human condition and the foundations for a just social order.

Islamic thought and culture has shown a similar ambiguity regarding Enlightenment ideals of rationality, liberty and equality. For long periods during the Middle Ages, Islamic thought and culture was clearly superior to the West in many respects including its knowledge of Greek philosophy, especially the works of Aristotle.   Some contemporary Islamic movements, however, have challenged Western Enlightenment ideals not only by headline-grabbing acts of terrorism, but more profoundly (if not as loudly) by the rejection of Western ideals as decadent, inherently exploitative and immoral. This is not entirely new. Marx had challenged Western capitalism as inherently exploitative and immoral.   But Marx saw the solution, not in the rejection of Enlightenment ideals, but in their fulfillment in a communist utopia. Important segments of Islamic thought, on the other hand, regard the solution as a rejection of the Enlightenment ideal of reason, and a return to faith and tradition.

Despite the ambiguous and less-than-complete dominance of the Enlightenment, it still has been the most prominent perspective in the West for several centuries, in the media, the universities, and among cultural elite's in general.

Furthermore, Western culture has been the dominant culture in the world for several centuries. From an outsider's viewpoint, Soviet communism and Western democracies were two variations of the liberal Enlightenment tradition. The collapse of Soviet Communism is not, on this view, the ultimate victory of the Western Enlightenment tradition. It only represents the internal collapse of one of the variations of this tradition.

Until recently, however, it has been possible to say without challenge that the Western liberal Enlightenment tradition represents the dominant perspective of the cultural elite of Western civilization. This is no longer clearly the case.

For example, the 1994 November/December issue of "Academe: Bulletin of the American Association of University Professors" is entitled "The Postmodern University" (read post-Enlightenment University).[2] That we are in a postmodern age is taken for granted not only by MacIntyre but by numerous others in prestigious positions. Thus, Enlightenment ideals are frequently under attack, not just by Islamic or Christian fundamentalists, extremist political movements, or philosophical thinkers on the fringes of academic life. These ideals are under attack by intellectual and cultural elite's who occupy important positions in our core institutions.

Rules Versus Virtues

Utilitarianism, Kant, and Rawls are typical examples of approaching the problem of ethical discourse within the Enlightenment tradition. With them, the problem of morality seems clearly to have been defined as the problem of identifying, grounding, and applying right rules. The utilitarian formula of the 'the greatest good for the greatest number', the Kantian 'categorical imperative', and the rules about equality developed in the Rawlsian 'original position', are all methods of discovering, generating, or testing rules. Virtuous behavior is treated as a secondary problem and is defined as the development of dispositions or habits to conform to those right rules.

This seems to be a natural way of posing the problem. We define our criminal justice system in terms of rules. Individuals are punished for disobeying rules not for the failure to be good persons. The question put to the jury is not, is this person a good person but has he or she broken a specific law under specific conditions. Rule of law is central to the freedoms we enjoy in a democratic society. Rule of law also makes possible our civil order. The rule of law regulates our property relationships, educational advancement, athletic competition, and all sorts of business and other institutional relationships.

It all begins in kindergarten or before. The alternative to defining morality with rules is to define the basic problem of morality in terms of virtues. This also is quite natural as a few examples and a little reflection will show.

My wife is an elementary school teacher, having taught kindergarten, and first and second grades over the years. She confronts the problem of defining right rules from the very first day of school.

Rule #1: "When lining up for the bathroom or going to and from lunch, keep your hands to yourself."

Rule #2: "When one student hits another, the proper thing is not to hit back but to bring the matter to the attention of the teacher for discipline."

These rules are not that different from rules applied in adult behavior. We are obliged to not shove, push, fondle, or touch others without their express permission. There are laws against it. If, however, these laws are broken, we are not permitted to retaliate or punish the offender (except in cases of self defense) on our own. We must leave that to the proper legal authorities and judicial procedure.

Much of the time, however, the moral training given by my wife has to do with the inculcation of virtues.

Sensitivity. "How would you feel if Suzy made fun of you in that way?"

Courtesy. "Line up without shoving." "Don't sneeze in your neighbor's face." "Wait your turn." "Thank Johnny for sharing his crayons with you."

Respect for proper authority. "You need to obey me when I tell you to do something, just as you do your parents." "We need to obey our teachers and principals." "We also need to obey police officers and bus drivers."

Prudence and caution concerning improper authority or behavior. "Don't go with strangers even if they seem nice and offer you candy." "If someone touches you in a place where you think they shouldn't, its okay to tell them no and then tell your parents or teacher."

Independence. "You can do that by yourself." "I'll help you so that the next time you can do that by yourself like a big girl." "Didn't Helen do a good job? She did it all by herself."

Commitment to community. "We can help each other learn." "We have to be responsible for our own behavior but also help our neighbor do what's right." "Jimmy when you distract Tommy, you make it hard for him to behave and learn."

What is being taught here--and it goes on constantly as any parent or public school teacher knows--is not the teaching of a system or list of rules but the teaching of habits, character traits, and attitudes. Parents, teachers, ministers and peers make the implicit or explicit assumption that a good person will have the proper habits, character traits, and attitudes and know where, when, and how to exhibit these traits without being specifically guided by an authority figure or a specific rule. In other words, there is an expectation that, within a certain framework, the individual will exhibit the virtue of *autonomy.*

One might even make the argument that if everyone both knew and had sufficiently internalized the proper virtues, then rules would be unnecessary. Rules are necessary only for those who because of ignorance or willful rejection of proper behavior are morally immature.

A less controversial assertion might be that rules are articulations of the virtuous life or the virtuous society. They are explanations of what it means to have virtuous attitudes, character traits or habits. This less strong assertion still asserts that defining morality in terms of virtues is primary, while rules are secondary.

Virtue Ethics and Biblical Ethics. The moral precepts that are part of the Ten Commandments are familiar to all and are generally interpreted as rules that everyone ought to follow. "Honor Thy father and mother. "Thou shalt not kill." "Thou shalt not commit adultery." "Thou shalt not steal." "Thou shalt not bear false witness." "Thou shalt not covet." [3] Whether the Ten Commandments are most properly interpreted primarily *as rules to be obeyed* or as expressions of *virtues to be cultivated* is a matter of much dispute.   Jesus, of course, summarized the entire law and the prophets in terms of the *virtue* of love--for God and one's neighbor.[4]   Nevertheless, that the Ten Commandments have been widely interpreted as rules is not a matter of debate.

Let us consider, however, a passage from the book of Galations in the New Testament. "The fruit of the spirit is love, joy, peace, long-suffering, gentleness, goodness, faith, meekness, temperance: against such there is no law"[5]

This is not a list of rules. It is clearly a list of virtues or character traits that every good Christian is supposed to exhibit in his or her day-to day-living. There is an explicit contrast in Galations with "the Law," which seems to be most appropriately interpreted as rules that, according to the writer, are not capable of enabling us to achieve salvation. There is a further contrast with the "works of the flesh," which are negative character traits that the good Christian is not supposed to exhibit. The writer of the book of Galations does not disparage the Law as such. The Law is to be respected but it cannot empower us or save us. Only grace can save us and only the Holy Spirit can enable us to live righteously. The function of the Law was to be a tutor, to make us aware of our sin and inadequacy and thus to make us aware of our need for grace.[6] The writer also affirms that the whole Law can be summarized in terms of the virtue of love. Love your neighbor as yourself.[7]

Thus, for the writer of the book of Galations, morality is not primarily about rules. As a matter of fact, to interpret morality as primarily about rules is to misunderstand the very nature of Christianity and to risk damnation. Morality is about dispositions, character traits, proper attitudes. It is about the virtues, the primary virtue being that of love.

Virtue Ethics and Plato and Aristotle. We need not, however, turn to the Bible to find an example in ancient literature of morality being treated as a problem of virtue rather than a problem of rules. Plato's *Republic*[8] is centered around the four cardinal virtues of 'wisdom', 'courage', 'temperance', and 'justice'. These are treated both as the virtues of a state and the virtues of individuals. Plato, despite his originality and penetrating insight, is obviously treating the problem of morality in the culture and tradition of his time. It is of interest, therefore, that it does not seem to occur to him to start with the problem of defining moral behavior as a problem of discovering and obeying right rules.

The *Nichomachean Ethics* of Aristotle is almost entirely devoted to a discussion of the character traits (dispositions to act or feel in a certain way) and the problems associated with the acquiring and cultivation of these character traits. Thus, we have discussions about what it means to be witty--rather than a boor or a buffoon, friendly--rather than obsequious or surly, modest--rather than shameless or shamefaced, generous--rather than a miser or a spendthrift.[9] The assumptions that underlie Aristotle's treatment are quite different from that of the writer of the book of Galations. What they have in common, however, is the way they define the problem. It is a problem of right character not of right rules.

Virtue Ethics, Culture War and Contemporary Philosophical Discussion. I will devote the bulk of this chapter to an exposition of Alasdair MacIntyre's critique of contemporary ethical theory. At this point I will simply note that MacIntyre's *After Virtue,* first published in 1981, created a tremendous stir in philosophical circles. Its central argument is that contemporary philosophical and public debate about ethics is fundamentally incoherent because it has become *divorced from any and all traditions and communities.* This divorce is associated with the fundamental assumptions of the Enlightenment. The Enlightenment perspective assumes that reason, including reasoning about ethics, can transcend all communities and grasp basic rules that are understood in the same way (although sometimes applied differently) by all persons regardless of their particular cultural heritage. MacIntyre argues that before we can talk coherently about morality, we must come to terms with our fundamental assumptions about what it means to be a person. Coming to terms with these fundamental assumptions will force us to define what we mean by being a good or evil person. This in turn will force us to define what we mean by basic virtues and vices. It is only after this task has been completed that discussion of moral rules and laws can make any sense.

But, according to MacIntyre, discussion of basic personhood and virtues can only be meaningful if carried on in the context of ongoing traditions and systems of communal relationships. The Enlightenment assumed that it is possible to grasp moral laws and rules that ignore both the continuity through time of traditions, and the concrete network of institutional and interpersonal relationships that constitute our present existence.   The Enlightenment, therefore, because of its rationalistic and individualistic assumptions, was anti-historical, and inimical to the sound social-psychological insight that the emphasis on education in the virtues entails.

MacIntyre followed the publication of *After Virtue* with two other important works.   The first was titled *Whose Justice?   Which Rationality?* In this work, he shows in great detail that the concepts of justice and rationality can make sense only in the context of a historical philosophical tradition. The second was *Three Rival Versions of Moral Inquiry: Encyclopedia, Genealogy, and Tradition.* 'Encyclopedia' represents the Enlightenment.   'Genealogy' refers to Nietzsche but treats Nietzsche as a forerunner and representative of postmodernism. By 'tradition', MacIntyre means the Thomistic tradition started by the great Roman Catholic theologian and philosopher Thomas Aquinas. These three books are all part of an extended argument by MacIntyre that attempts to show that meaningful thought, especially about ethics and culture, occurs only in the context of traditions. MacIntyre affirms that failure to recognize this fact has made discourse about ethics in our society incoherent.

Virtue Ethics, and Contemporary Political and Cultural Debate-- The Work of William Bennett. As I indicated above, MacIntyre's *After Virtue* has sparked a considerable discussion on the development of the virtues in philosophical circles.   This debate, however, has entered into more popular literature and into contemporary political debate.   One of the most recent and popular of evidences of this is William Bennett's *The Book of Virtues, A Treasury of Great Moral Stories.   The Book of Virtues* contains commentary by Bennett on stories and excerpts from great works of literature. Some of these make for quite sophisticated reading but many, if not most, are myths, fairy tales, fables and short stories suitable for reading to small children. This is Bennett's point. We teach morality by example.   These are examples taken from our daily lives and from the stories we read to our children and to ourselves.   We learn about virtue by being exposed to examples of virtuous acts and virtuous characters in real life and in literature.

The publishing of this book is a rare phenomenon.   It is a best selling book on ethics written by Ph.D. in philosophy who, at one point, was mentioned as a possible presidential candidate on the

Republican ticket. Bennett, like MacIntyre, a Roman Catholic, was Director of the Office of National Drug Control Policy under President Bush. He was Secretary of Education and Chairman of the National Endowment for the Humanities under President Reagan. Bennett is also a protégé of John Silber. Silber, a Kant scholar, is a former president of Boston University and ran unsuccessfully for governor of Massachusetts.

One of Bennett's other books is entitled *The De-Valuing of America: The Fight for Our Culture and Our Children* Unlike *The Book of Virtues, The De-Valuing of America* is a polemical work with clear political implications. It is clear from Bennett's work that he sees debate about ethics as directly related to political conflict but also to the broader category of cultural conflict that encompasses both political and ethical debate. Whatever disagreements there may be between Bennett's work and the more specialized scholarly treatment of MacIntyre,[10] Bennett's concerns place him squarely in the company of MacIntyre and others who view ethical discourse and cultural critique as necessarily related.

Culture Wars--Tradition Wars

MacIntyre and Tradition. Exposition of MacIntyre's theory is complicated by the intentional breadth of his perspective. Contemporary Westerner's have a tendency to define justice in narrow legalistic terms. For us, justice is something that happens or fails to happen in a court of law. It is carried out in the enactment of laws by legislators. We tend to see justice as confined to the concept of 'distributive justice'. Justice, for MacIntyre, is established only in part by the concept of distributive justice or the issue of the just or fair distribution of the goods of society. Rawls is clearly concerned primarily with distributive justice when he argues in favor of the 'difference principle'. He defines the functioning of the difference principle in the context of laws controlling the equal or fair distribution of wealth.

Unlike Rawls, MacIntyre is concerned with more than just the problem of distributive justice. It is typical of the Enlightenment perspective to conceive of the problem of justice as a problem of the fair distribution of the goods of society among *autonomous* individuals. Part of MacIntyre's fundamental critique of the Enlightenment, however, is to reject the view that society is nothing more than a network of cooperative relationships between autonomous individuals.

This difference in the concept of society, I believe, helps explain the profound differences in approach that we witness in reading Rawls' *A Theory of Justice* and MacIntyre's *Whose Justice? Which Rationality?* MacIntyre appears, by 'justice', to mean the vary structure of the social order, including the relationships among individuals but also including the *self-definition of persons* within a particular social order. Justice for him is broader than the problem of distribution of scarce resources or the imposition of appropriate penalties for failure to comply with societies laws and rules.

The illustration of the systemic character of the problem of rearing the next generation. This can be illustrated by a problem with which MacIntyre does not deal directly, but is implicit in all his writing and is very much at the center of the culture war debate. This is the problem of the rearing of the next generation.

The problem of rearing the next generation is related to a whole assortment of other issues. These include our concepts of individualism and community, our fundamental religious convictions, an economy that requires women to work outside the home and also causes families to be geographically separated, our convictions regarding freedom of speech, and the pervasive impact of the media. Political conflict, medical advances especially as they relate to sexuality, the welfare system, feminism, the gay rights movement, the educational system, the increasing ethnic and cultural diversity of our population, the explosive growth of technology also impact on this issue.

Even this partial listing of the issues and institutional arrangements related to child rearing emphasizes two points. Meaningful and cogent discussion of 'family values' must take place not in isolation from other issues but only from a perspective which is *broadly systemic.* Secondly, debate about family and related issues necessarily involves debate about fundamental philosophical and religious assumptions.

Whether our society in the next several decades will reach a consensus regarding child rearing that is pragmatically workable and philosophically coherent is at least problematic. We, of course, may continue to just muddle through for decades. The rearing of the next generation is such a fundamental task for any society, however, that failure to deal adequately with this task makes the very survival of such a society questionable. The survival of a society that has not resolved fundamental issues related to rearing the next generation is in doubt even if the society does not have to compete with a society that has solved these problems. It becomes even more serious where competition is required with a society that has resolved this problem

Traditions within traditions and the culture wars. Western culture may be distinguished from Chinese, Indian, or Islamic culture. Western culture itself, however, may be viewed as a mixture, more or less integrated, of a number of different cultural traditions. The same may be said of Chinese, Hindu and Islamic cultures, however, monolithic and integrated they may appear to our unsophisticated Western eyes. What goes on all the time within cultures, both our own and others, may be viewed as a conflict of traditions.

There are different competing traditions regarding the rearing of the next generation within our contemporary American society. When there is one clearly dominant tradition or when the traditions have a great deal in common, the sense of their being cultural conflict may be diminished or even largely absent. What seems to distinguish our present situation is the absence of a clearly dominant tradition, on the one hand, and the presence of a sharp contrast among competing traditions on the other.

In addition to this, however, our society has experienced such rapid change that each tradition seems to be experiencing a crisis of meaning within itself. All of this has lead to large numbers of people becoming alienated from traditions to which they once adhered without becoming integrated with an alternative tradition.

Some Alternative Solutions to Culture War

Philosophically there would seem to be at least five differing responses to the crisis engendered by this phenomena. One response has been mentioned above. We may just *muddle through.* The second is that offered by the *Enlightenment.* We may appeal to a tradition transcendent set of criteria capable of being grasped by all well informed and rational individuals regardless of their tradition or heritage. This is the solution that has come increasingly under attack by MacIntyre but also by others. A third response is that of *cultural relativism.* We may take the division within our own society as evidence of cultural relativism and accept the fact that there can be no *rational* resolution of the differences between different cultural traditions. A fourth response is the e*motivist* one which we will explore more fully in the immediately following section. The emotivist alternative, of course, also offers no *rational* resolution of basic conflicts. If we are not satisfied with just muddling through and if we reject the Enlightenment, cultural relativism, and emotivism then we may choose a fifth alternative of the prospect of *continuous unresolved conflict.* A sixth choice is conflict resolution by various forms of *coercion and manipulation.* One tradition may overpower the others, completely destroying or marginalizing them, but this is the only alternative to continuous unresolved conflict. Marxist social criticism affirms that coercion and manipulation is the only real basis of social order in every society, at least until we achieve the revolution of the proletariat Those who think otherwise are living under an illusion.

Some may look upon this sixth alternative of peace through victorious warfare as a regrettable but still acceptable alternative. There are not only moral problems with this solution but pragmatic ones. In the first place, all parties to the cultural debate in Western society, secular humanist, fundamentalist, so called main stream religious bodies, and those who do not identify themselves clearly with any group are committed to the democratic process, the inherent rights of individual freedom of action and discussion, and persuasion rather than manipulation. This, of course, does not prevent them from suspecting and accusing their opponents of not being committed to or practicing these ideals. Nevertheless, these ideals are very deeply entrenched in the Western cultural tradition. Any group self-consciously and openly denying these ideals would create difficulties for holding the allegiance of its own followers and successfully suppressing its opponents. Secondly, there seems to be a contradiction in affirming democratic ideals on the one hand and the *morally legitimate* coercion or manipulation of minorities on the other hand. The civil rights, feminist, and gay rights movement, have of course, all made this point. So has the religious right.

The above observations raise concerns related to the title of this book and the cultural phenomenon that it addresses. The term 'culture war' suggests coercion and manipulation rather than persuasion. It is odd to speak of a 'war of persuasion'. Philosophers typically have preferred to identify themselves with the persuasion of sweet reason rather than either harsh coercion or deceitful manipulation. At the same time, philosophers have accused other philosophers of manipulation since the time of Socrates and the Sophists. MacIntyre rejects all of the alternatives listed above. We will have a better understanding of his position as we examine his specific reasons for doing so.

MacIntyre and Cultural Relativism

The appearance of relativism in MacIntyre's though. A reader who knew only the title of MacIntyre's *Whose Justice? Which Rationality?* would think that this was a book in defense of some variety of relativism. A superficial skimming of the book might suggest that it was a defense of cultural relativism. MacIntyre reviews the concept of justice, and of the rationality associated with the defense and development of various concepts of justice, as they appear in different cultural traditions. Again and again he illustrates in detail and depth the dramatic differences in the concepts of justice in various traditions, and the different concepts of reason that are used to defend these different concepts of justice. Justice and rationality vary dramatically among traditions. They change and develop dramatically within traditions over time. To illustrate this, MacIntyre takes us through the Platonic/Aristotelian tradition beginning with a discussion of Homer. He moves on to the Augustinian/Thomistic tradition, the Scottish Enlightenment, and to Liberalism as an example of just another tradition. All of these are presented as having different concepts of both justice and rationality. All of this, at first glance, looks like cultural relativism.

Furthermore, MacIntyre repeatedly argues throughout the book that the Enlightenment tradition is dead. Part of his argument is that the Enlightenment is just another cultural tradition with its own *relative* cultural definition of rationality and justice. This argument is important for the issue of cultural relativism since it has been argued for centuries by those in the tradition of the Enlightenment that reason gives us the *only* transcendent perspective, culturally and individually, by which human beings may evaluate individuals and cultures. Other opponents of the Enlightenment are arguing that the Enlightenment was the *only* alternative to cultural relativism. The Enlightenment is discredited, therefore cultural relativism is demonstrated to be true.

MacIntyre looks, at a first superficial reading, as though he agrees with these relativist opponents of the Enlightenment.

The alternatives to cultural relativism seem to be reason (as represented by the Enlightenment) or revelation (as represented by one of the world's various religious).

There are, of course, millions who believe in religious revelation as a source of culturally transcendent truth. Unfortunately, there is enormous disagreement among religious traditions regarding the fundamental nature of this transcendent truth.

Modernity, as the Enlightenment is sometimes called, was viewed in various ways as a solution to this religious diversity. (1) For many, reason replaced revelation. (2) For others, reason was offered as the best defense of a particular religious revelation. (3) For still others, reason was offered as both a defense of and a correction to the excesses proposed by religious revelation. Adherents to a particular religious faith used reason and the Enlightenment ideal to distinguish between true and false claims made by revelation and then proceeded to defend the revised revelation which had been modified according to rational criteria.

The rejection of the Enlightenment ideal of a universally transcendent reason precludes the use of any of these approaches as a solution to the problem of achieving religious unity. It also, of course, precludes the use of reason (as defined by the Enlightenment) as a means of resolving cultural conflict insofar as that conflict has its source in religious diversity.

For MacIntyre, neither the Enlightenment, nor religious revelation (apart from a religious tradition) provide an alternative to cultural relativism. This is because revelation, like reason, comes to us in the context of an historical tradition. What then is MacIntyre's alternative to cultural relativism?

MacIntyre and tradition as an alternative to relativism. Whether MacIntyre adequately escapes the criticisms of the cultural relativist is open to dispute. That he personally the rejects both cultural and individual relativism, however, is clear. The basis of his rejection is also clear. MacIntyre affirms that there is no conception of justice, reason, or for that matter, revelation independent of some historical tradition. He also affirms, however, that it is possible to demonstrate that some traditions are morally and intellectually superior to others.

It is also possible, according to MacIntyre, for a person raised in and committed to one tradition to be able to understand a tradition to which one is not committed. This is the epistemological claim that MacIntyre makes over against the radical cultural relativist who insists that individuals from one tradition cannot even understand another tradition..

Before we can evaluate the basis of MacIntyre's rejection of cultural relativism, we need to understand his assumptions concerning the relationship between intellectual and social traditions. I will attempt to clarify these assumptions before considering MacIntyre's specific criteria for demonstrating that one tradition has shown itself superior to another on philosophical grounds.

By tradition, MacIntyre means a set of more or less coherent intellectual cultural relationships existing over time. Tradition, for MacIntyre, is broadly conceived. Among the examples he explicitly considers are: (1) the Classical Greek tradition including Homer, Periclean Athens, Plato and Aristotle; (2)the Augustinian/Thomistic tradition; (3) the Scottish Enlightenment (17th and 18th century) which includes the jurist Stair, theological developments during this period, and the philosophers Hutcheson and Hume; (4) the Western Enlightenment tradition in general and; (5) Nietzsche as representative of the beginnings of postmodernism. Intellectual and social traditions are intimately related such that a crisis for one is likely to create a crisis for the other. Thus, although MacIntyre concerns himself with the analysis of intellectual traditions, he is concerned very broadly with the analysis of culture and the occurrence and resolution of crises within cultures.

As the above remarks indicate, it is possible for an intellectual tradition and a social cultural tradition to experience a crisis. This can come about in a number of ways. (1) Over a process of years, decades, or even centuries, a particular intellectual tradition can uncover inconsistencies, areas of incompleteness or other intellectual difficulties. This may result from later generations of scholars discovering problems that earlier generations had missed. (2) Social upheaval can create problems for a society that the dominant intellectual framework is incapable of dealing with in its present form. (3) A society may suddenly be confronted with an alternative conflicting intellectual framework that challenges the dominance of the existing paradigm. (4) An intellectual framework may be challenged by some combination of (1-3).

Even individuals who are not beginners in philosophy may find the above somewhat abstract. I will give some examples. Some of these are given by MacIntyre. All of them are, I believe, consistent with his discussion.

The Babylonian captivity of the children of Israel created a cultural, spiritual and intellectual crisis for the Jews. They were forced to face the problem of how their God who was Lord of the universe could allow the defeat of His people. A number of the Old Testament books are written to make sense out of this dilemma.[11]

St. Augustine dealt with a similar problem. Christianity became the religion of the Roman Empire in 381 AD. In 410 AD. Rome was sacked by pagans. Augustine's City of God was written as a response to the pagan critics of Christianity who claimed that the defeat of Rome meant that Christianity was a false religion.[12]

In the eleventh and twelfth century there was a tremendous recovery in the West of the works of Aristotle through efforts of Muslim (read pagan infidel) scholarship. This represented a tremendous intellectual challenge to Christian intellectuals who revered Aristotle but were far behind their Muslim counterparts in the research, understanding and integration of his work with their own faith.[13]

Within the natural sciences, Thomas Kuhn has documented the crisis within astronomy created by the discovery that the Ptolemaic theory that the sun revolved around the earth failed to account adequately for an enormous amount of the behavior of heavenly bodies.[14] Other authors, in part inspired by Kuhn have written of intellectual crisis occurring within the social sciences.[15]

Everyone is familiar, many of us first hand, with the crisis in medical ethics. This crisis has occurred not so much from any sources external to medicine but from advances in medical science. Progress in medical science has created ethical dilemmas that did not exist a generation ago.

It would be easy to multiply examples of social and intellectual crises within cultures, academic disciplines, professions, etc. MacIntyre thinks that we are undergoing a tremendous upheaval within our present culture represented by the phenomena of postmodernism. In affirming the existence of this crisis, he is hardly alone.

It is important to emphasize here not only that traditions may undergo crises but that participants within traditions are capable of recognizing the existence of crises. Furthermore, they are capable of recognizing a resolution of a crises or the failure of their own traditions to resolve a crises. This leads us to consideration of the criteria for demonstrating that one culture is morally superior to another.

MacIntyre's criteria for one tradition to philosophically defeat another on rational grounds.[16] MacIntyre lists a number of criteria for one tradition to show that it is more rational than another. To summarize these criteria we will identify a tradition as T1 and the alternative tradition that shows itself more rational than the first tradition as T2. Let us assume that T1 has one or more problems that we will identify as Pa, Pb, Pc, etc. The criteria for rational refutation may be summarized as follows. (1) T1 generates a problem that is both social and intellectual. (2) T1 is unable to solve the problem with its own intellectual and cultural resources. (3) T1 is not able to explain the problem that confronts it. (4) T2, explains why Pa occurred in T1. (5) T2 explains why T1 could not have possibly resolved the problem Pa. (6) T2 provides a resolution of Pa that T1 is forced to accept as a more reasonable resolution of the problem than any that it has provided from within its own tradition.

These criteria may be summarized in less technical terminology. MacIntyre is maintaining that adherents of a tradition are able to recognize when they have a problem that their tradition cannot resolve but a competing tradition is able to resolve. This means that with respect to that problem, at least, the alternative tradition is able to show on rational grounds that it is superior to their own.

MacIntyre does not give a specific number of problems that are required for one tradition to be judged clearly superior to another but the basic criteria are clear. If one tradition is in competition with another, the more important the problems that can be solved by the other tradition and the greater the number of these important problems, the more likely we are willing to say that the latter tradition is more rational than the former.

Let me try to illustrate his position by reference to something with which we are all familiar, for example, the workings or non-workings, as the case may be, of a computer. My knowledge of computers is limited. Still there have been periods when I have thought I understood computers. Sometimes, however, they do not work the way I want them to work. I cannot fix the problem, and I don't even know how I got into the problem in the first place. Resolving the problem is important. I cannot continue my writing until it is fixed. I am in a state of crisis. I thrash about and try random strategies in an unintelligible fashion. I pray. It does not work. I suspect that I am making some fundamentally wrong assumptions about the workings of computers. I suspect that I need a more sophisticated or perhaps radically different understanding of at least the computer program with which I am trying to work.

I turn to a person presumably more knowledgeable than I about such matters. I usually get one of four results, either (1) no help at all, or (2) a simple solution consistent with my basic assumptions about the way computers work. The friend explains to me in terms of my assumptions what I need to do to avoid the problem next time. This is a rational explanation that doesn't require me to change my world view regarding computers. (3) Sometimes I get help that is not rational at all even though it works. My friend presses some keys and fixes the problem. When asked how she fixed it, she tells me she doesn't know. When asked how I got into the problem in the first place, she tells me she doesn't know. When asked what I should do to avoid the problem in the future, she tells me she doesn't know. My friend is obviously more skilled than I at fixing problems, or her prayers regarding computers are more efficacious, or she has a magic touch, but, in any case, she does not offer a rational refutation concerning my basic assumption about computers (i.e., that they are inhabited by mischievous and sometimes evil gremlins).

(4) Sometimes, however, a fourth alternative occurs. My friend fixes my problem and then proceeds to explain to me why the problem occurred. Not only that, she explains why, given the assumptions I was operating on, it had to occur. She even goes on to explain why I could never have solved the problem using my basic assumptions. She then proceeds to give a rational account of a resolution of the problem in terms of her different set of assumptions. This account makes sense to me and I am forced to give up my old set of assumptions. I keep the gremlin hypothesis ready in the background, however, just in case another crisis arises.

The above is, of course, only an illustration but one that is instructive. It illustrates MacIntyre's argument in a couple of respects.

My friend's understanding of computers is greater than mine but what she offers is only an interpretation of computers that is *more rational* than mine. She neither offers, nor pretends to offer, the *ultimate* rationality with respect to computers. New software and hardware is coming out all the time. New problems arise periodically. What we have here is *not relativism* with respect to computer operation. Some interpretations are more rational than others and can be shown to be more rational. On the other hand, neither do we have rational absolutism, if by absolutism one means a final answer that is necessarily capable of withstanding all criticism and will inevitably remain forever superior to all challenges and solve all problems.

The above remarks illustrate MacIntyre's position. One tradition may defeat another by showing itself to be more rationally coherent than another. One tradition may show itself to be more rationally coherent than all the available rivals. It cannot, however, show itself able to solve all future problems or to be rationally superior to all possible future rivals.

Let us take another example. This time we will refer to the problem of rearing the next generation. Not so long ago American society had a paradigm for child rearing that most people, including the social, intellectual and political elite regarded as normative.

The ideal included the following: (1) a two parent family, (2) committed to a life long relationship, (3) living in reasonably close proximity to an extended kinship unit, i.e. available grandparents, aunts, uncles, cousins, etc., (4) a mother who did not work outside the home at least during the pre-school years of the youngest child, (5) a neighborhood that was small enough to be relatively personal, including a neighborhood grocery, pharmacy, hair stylist, school, churches, recreational facilities, etc., (6) a high degree of agreement among the various institutions with respect to basic moral values, (7) media that was perceived as supportive of the basic values of family, church, school, neighborhood, etc.

All of these ingredients were not always present. The sometimes existed only to a limited degree. Nevertheless, many of the structures were present for a significant portion of the population. Now it is certainly the case that many of these structures are not present for a very significant portion of the population to a significant degree. Furthermore this is perceived to be creating a crisis for our society.

But what does the breakdown of these structures have to do with an *intellectual* tradition? MacIntyre, because he sees intellectual and social tradition as intimately related, would see intellectual assumptions being challenged by social economic forces, or, in some cases, challenging these forces. For example, economic changes have encouraged, and in many cases required, women to work outside of the home prior to the youngest child becoming school age. But there is not only economic necessity. We have come to believe that women, in order to achieve maximum fulfillment as persons should have careers other than, or in addition to, wife and mother. This is not just an economic change. It represents a significant shift in values.

We have developed an economy that increasingly provides opportunity for persons to be geographically and socially mobile. We identify this mobility with freedom and call it good. The economy also frequently requires that individuals and families be uprooted in order to survive. This creates alienation and we call that bad.

Corporations transfer people to different parts of the country and sometimes different parts of the world. Employees may leave a particular corporation but transfer to a different city in order to pursue a given career track. Two hour commutes to and from work are not uncommon in our highly mobile society. Mobility creates opportunity for professional growth, economic advancement, cultural enrichment, and self-realization. It also makes it less likely for more and more people that they will live and work in the same neighborhood, or that they will live in the same neighborhood all their lives. The neighborhood grocery is becoming a thing of the past. So is the neighborhood school and the neighborhood church. All of this has meant that parents can rely less and less on the support of the neighborhood in the rearing of children. Grandparents and relatives are less available to help.

The decreasing of restrictions on divorce has doubtless liberated many men and women from dysfunctional marriages. It has also contributed greatly to the impoverishment of women and children.

All of this has raised many social and economic problems. It has also raised problems of social justice. Is the present welfare system moral and just because it meets the needs of the needy, or is it unjust because it encourages children to have children that they are not able to care for? What is the responsibility of business to help employees meet their responsibilities as parents? Is abortion an acceptable means of birth control that society should endorse or even allow?   Should homosexuals be allowed to adopt children?   Should white parents be allowed to adopt Afro-American children?   Should we decrease the amount of resources expended on neonatal care?   What is the responsibility that children have for the care of their parents?   What is the meaning of 'family'?   Of 'motherhood'?   Of 'fatherhood'?

These are moral issues having to do with social justice.   There is not a consensus in our society regarding how society should deal with them.   There is frequently not even consensus within various traditions within our society on these matters.   Where we do achieve consensus on one issue or another there is frequently not agreement on the *grounds* of that consensus.   Individuals and groups *happen* to agree but are not able to give a rationally coherent account of why they have come to this or that moral conclusion.   Sometimes they cannot even give a rationally coherent account for themselves.   Frequently the account they find satisfying makes no sense to people outside their particular religious tradition, professional group, social class, or political party.   Furthermore, these moral issues have arisen within the context of our society and are frequently a result of the pursuit of goals that we as a society have considered and still do consider good and moral.

Whether or not the Enlightenment tradition will be able to provide the resources (within its own tradition) to solve the problems cited above remains, of course, to be seen.   It is clear, that significant groups--as diverse as Christian fundamentalists and non-fundamentalist Christians, various branches of Islam, and significant numbers of social and intellectual elite's of no particular religious persuasion--think that it cannot.

The relevant test here for MacIntyre would not be that critics of the Enlightenment affirm that it cannot resolve the problem but that adherents of the Enlightenment perspective themselves recognize their inability to solve the problem.   It is this realization that constitutes a crisis.   Furthermore, a deep crisis would require that the Enlightenment tradition not only cannot solve the crisis but cannot give a rational account concerning why it occurred in the first place.

For the Thomistic tradition or any other tradition to show itself rationally superior to the Enlightenment tradition, several additional requirements would have to be met.   The Thomistic tradition would have to show why the Enlightenment tradition failed and must necessarily have failed. It would have to provide a solution to the problem. This, of course, would mean not just showing that the Thomistic tradition provided a rational solution to the problem of rearing the next generation in 1274, the year of St. Thomas's death. It would have to be shown that the tradition provided a solution to those problems in the present set of circumstances. This is, of course, a very different thing.

The Enlightenment, Emotivism, and Contemporary Culture

We will return to a discussion of MacIntyre's relationship to cultural relativism at the end of this chapter. We will develop a clearer view of MacIntyre's view of rationality after we have considered his views on emotivism. To summarize briefly, we may say that MacIntyre rejects emotivism as an ethical theory and a theory of language. He affirms, however, that emotivism is descriptive of the ethical discourse of Western culture. Western culture is an emotivist culture. Furthermore, emotivism is the logical outcome of the Enlightenment view of rationality.[17]

For MacIntyre the essential characteristic about emotivism is that it assumes that rational discourse about ultimate ends is impossible. Furthermore, to the extent that emotivism is embedded in a culture, it actually makes rational discourse about ultimate ends impossible. MacIntyre affirms that both Kant's rationalistic non-consequentialism and the consequentialism of utilitarianism break down into emotivism and were destined to break down into emotivism once they were introduced. In this sense, MacIntyre affirms, Ayer has the better of the argument over against both Kant and the utilitarians. This is true even though Ayer's own position cannot be given a rationally coherent grounding. MacIntyre's reasons for these assertions will be given below.

Two Concepts of Reason: Mechanistic and Teleological Explanation. We have introduced the distinction between teleology and deontology in a previous chapter.[18] In this treatment, teleology was identified with consequentialism and deontology with its opposite. Utilitarianism was treated as a variety of teleology or consequentialism because what is morally right was determined by what results in the greatest good consequences for the greatest number. Deontology was identified with Kant because in his ethic, correct moral action is determined independently of consequences. For Kant, we are responsible to act rationally quite independently of whether this leads to our own happiness or that of others. This distinction is all right as far as it goes, but to interpret MacIntyre it is necessary to explain a much richer sense of teleology most closely identified with Aristotle.

A simple illustration will help to clarify the difference between mechanistic and teleological explanation in the sense that MacIntyre wants to emphasize. I want a good car, and I want a good life. I want my car to go well and I want my life to go well. I therefore want to know what it takes to get and keep a car that goes well. I therefore want to know what it takes to get and keep a life that goes well. What does it mean to explain what makes a car go well? How does this differ from what it means to explain what makes a life go well? 'Good', 'going well', 'know', and 'explain' seem to be used in these sentences in ways that are both similar and different. The differences seem not just to hinge on the fact that persons and their lives are more complicated than cars.

An explanation of what we mean by a 'good car' seems to be available in terms of what we may call a mechanistic explanation. My car is not running smoothly. I take it to the mechanic and he replaces the spark plug wires, and this fixes the problem.. I usually am not interested in the details as long as the car runs properly but the mechanic is able to give them to me if I am interested. It has to do with electric fire getting to the spark plugs and to the pistons to enable internal combustion to take place and drive the piston rods, etc. This seems to be all that there is to it. By and large our society believes in mechanistic explanation and finds it non-controversial. Although we do not often put it this way, we can describe mechanistic explanation as a series of hypothetical imperatives or synthetic a posteriori propositions that describe how machines, biological organisms, and, frequently, social institutions work. We do not believe that mechanistic explanation can tell us how to have a good life. We do not believe that mechanistic explanation can tell us how machines, biological organisms, or social institutions ought to work. We are, however, uncertain as a society, that there is any other type of explanation (non-mechanistic explanation) that can tell us about the good life.

This seems to be the situation. Mechanistic explanation offers rational explanation in terms of if/then statements like "If the ignition system is working properly, then the engine will run." It does not offer rational explanation in terms of ultimate ends or purposes. Mechanistic explanation is a rational explanation that can explain the working of machines and human behavior to the degree that human behavior is subject to what we may call either hypothetical imperatives or synthetic a posteriori propositions. Mechanistic explanation cannot explain human behavior to the extent it is not subject to explanation by synthetic a posteriori propositions. Furthermore, there is no societally agreed upon non-mechanistic explanations. There is not even agreement that such explanations exist. This seems to describe emotivist assumptions about the possibility of reasoning. What is a possible alternative? MacIntyre tells us that, prior to the Enlightenment, there was a common teleological perspective interpreted in the framework of Aristotelian philosophy.

Let us now attempt to clarify the Aristotelian concept of teleological explanation. For Aristotle a complete casual explanation of an event included consideration of four causes. These included material cause, formal cause, efficient cause and final cause. Lets take my idea of a good car for an example. Cars are made out of steel, plastic, leather, cloth, etc. These materials are created from more basic things like iron ore, oil, animal hides, cotton, etc. These products are created or formed according to certain structures and they fit together according to certain other forms or structures. Thus, we have basic materials which may be created from more basic materials. Some of these materials are the *material cause* of the automobile. The basic materials and the automobile itself are created according to a form or pattern that we will call the *formal cause* of the automobile. Were it not for the materials and the form or structure there could be no automobile.

Of course, someone has to construct the automobile using the materials and the pattern that gives the automobile its structure without which it would be not an automobile but a pile of scrap. That someone or those someone's who put the automobile together are the *efficient cause* of the automobile. Aristotle's efficient causality is not exactly identical with mechanistic causality as conceived in the modern world, but it comes close. The point is that Aristotle would say that without material and formal causality, efficient causality would explain nothing.

But Aristotle would also point out that an automobile in a world where there were only fields, deserts or forests would be incomprehensible. There must be driveways, streets, roads and highways. There must be cities and towns to go to and economic and social structures that make it meaningful to go there. There must be legal structures that govern property rights and traffic laws associated with automobiles. Automobiles require fuel, and fuel comes from foreign nations by pipelines and ships. A whole complex of international relations is necessary to fully explain the existence of the automobile. These structures all have material and formal causes of their own that are interrelated in complex ways. Included in these physical and institutional structures are, of course, alternative modes of travel and communication that cost more or less, pollute more or less, or that take more or less time to use than automobiles.

Automobiles enhance our happiness. They also kill thousands in accidents. They enrich our lives by making communication, sociability, and economic progress possible. They provide, in some cases, relatively cheap transportation. In some cases, they require a disproportionate amount of our income. They make possible a social structure that causes millions to spend billions of hours in traffic jams. The internal combustion engine in my car is related to the engines that have made modern warfare possible.

All of the uses to which automobiles are put are related to purposes that people have -- bad purposes, good purposes, better purposes, the best purposes. From Aristotle's point of view, the complete explanation of the automobile would require in addition to material, formal, and efficient causality the concept of final causality. What is the end, the purpose, the telos of the automobile? A full explanation includes the concept of purpose. Whether cars are good, whether a particular type of car is good, whether a particular car is good for a particular person requires analysis of purpose in the context of an interlocking web of relationships that includes a sense of the final purpose in life.

This perspective will appear strange to the modern mind. That, however, is because the modern mind has been trained to think of explanation exclusively in terms of mechanistic processes. Westerners also have been trained to believe in progress and to define progress in terms of the increasing power to understand physical and social relationships in terms of the accumulation of power to manipulate and control these relationships. In other words, we define progress in terms of increased understanding and use of mechanistic explanation. But our basic assumptions would appear strange to the Ancient world of Aristotle and the Medieval world of Aquinas. These assumptions also appear strange to much of the contemporary non-Western world. There are, of course, remnants of this Aristotelian world view, or at least similarities to it, even in the West.

There is concern with air pollution. Occasionally a city planner will arise who is concerned with the destruction of community that has occurred because of the automobile. The Amish, who reject the use of automobiles altogether, still thrive in various pockets of rural America. There are still pious people who wonder whether God wants them to own a car or a house or one that expensive or large. Such city planners, however, or people concerned about the ecology, or Amish folk or pious Christians or Jews, are considered odd.

The point I am making here, of course has nothing particularly to do with automobiles. I could have chosen as an example a house, a book, a business, or a tree. The point is that, for Aristotle, the existence of anything in the universe can only be fully intelligible if it is considered in the context of material, formal, efficient and *final* cause. Teleological explanations are the only ones that make sense out of the totality of our experience. Furthermore, teleological explanations must include the individual thing in a hierarchy of relationships. Purpose, for individual human beings, makes sense only in the context of communities. Human communities make sense only in the context of ultimate meaning for humans and the universe.

The concept of teleological explanation has relevance for our analysis of the so called is/ought distinction. Modern ethical discourse has assumed a sharp distinction between descriptive statements which claim that such and such a state of affairs *does* exists, and normative statements which claim such and such a state of affairs *ought* to exist. As we have seen, A.J. Ayer affirms this distinction and draws the conclusion that normative statements are meaningless. Kant affirms the distinction but affirms that normative statements are meaningful because they represent synthetic a priori statements which differ from descriptive statements. MacIntyre points out that the is/ought distinction was not assumed by Greek thought in general, and Aristotelian thought in particular. This is because of Aristotle's teleological perspective which included formal and final cause as part of the description of any phenomena.[19] For Aristotle, a full description of the thing must include its relationship to the final good, but also its relationship to the network of interrelated structures, both above it and below it, in a hierarchy of ends. In other words, a full description includes a description of the purpose of a thing and its relationship to the purposes of other things and the relationship to ultimate purpose. Brute 'facts' don't exist. 'Facts' exist only in rich and complicated contexts that must include purpose. Purpose is not an add-on to an already existing reality. It is part of the very nature of that reality.[20]

There is, of course, another assumption that was made in the framework of the Aristotelian perspective and also in the Christian Thomistic Aristotelian perspective. This is the assumption that the universe has a purpose that is ultimately good. A 'fact' therefore, cannot be understood apart from its place in the universe which has a final end or purpose that is good. From this teleological perspective the fact/value distinction or is/ought distinction disappears. We cannot evaluate what a phenomenon is apart from its relationship to these networks of ends, and to the final or ultimate end. We cannot separate 'is' from 'ought' in any adequate explanation of any phenomenon.

This is a strange way of thinking for those of us raised in modernity. We are used to thinking of reality in atomistic fashion as composed of separate individual things. We have not, however, entirely lost our ability to think in terms of higher purposes as perhaps a few negative examples may show. Did they have 'good' ovens at Buchenwald? Were any of those who actively took part in the execution of the victims there happy and fulfilled? The mind recoils at answering these questions in the affirmative. They doubtless had very hot ovens at Buchenwald. They may have operated very efficiently. They may have achieved the purposes for which they were designed to a high degree of reliability. One wants to say, however, that to call them 'good' or 'gut' is to misuse the English or German languages or indeed any language that we would be willing to call human. Our unwillingness to call them good seems to be related to an ability to define reality--even ovens--in terms of purpose. We have not entirely-- at least many of us have not entirely--lost our ability to think teleologically.

What about the question of happy and fulfilled guards at Buchenwald? Let us suppose that there were some at Buchenwald who were able to go about their daily work experiencing feelings of intense pleasure, and a complete absence of guilt or shame. Let us further suppose that they believed sincerely that they were serving humanity and achieving a state of personal perfection and self-realization. Would we be willing to accept their report, however sincere, that they were happy? A negative answer to this question seems to be intelligible on one of two bases. We could respond as emotivists. Here the claim would be that our early socialization makes it impossible for us to link the positive feelings we associate with the word happy with the negative feelings we associate with the killing and torturing of persons we regard as innocent. But on the emotivist perspective our unwillingness to associate these two concepts can have no rational justification. It is simply due to an accident of our socialization that our emotions came to be associated in this way. Some of the Nazi's at Buchenwald were subject to different emotional associations. We may be able to 'explain' our different emotional associations giving some sort of mechanistic causal analysis. We cannot, however, meaningfully disagree.

Another alternative response would seem to be something like the following. Happiness for human beings does not just have to do with feelings of pleasure, the absence of the feelings of guilt and shame, or even the individual's own perception of fulfillment and self-realization. Happiness has to do with becoming the kind of person one really ought to become. Happiness has to do with achieving one's appropriate end. Happiness has to do with relating to others in ways that enable one to be in accord with the ultimate values of the universe and contribute to others achieving this same end. This answer, however, is the answer of one who is thinking teleologically. This answer entails defining what it means to be truly human in terms of the final end or ends for human beings and the final end or ends for the universe. This answer entails a rejection of the fact/value distinction. This answer requires us to talk about what it means to be human in ways that transcend the individual preference of autonomous individuals. This is true because if we go much further in our discussion of *true* happiness we will find that we are deeply embedded in the assumptions of some on-going tradition that deals with the meaning of human existence.

Politics, Autonomy and the Good

The Ancient and Medieval concept of political community. For Ancient and Medieval man both Aristotelian and non-Aristotelian political communities were moral communities. Part of one's definition as a human being was wrapped up in one's membership in a political community. To ask what it means to be a good person necessarily included the question of one's role and contribution to the political community. Moral thinking entailed teleological thinking and part of one's telos included being a good citizen of a particular community.

Despite significant differences, Kant, the utilitarians, Rawls, and the tradition of Modernity (or the Enlightenment in general) start with the assumption of the autonomous individual. We all may be born into a community or complex network of communities. We all may be intellectual heirs of a tradition forged in communal evolution and conflict. According to these thinkers, we nevertheless, are capable of thinking of ourselves as persons apart from communities. Communities, in turn, are voluntary associations of autonomous individuals. Aristotle would have thought that this assumption is not only false but ultimately unintelligible. So does MacIntyre.

What is politics for the Enlightenment tradition? Rational autonomous individuals make judgments about the good for themselves and others. They create *personal* ends and enter into political associations in order to achieve these ends. They create 'social contracts' to enable them to pursue these personal ends. Of course, the proponents of the contract theory do not assert their viewpoint as actual historical accounts of the formation of political communities. People on many occasions make new economic contracts and form new businesses. We are, however, born into cities, towns, states and nations that already have ready-made laws and rich traditions. But what is affirmed by Enlightenment thinkers is that it is possible to think of oneself as an individual apart from a political community, and, furthermore, that such a perspective is the only proper one by which to evaluate political associations. The implication of this is that individuals who have different (or perhaps *accidentally* similar) final ends come together to form political associations to enable them to better pursue their individual and various views of the *telos*. From this point of view, political associations are just that -- associations.

They are not communities of shared values. Individuals may think teleologically but it is increasingly difficult to think teleologically within the context of contemporary political communities.

Does Kant provide an answer to the problem of community? MacIntyre doesn't think so. Kant proposes an absolute that provides a standard by which all political entities must be judged. One must treat others always as ends in themselves and never simply as means. One must act as a law-making member in a kingdom of ends in themselves. Just laws respect rationality, autonomy and the personhood that they represent. MacIntyre's specific treatment of Kant in the three major works we have quoted from is relatively brief.[21] Several arguments, however, would appear to be relevant here.

Most importantly, the categorical imperative is so abstract that it is subject to multiple interpretations in any concrete situation. To the degree that Kant avoids making this self-evident, it is because he implicitly draws on assumptions about right, wrong and virtue which are drawn from his own Christian, Lutheran culture. Though Kant and his readers often refused to recognize their debt to this culture, his interpretations of the implications of his theory were accepted because they were heirs of these same assumptions. Anyone who self-consciously rejects these traditional assumptions or who is heir to a tradition significantly different from that of Kant will find the implications drawn from his moral premises implausible. This is true even though they may accept the same premises that Kant affirms.

When different interpreters draw conflicting implications from Kant's premises there appears to be no way of resolving this conflict except by appeal to background assumptions given in one or another tradition. But Kant has explicitly rejected tradition, and what MacIntyre calls the rationality of tradition, as a reliable source for founding ethical judgments. Thus, there would appear to be no *reasons* one can give to resolve the differences in implications. We have thus started with an ostensible principle of rational absolute morality but slid into emotivism.

Does utilitarianism provide an answer to the problem of community? Utilitarianism from one perspective seems to be the opposite of Kant's deontological theory. MacIntyre, however, views them both as different variations on the same theme. Both affirm the existence of the autonomous individual which he refers to as an *invention* of modernity.[22] Utilitarianism leads to emotivism as well. The principle of the greatest good for the greatest number is only intelligible if we have clear and reliable concept of the good. It may work reasonably well if all or most of the members of a society *happen* to have a relatively common conception of the good. When this fails to be the case, however, utilitarianism does not give us the resources to rationally resolve differences. We are left with unresolvable conflict, coercion, or manipulation as alternatives. Associations of autonomous individuals, by definition, do not have a basis for rationally resolving conflict regarding the good. In other words, we are back to emotivism again.

'Good,' for MacIntyre, is defined in the context of communal relationships. Communal relationships essentially entail common moral commitments. A man or a women is a person occupying roles functioning in various ways in a complex social order. We cannot intelligibly ask, whether X is a good mother, physician, business woman, lawyer, judge or juror unless we know what mothers, physicians, business women, lawyers, judges, or jurors are supposed to do and be.

We cannot ask what these roles are supposed to entail unless we know what a good society is supposed to be. To answer these questions we must know what it means to be a good person living in a good society. To say what a good person and society is supposed to be, we must know what it means to be human. Reasoning about such things, argues MacIntyre, goes on within historical intellectual traditions and only within historical intellectual traditions. If a society happens to have agreement on these subjects, it will be possible to agree on what is the greatest good for the greatest number. If it doesn't happen to have such agreement, then utilitarianism gives us no basis for the intellectual resolution of the conflict.

Does Rawls provide an answer to the problem community? I have already spent a considerable amount of time discussing Rawls in relationship to these issues in the last chapter. There I argued that the later Rawls *may* be interpreted as a cultural relativist. Rawls also seems to be making fundamental sociological assumptions about the nature of the Western intellectual tradition that MacIntyre rejects. In particular, Rawls assumes that there is a relatively coherent Western intellectual tradition. Utilitarianism has given one articulation of the theory of justice inherent in that tradition. Rawls believes that he has given another articulation that is more accurate, more coherent and more likely to preserve the best within that tradition. Therefore, his theory of justice is superior to the utilitarian one. But he thinks, and this the important point, that this tradition, although in need of shoring up, is pretty much intact. To the extent that he is right, either cultural relativism or emotivism may provide the basis for a coherent and harmonious social order. MacIntyre on the other hand seems to believe that the Western Enlightenment tradition that Rawls represents is breaking up. To the extent that MacIntyre is right, Rawls' attempt to develop a theory of justice that at its core avoids all teleological judgments is doomed to fail. It will fall prey to emotivism in a culture where coherent rational and emotional life is breaking down. His theory rests on grounds that provide him no rational basis for defending it when it comes under attack. Once again the alternative seems to be emotivism. This, however, is an emotivism that is occurring in not only an intellectually fragmented society but in an emotionally fragmented one.

Of course, neither the early Rawls, who seems to espouse moral absolutism, nor the later Rawls, who appears to be a cultural relativist (at least regarding the relationship of comprehensive perspectives and political theory) has room for the kind of communal and teleological thinking that MacIntyre is defending. Rawls consistently represents the tradition that regards the autonomous individual as the primary basis of justice and the social order. Furthermore, for Rawls, political society is an association of individuals who presumably have different ultimate ends. As we have indicated earlier, however, the Rawlsian conception of personality seems to exclude even individuals who have a single ultimate end.[23] Rawls allows that individuals in the original position may regard themselves as possibly being the representatives of groups when they shed the veil of ignorance and become fully knowledgeable members of a political order, but this possibility remains undeveloped in his theory.[24]

Contemporary culture, the emotivist self and the problem of community. MacIntyre argues not only that various political theories fail to give us an alternative to emotivism.. He further argues that emotivism is embedded in our culture in a pervasive sense. Two examples he gives are the bureaucratic self and the therapeutic self.[25]

Typically, we think of bureaucracy and therapy as two different sorts of social phenomena with different perspectives.   According to MacIntyre, however, they share a common commitment to an explicit emotivism. Rationality in a bureaucracy has to do exclusively with the efficient relationships of means to ends. It is not appropriate to raise, *within* the context of the bureaucracy, the rationality of the ends themselves. This means that if the individual is operating within a public bureaucracy, that the ends for the bureaucracy are supposed to be given to the organization by the political process.   We have, however, already indicated that the political process seems ill equipped to rationally consider the ends that it presumably is to give to the bureaucracy.   If the bureaucracy within which the individual is operating is a business bureaucracy, then the ends again are already given. The end is profit--the bottom line. Rationality has to do with the most cost-effective means of reaching the maximum long and short term profit. There may be an assumption that what is good (rational) for the company is good for the public. This may in fact be the case, according to one or more perspectives. Rational consideration of the ultimate ends of the company, however, are ruled out of bounds.

What about therapy? Successful therapy is presumably about the adjustment and reconciliation of the desires and feelings of the individual with the social reality within which the individual must operate. The 'good' therapist helps patients adjust their own goals or the goals of a particular social context in which they operate. The latter may be accomplished by transforming a social context, becoming less emotionally vested in the social context or changing contexts altogether. The point is that 'rational adjustment' is the goal, not a 'rational evaluation of the ultimate aim' of either the individual or society. MacIntyre need not deny that on occasion both bureaucracies and individuals dispensing or seeking therapy undergo radical soul searching about ultimate ends.   What he does insist, is that the dominant model takes ends as given and gives rational consideration to means alone.[26]   Where rational debate or discussion about ends is impossible, we have emotivism, if not in theory, then in practice. In other words, only analytic a priori or synthetic a posteriori propositions may be considered. Normative statements are excluded.

Secular Humanism and Fundamentalism

It should be clear from the above analysis that MacIntyre is neither a secular humanist nor a fundamentalist. What may not have been clear up to now is that his rejection of both perspectives is related to emotivism.

Secular humanism represents, on the one hand, a rejection of the authority of revelation and tradition, on the one hand. On the other hand, it represents the affirmation of the authority of reason and scientific method to both the physical universe and the moral and social universe. It thus stands as a clear affirmation of the Enlightenment ideal of the authority of a transcendent reason. This is not to say that there have not been some who have identified themselves with both cultural relativism with respect to morals and secular humanism at the same time. In the main, however, secular humanists have not been epistemological relativists. Rational scientific knowing is consistently held by secular humanists to be superior to any other mode of knowing. Furthermore, it would seem to be the case that secular humanists cannot consistently be moral relativists. A culture deeply committed to reason and science is held by them to be superior to cultures not so committed or less committed to these ideals. Religious people living within contemporary culture are showing a failure of will and are falling back into superstition. For those who should know better, this is a moral and spiritual failing. In this respect, they are not unlike the Christians who regard those who have heard the Gospel and have still rejected it as having spiritually and morally failed.

If, however, the Enlightenment is dead then so is secular humanism. Secular humanists, therefore, have not escaped emotivism. They are no more capable of reasoning about ultimate ends then any other adherents to the Enlightenment.

What about fundamentalists? Are they emotivists as well? MacIntyre does not say so directly but it is clear from his discussion that he does not think that fundamentalism has successfully escaped the emotivist culture. In the opening pages of his *Whose Justice? Which Rationality?*, MacIntyre refers to fundamentalists and evangelicals as fideists.[27] In these same pages he refers to the fact that there are many secular fideists as well. The difference between the fundamentalists and the secular fideists is that the fundamentalists are honest about their fideism whereas the secular fideists are not. MacIntyre is not a fideist but he obviously prefers honest fideism to dishonest fideism.

What does MacIntyre mean by fideism? MacIntyre is not using the term in a technical sense here, but what he seems to mean by fideism is the commitment to a set of beliefs that can be apprehended by faith and not by reason. As such they are held to be true based on faith and can neither be defended successfully nor refuted by rational argumentation. Fideists do not see this lack of relationship to rational argumentation as a weakness. Faith does not need the defense of reason.

How is fideism related to emotivism? Obviously the fideist does not accept the emotivists theory of meaning. The fideist believes that the affirmations of faith are true statements of fact and are not merely meaningless expressions of emotion. The fideists is like the emotivist, however, in maintaining that the propositions of the faith and the ethical assertions that follow from them are not capable of rational defense. Thus, in an argument with an opponent, the fideist is in no better position than the emotivist to give a rational defense of ethical assertions.

Secular fideists are less honest than the religious fideist and less self-conscious. They believe that their affirmations are based on reason since, by definition, they have rejected faith as a source of knowledge. Persons who pretend to themselves and others to be defending a position on rational grounds when in fact they have no rational grounds for their position are using ethical assertions in exactly the way Ayer says that we all use ethical assertions. They are simply expressions of emotion and attempts at manipulation. They cannot be legitimate attempts at rational persuasion.

Thus, the secular humanist is accusing the fundamentalist of fideism that is in practice the equivalent of emotivism. Fundamentalists, for their part, accuses secular humanists of being fideists, but dishonest ones. Clearly, the room for the use of rational persuasion to alleviate cultural conflict is limited given these assumptions.

Is MacIntyre's characterization of fundamentalism as fideism accurate? I think that it is not entirely accurate. At least many who would be willing to call themselves fundamentalists would not accept his characterization as accurate. Many in the historic fundamentalist tradition have been willing to use argument in defense of their faith propositions. Interestingly enough, however, they have often accepted

Enlightenment assumptions about reason and proceeded to defend their faith propositions on the basis of these assumptions. From MacIntyre's point of view, a fundamentalist rejection of fideism based on Enlightenment assumptions about reason is bound to fail.

There is also no question that there is a strong strain of anti-traditionalism in Protestantism in general and in fundamentalism in particular. Fundamentalists often talk as though tradition is not only not necessary to interpret the Bible. It even gets in the way. Fundamentalists tend to believe that the Bible is both directly intelligible to the modern mind and directly applicable to our modern situation without benefit of an authoritative church or thorough understanding of two thousands years of theological reflection. These are, of course, only tendencies. They are, however, genuine tendencies. It appears therefore, if rationality can occur only in the context of a self-conscious tradition, that fundamentalism is not in a strong position to challenge the emotivism of our culture on its own terms.

MacIntyre and the Culture Wars

MacIntyre's solution to the problems of our emotivist culture are not as clear as his analysis of the problem. I think it is safe to say that his answer would include both a rejection of Enlightenment assumptions about individuality and a commitment to enter into the market place of ideas as a representative of a tradition ready to propose, from the point of view of one's own tradition, solutions to concrete problems faced by all members of society. This would require a great deal of hard work. Under Enlightenment assumptions, each individual is required to leave his or her own tradition at the door before entering the room where public debate takes place. One does not need to master the history and thought of the tradition of another. One does not even have to master the history and thought of one's own tradition. One certainly does not need to accept the burden of interpreting one's own tradition to another before meaningful dialogue can take place. After all, on Enlightenment assumptions, tradition is not only unnecessary, it gets in the way.

If MacIntyre is right, multiculturalism may turn out be less fashionable when people discover how hard it turns out to be. Simply developing a taste for grits, Polish sausage, and sushi just is not going to cut it. Where will these dialogues take place? Where will people be trained to the level of sophistication necessary to carry on such dialogues? The modern university with its commitment to a combination of Enlightenment rationality and emotivism seems like an unlikely breeding ground for the training of the kind of understanding necessary to make such dialogue possible.

MacIntyre's Project: Some Reservations and Suggestions

There are several concerns that emerge in our consideration of MacIntyre's project. In the first place, we do not have a clear articulation of a program for developing a moral system or reforming society. Utilitarianism, Kant and Rawls all raise numerous unanswered questions. Nevertheless, it is reasonably clear, in a general way, how one might proceed in developing a program in accord with their principles. MacIntyre's critique of these other positions is rich, profound, insightful and frequently brilliant. The alternative he proposes, however, is not fully developed.

Secondly, rationality and justice can be defined only in the context of intellectual and cultural traditions. The Enlightenment tradition has proved to be just that--another tradition. Granting that the Enlightenment is just another tradition is in itself an admission of failure, since the Enlightenment claimed to be an alternative that transcended all tradition. Thomism is offered as an alternative to both the Enlightenment and Genealogy or postmodernist deconstructionism. Thomism, however, is only one possible alternative among many others. This raises numerous problems. Does our culture provide the resources for the nurturing and development of Thomism or for that matter any other intellectual cultural tradition? MacIntyre affirms that we live in an emotivist culture. This strikes me as a non-controversial affirmation. What MacIntyre means by this affirmation, however, is that an emotivist way of thinking is deeply imbedded in our most basic institutional structures. It is emotivist institutional structures in which we live and move and have are being. The barbarians are not just at our gates. They live in our hearts. How therefore, can we create in the modern world, institutional structures that can support any tradition at all? This is as much a sociological question as a philosophical one. It is one, however, that MacIntyre cannot avoid. His critique of contemporary culture is as much sociological as philosophical.

In the third place, there is the problem of the relationship of philosophy to revelation and theology. Even Rawls has a relatively explicit answer to this question. He does not rule out a transcendent revelation or theology defined as the enterprise of articulating that revelation. He defines this as irrelevant to his project. Rawls believes that a political theory can be formulated without making commitments to the ultimate nature of reality. He sees no need to develop a comprehensive theory. In fact, for Rawls, the avoidance of a comprehensive theory is the key to the resolution of cultural conflict. This is just the opposite of MacIntyre's position. For MacIntyre, the development of a comprehensive theory that makes explicit commitment to ultimate ends is the only way that a coherent conception of rationality and justice may be developed.

Thus, even if MacIntyre had made no commitment to develop an explicitly Christian perspective, he would be required by the logic of his approach to deal with the issues raised by problem of revelation. He could deny its reality as the secular humanists do. He could affirm that reason and revelation provide separate and non-interactive tracks to the same reality as some religious thinkers have done. He could develop a thesis regarding the interrelationship of reason and revelation. He could not consistently ignore the issue of the relationship of reason and revelation. As a Thomist, however, he clearly cannot ignore this problem. MacIntyre's failure to develop a theory of the relationship of reason and revelation must therefore be interpreted as a piece of unfinished business in the context of his philosophical perspective.

Finally, for MacIntyre, there are the very formidable intellectual difficulties necessarily associated with any cultural critique. This seems to imply an intellectual elitism of significant dimensions. Utilitarianism, Kant, Rawls, cultural relativism, emotivism, fundamentalism and secular humanism (as represented by the magazine Free Inquiry) all represent themselves as fundamentally accessible to persons of average or slightly above average intelligence and education. One does not need to be a first class scholar in intellectual and cultural history in order to understand one's own perspective and how it differs from competing alternatives. MacIntyre's criteria for evaluating alternative perspectives seems to require this expertise. At the same time, MacIntyre insists that theories of rationality and justice need to be supported by a rich, varied and comprehensive institutional structure.   MacIntyre seems on the one hand, to reject abstract theoretical discourse available only to a few philosophical elites well versed in the history and thought of numerous cultures. On the other hand, he seems to define the criteria for cultural criticism in a way that would be possible only for such elites MacIntyre presents us with a project yet unfinished. Whether the difficulties noted above along with others can be surmounted awaits future articulation of this project either by MacIntyre or others willing and able to take up the task that he has begun.   MacIntyre might respond to this criticism by an emphasis on what is the proposed strength of his position. MacIntyre insists that ethical and intellectual understanding must take place within the context of a community.   It is, by definition, according to MacIntyre's understanding not the work of a solitary thinker, however brilliant.   What MacIntyre must call for is the work of entire community where there will be a division of labor. This will include a division of labor among scholars. It will also include the work of non-scholars who are working out the ethical implications of their respective professions and situations.   This still leaves open various questions about the nature and structure of this community with its various sub-communities. Macintyre might further reply that what he presents is only a preliminary sketch of the task before us and that others may be enlisted to spell out the details of this preliminary sketch.

Notes

[1] Immanuel Kant, *The Critique of Pure Reason*, p.29.

[2] Academe: Bulletin of the American Association of University Professors, November/December 1994, Volume 80, Number 6. See especially Richard Rorty "Does Academic Freedom Have Philosophical Presuppositions?" pp. 52-63.

[3] Exodus 20:12-17

[4] Matthew 22-35-40

[5] Galations 5:22-23.

[6] Galations 3:19-25.

[7] Galations 5:14.

[8] Plato. *Republic, Great Dialogues of Plato,* See especially Book VIII, pp. 341-369.

[9] Aristotle. *The Nicomachean Ethics,* pp. 55-75.

[10] Compare *Whose Justice?* p. 386 and *Three Rival Versions,* pp. 204 and 228.

[11] The basic thesis offered is that Israel's captivity does not represent a defeat of Jehovah but rather the punishment of Israel for her sins.

[12] St. Augustine, *The City of God.* Augustine distinguishes between the City of God and the City of Man. Rome (the City of Man) has been defeated but the Church (The City of God) is still triumphant. Augustine, of course, refers to both the Old and New Testaments to buttress his argument. The concept of the distinction between church and state and the debate about the nature and extent of the separation between the two has been around for centuries.

[13] MacIntyre, *Whose Justice.* pp. 164-208.

[14] Thomas Kuhn. *The Structure of Scientific Revolutions.*

[15] See Alvin Gouldner. *The Coming Crisis in Western Sociology.*

[16] MacIntyre, *Whose Justice?* pp. 364-5. There are a number of places where MacIntyre discusses the criteria for one tradition showing itself to be more rational than another. The above cited pages are perhaps the clearest in his major works.

[17] Most of the discussion in this section is a summary of the extended argument given by MacIntyre in his After Virtue. See especially chapters 1-7.

[18] See chapter V, pp. 85-87.

[19] *After Virtue,* p. 84.

21 Compare especially *Ibid.,* pp. 43-50.

22 *Ibid.* p 61.

23 See Chapter VII, pp. 167-8.

24 See Chapter VII, pp. 175-6.

25 *After Virtue,* pp. 23-35.

26 See Robert Bellah et al. *Habits of the Heart.* where similar concerns are raised.

27 *Whose Justice?* pp. 5-6.

Chapter IX

Concluding Remarks on an Ongoing Conflict

Where do we go from here? The answer to this question depends on where we hope to end up. If the goal is to end cultural conflict by the complete annihilation of all opposition then one set of strategies will be appropriate. We should rationally persuade those we can rationally persuade, manipulate those we can manipulate, coerce those we can coerce, discredit those we can discredit, marginalize or render irrelevant those we can marginalize, and eliminate those we can eliminate. This is a recipe for a culture war. If it need not necessarily be a physically violent war, it will inevitably be psychically violent. The word 'war' suggests destructive conflict. In war there may or may not be winners but inevitably there are losers. Conflict, on the other hand, leaves open the possibility of constructive enrichment. The process may be difficult but it doesn't have to be destructive. The challenge of our time is not to eliminate all conflict. That is impossible. It would also, I believe, be undesirable.[1] The challenge is to eliminate *violent* conflict.

Cultural relativists assume that if we embrace cultural relativism and repudiate all forms of universalism that this will lead to tolerance and hence peace. Emotivists are not as explicit in their strategy for the abolition of destructive conflict. An emotivist program for peaceful conflict resolution would, however, rest on the following assertions Commitment to a scientific view of language will cause us to recognize that value statements are meaningless. This recognition will do away with meaningless debate and free us to concentrate on those issues that can be solved by the application of scientific method to social discourse. This may not lead to complete harmony but it will contribute to that end. The egoistic, hedonistic, utilitarianism of a Bentham, on the other hand, offers the basis of a comprehensive social science and ethical theory. Bentham attempted to articulate both a vision for what the good society ought to be and a social science theory that would allow us to achieve that vision. Peaceful conflict resolution could be achieved by stripping away our illusions about human motivation and applying a rational scientific methodology to human relationships. Thus, both Bentham and the emotivist A. J. Ayer would see the resolution of violent conflict through the commitment to scientific method. They differ on their view of the relationship of scientific discourse to ethical discourse.

Kant's vision for the resolution of social conflict is also clear. In a world where everyone acted as if they were 'law making members of a kingdom of ends' the autonomy and hence the basic dignity of every person would be respected. For Kant, this also means the application of rationality to ethical problems although he distinguishes between the type of 'rationality' which we apply to ethical discourse and the type we apply to physical phenomena. Such a world would be devoid of destructive conflict if not devoid of all conflict.

Rawls believes that a commitment to social justice and harmony requires the rejection of all these alternatives. The early Rawls and perhaps the later Rawls is neither a cultural relativist or an emotivist. But he disagrees with utilitarianism on at least two grounds and with Kant in at least one important respect. The utilitarianism of Bentham and Mill is inadequate because it allows the greatest number to achieve their good at the expense of the minority. Thus, his charge is that utilitarianism is compatible with exploitation. But their views are also metaphysical or what Rawls later refers to as a comprehensive doctrine. Rawls makes similar claims regarding Kant. Though he is attracted to

Kant in many respects and in is in some sense a Kantian, he does not want to offer a comprehensive perspective in the sense that Kant affirms.

What is wrong with compressive doctrines as a foundation for political justice is that they make claims about the totality of human existence and not just the political realm. They make claims about what is ultimately true, and good, and knowable. In this sense they are or function as 'religious' perspectives A comprehensive perspective when it is put forth as the foundation of a political order becomes inevitably discriminatory of other alternative comprehensive perspectives. To the extent that one comprehensive perspective becomes implemented in the political realm, incompatible comprehensive perspectives become disenfranchised. Rawls does not use this language exactly, but it is consistent with his viewpoint to say that if one 'religious' perspective is made the foundation of a political order than complete freedom of religion in that society becomes an impossibility. In the terminology we have been using in this book, religious and hence cultural war is inevitable in a society that includes adherents to more than one comprehensive perspective. Rawls does not discuss fundamentalism or secular humanism but they would both seem to be comprehensive perspectives that vie for political implementation. Given Rawls' assumptions, to the extent that the policies these respective perspectives would implement are incompatible (and they both regard their perspectives as incompatible) cultural war seems to be the only possibility.

Rawls solution is to create and found political justice on a zone that is neutral with respect to comprehensive perspectives whether associated with traditional religions or secular philosophical assumptions. This is his solution to the problem of avoiding 'culture wars'. The viability of his whole project then rests on the answer to two questions. Do his own assumptions rest on a metaphysically 'neutral zone'? If Rawls can be shown to have failed in his attempt to create a 'neutral' zone', a second question arises. Is it even possible to create such a 'neutral zone'? I have argued in this book that Rawls has not succeeded in his attempt at neutrality. The view of self that he sees as entailed by his political theory seems clearly to affirm assumptions about selfhood that make claims about the ultimate nature of personhood. Furthermore, this view of personhood seems to clearly exclude an extraordinarily wide spectrum of viewpoints, ranging from

John Paul Sartre to Mother Teresa. If this analysis is correct, than Rawls' viewpoint is neither inclusive or tolerant. As such it does not offer a perspective that will help us avoid culture wars. As a matter of fact, it would seem to increase the possibility of culture war. This is because to the extent that Rawls' claim to neutrality is perceived as false, any attempt to impose his perspective on the grounds of its pure neutral rationality will be seen as arguing in 'bad faith'.

If one concludes that Rawls has failed to provide a perspective that is both metaphysically neutral and at the same time rational, it does not follow that it would be impossible for anyone to do so. The claim that such neutrality is impossible, however, is precisely the one that MacIntyre makes. MacIntyre's claim is, of course, an epistemological one. Since there is no such thing as tradition transcendent rationality, Rawls cannot have discovered or articulated such a rationality any more than Bentham, Mill or Kant. His claim to have done so rests on Enlightenment assumptions about the nature of rationality. Such a view of rationality was destined to break down into emotivism and deconstructionism. Emotivism and deconstructionism despite their apparent differences lead to the same conclusion. Given emotivist assumptions, affirmations about basic values cannot be attempts at rational persuasion. They can only be attempts at manipulation or a form of intellectual bullying. Once this is unmasked the only alternative would seem to be a culture war.

MacIntyre's solution is to recognize and openly admit the rationality of traditions. If there cannot be a tradition free rationality there can be rationality within traditions. If we have the resources and the commitment, we can become conversant with multiple traditions and conduct a debate among the various traditions. This is an open invitation to cultural conflict but would make it possible to avoid cultural war. There are at least three separate issues here. In the first place, we may inquire about the adequacy of MacIntyre's criticism of the Enlightenment project and emotivism and deconstructionism which he regards as the results of the failure of that project. Secondly, there is the separate issue of adequacy of his own alternative to these various movements. It is, of course, possible that MacIntyre may be right in his criticism of the Enlightenment but still not have offered us an adequate theoretical alternative. Thirdly, we may ask what it would mean to implement MacIntyre's alternative in the form of a practical program. MacIntyre seems to have said little about this third problem.

It may be that one might agree with MacIntyre's critique of the Enlightenment and the adequacy of his theoretical alternative but still regard the concrete implementation of that program in contemporary Western society as hopeless. I will deal briefly with these three issues

That the Enlightenment is under serious attack in academic circles is beyond question. It is also beyond dispute that emotivism grew out of the movement known as logical positivism and the logical positivism represented an attempt to found philosophy on scientific principles which in turn are indebted to Enlightenment ideals. Thus, there seems to be a direct line from the Enlightenment to emotivism. That this was or is the only possible line is a matter of dispute. Defending or attacking MacIntyre's thesis here would involve us in a complex debate in intellectual history that would take us beyond the scope of this book. Similar things might be said about deconstructionism and its relationship Nietzsche. Nietzsche, of course, considered himself to be in direct revolt against Enlightenment ideals rather than as a logical extension of those ideals. On the other hand, the assertion that we presently live in an emotivist culture is a descriptive sociological claim as much as a philosophical one. I am very much inclined to think that this is an accurate statement. As a matter of fact, one of my principle reasons for writing this book on ethical 'theory' is my dissatisfaction with much of contemporary ethical debate that seems to be long on exhortation and the use of emotionally laden assertions and short on rational persuasion. One reason for choosing to compare to relate the ethical theories considered to the topic of 'culture war' and the positions of fundamentalism and secular humanism is my hope that the careful consideration of these theories might to some degree cast the light of cool rational reflection on an area where emotional rhetoric frequently seems to hold sway. Nevertheless, although it seems obvious to me that MacIntyre is right in describing our culture as emotivist, his claim is an empirical one that would benefit from careful sociological analysis. In any case, we need to distinguish the two very different claims that are being made by MacIntyre. One claim is that the Enlightenment has degenerated (as it was destined to do by its own logic) into emotivism and that emotivism has been intellectually repudiated. Since the enlightenment leads to emotivism and emotivism has been discredited, the Enlightenment has been discredited. His second claim is the empirical one that despite the fact that the emotivism has been intellectually discredited, that it is socially and culturally still dominant. I have indicated in this book my own thesis that the phenomenon of 'culture war' is directly related to the cultural dominance of emotivism.

What about the adequacy of MacIntyre's alternative of the rationality of traditions? I have indicated some reservations about the alternative in the chapter on MacIntyre. Among these are: MacIntyre's failure to develop a systematic approach to ethics; the problem of creating, in a culture characterized by emotivism, institutional structures to support and articulate the meaning of the tradition; the relationship of reason and revelation; and the seeming requirement that, given MacIntyre's epistemological assumptions, only a relatively few intellectual elite's would be capable of the comparative analysis of various traditions. These criticisms are of different types and degrees of seriousness.

It seems to me that the most important theoretical piece of unfinished business for MacIntyre is the clear articulation of his views on the relationship of reason and revelation and the implications of this for theology. Given his assertion that he is articulating a Thomistic philosophy, I do not see how he can legitimately avoid this task. Here it might be useful for him and his readers to examine and enter into dialogue with the Reformed tradition particularly as it is represented by the tradition of Abraham Kuyper, Dutch theologian, newspaper editor, former prime minister of the Netherlands and founder of The Free University of Amsterdam. The most philosophically sophisticated representative of that tradition is the philosopher Herman Dooyeweerd whose four volume work entitled *A New Critique of Theoretical Thought*, as the title suggests, also gives an extensive critique of Enlightenment assumptions.[2] Dooyeweerd rejects the Enlightenment assumption that theoretical thought can provide a religiously neutral standpoint from which to interpret human experience. Theoretical thought is one mode of knowing which must be set alongside other spheres of human experience. The attempt to interpret all spheres of human experience in terms of theoretical thought has the effect of a radical reductionism which denies other dimensions of reality their rightful legitimacy in the created order. For Dooyeweerd this reductionism creates all kinds of distortion in both our theoretical activity and our social relationships. Put in the context of our discussion, this has the effect of making legitimate and constructive cultural conflict difficult and encourages culture war. Even a superficial summary of Dooyeweerd's thought would require an additional chapter to this book which I will not attempt here. I mention Dooyeweerd as an example of another philosopher committed to the development of a philosophy which engages the issues of Enlightenment presuppositions, cultural critique and religious values. The Kuyperian tradition has contemporary proponents committed to the analysis of the Western political system in general and the American scene in particular.[3]

I will turn now to the other problems I have noted in MacIntyre's project. I have referred to his failure to develop a systematic ethics; the problem of developing institutional structures to sustain traditions of rationality, justice and culture; and the seeming requirement of intellectual elitism in order engage in the kind of cultural critique he appears to advocate.

The key to the other two issues would seem to be the problem of developing and sustaining institutional structures to sustain traditions of rationality, justice and culture. MacIntyre might defend himself against the criticism of failing to develop a systematic ethics by affirming that in advocating Thomism he is already heir to and part of a rich intellectual and culture tradition with institutional structures already in place to sustain that tradition. He doesn't have to create the Roman Catholic Church, Catholic colleges, universities, churches, intellectual associations and the rich heritage of ethical reflection represented by the Thomistic tradition. By the same token, it may be argued that although Thomism as an intellectual tradition is obliged to confront a variety of intellectual traditions, each individual Thomist is not obliged to master every alternative tradition. It is of the essence of MacIntyre's position that the growth, development and maintenance of a culture is a communal enterprise. Not all members of the community are required to be philosophers. Not all philosophers are required to be geniuses. Thomism, therefore, no more implies intellectual elitism than the Western liberal Enlightenment tradition. As a matter of fact, given the individualistic assumptions of the Enlightenment, the implications of Thomism may be far less elitist.

The above arguments, however, do not release MacIntyre from the obligation of articulating in more detail how the fruitful encounter of various traditions is to take place. Nor do they, it seems to me, deal adequately with the issue of the relationship of reason and revelation. Most traditions in fact, claim revealed truth in some form as a part of the tradition. The Enlightenment is a notable exception in this regard.

Concluding Comments

For many, if not most, of my readers this book will be the first and perhaps last encounter with philosophy in the technical sense of that term. It will not, however, be the last encounter with philosophy in the less formal sense. Affirmations, counter affirmations, expositions and arguments about the nature of reality, how we may know that reality, the nature of human personhood, the good life and the good society are encountered every where -- in sermons, films, editorials, classrooms, political debates, hospital bedsides, law courts and dormitory bull sessions. For better or worse, we live in a time that is unsettled with respect to our most basic assumptions about human existence. Someone once said that "war is to important to be left to the generals." Likewise, questions about the meaning of life are too important to be left to the philosophers.

What has been offered in this book is an example of a critical analysis of some basic thinkers and theories about the nature of the good life and the good society. It is hoped that the reader's ability to engage in critical analysis has been enhanced and that this enhanced ability will last a life time. Whether or not one remembers the details of the theories presented and the specific arguments for and against those theories is of secondary importance. I would even go so far as to say that it matters very little. Careful and reasoned confrontation with the issues raised in this book, however, matters a great deal.

How that confrontation takes place in our society also matters a great deal. 'Cultural conflict' is inevitable and is frequently constructive. 'Cultural war' is more problematic. In some cases it may be inevitable. Depending upon how it is carried on, it may even be constructive. I am not so presumptive as to think that the reading of this book will turn cultural war into cultural conflict. The turning of "swords into plowshares" is the proper task of someone far greater than I, using methods far more powerful than philosophical arguments. I would, however, make three basic observations that have been implicit throughout the discussion of this book.

In the first place, I have noted from the very beginning Arthur Holmes' insight that a useful distinction can be made between the base, principles, rules and case application of an ethical theory. These distinctions are relatively easy to grasp in principle, although in concrete arguments they may at times be difficult to sort out. Serious attention to these distinctions can have profound implications on the nature of cultural conflict. Much of the debate surrounding the so called 'culture wars' assumes that difference at the base level necessarily implies disagreement at the principle, rule and case application level. This assumption has a negative impact on the possibility of dialogue and cooperation between different groups. It may be, with respect to some issues, that disagreement goes all the way down so that disagreement at the base level precludes agreement at any level. I would not want to trivialize the differences between Christians, Jews, Muslims and those who reject the alternatives offered by all organized religions. Neither do I wish to trivialize the differences among various traditions among the worlds great religions. On the other hand, with respect to many issues and in many contexts there is what Rawls referred to as an 'overlapping consensus'. This overlapping consensus may occur at the principle, rule or case application level or in all three. When it does occur, we have the possibility of cooperation and dialogue instead of cultural war. This leaves open the possibility that although wrong, one's opponent is not completely wrong. It also leaves open the possibility that although one is right, one may not be completely right.

Secondly, the issue of the exclusion of comprehensive doctrines from political debate seems to me to invite destructive conflict rather than ameliorate it. I have taken some pains to show that Rawls seems to have failed to develop a political theory that is metaphysically neutral. On the contrary, it seems to me, that his view of selfhood draws upon a comprehensive world view that excludes not only most, if not all, of the world's religions but numerous varieties of secular humanism. I have no question regarding Rawls' sincerity, but I question the success of his project and the likelihood that others are likely to be more successful. I do think that 'overlapping consensus' is possible with respect to a wide variety of important issues. The best way to achieve this 'overlapping consensus', however, is to clearly and self-consciously introduce a variety of comprehensive doctrines into the political market place of ideas where they can be examined with respect to their ontological, epistemological and their practical day to day implications. The continued attempt to separate discussion of ultimate commitments from the discussion of social justice will, I believe, be unsuccessful. It will make the dialogue more impoverished and superficial than need be the case. It will invoke charges and counter charges of dishonesty and unfairness. It will encourage the reduction of political debate to sound bites, character assassinations, and ad hoc and peripheral issues.

Finally, I think there are significant implications for the way one carries on philosophical discourse, especially about ethics and social philosophy. Undergraduates who take their first and frequently only course in philosophy are often encouraged to 'bracket' their own religious beliefs and historical and cultural traditions. 'Thinking critically' is introduced as requiring the putting aside of all the presuppositions about the meaning of life that one has brought to the classroom and the adopting of an intellectually 'neutral' approach to all those things that up to now have mattered most. MacIntyre has raised formidable epistemological objections to this way of defining the philosophic enterprise. I have stated my reservations about his answers to many of the problems he raises. I am more sympathetic to his critique of the Enlightenment tradition. It seems to me that what undergraduates have been asked to do for decades is not to abandon their various traditions for a tradition free perspective but to abandon their traditions for an alternative tradition that masquerades as epistemologically neutral. This way of posing the problem invites several non-constructive responses. Some undergraduates disengage from the intellectual enterprise, memorize what the professor and the text affirm and give it back on the final exam pretending until after the grades are in that the views they express are their own. Others adopt a superficial relativism or emotivism and leave their one and only course in philosophy convinced that reasoning about these issues is impossible, at least for them, and irrelevant to their lives. In the overwhelming majority of cases whether the philosophy course is taught in public or private colleges, this is not an outcome that the professor desired.

Philosophy should be dedicated to helping students engage the views of rationality and justice they have inherited from their traditions as well as the views of alternative traditions. If MacIntyre is right, and I think that he is, then a life long commitment to the bracketing of one's own and all alternative traditions is not the proper goal of philosophy. Secular humanists, Christians, Jews, Muslims and others should be encouraged to engage their own comprehensive world and life views and to critically and sympathetically examine alternative perspectives. Many students come to the study of philosophy as heirs of rich intellectual and cultural traditions of which they have only a very limited and superficial knowledge. They may choose to abandon those traditions but this should be done only after an informed and critical examination of their own tradition and the alternative that they intend to adopt.

Tapping into the resources available for this informed and critical examination in many cases may not be readily available. Students have other demands than the study of philosophy or religion. There are, however, various resources. One's minister, priest or rabbi is more likely to be more open to dealing with doubts and questions then may be supposed. Church related colleges abound with faculty committed to the kind of engagement described. Public universities and colleges also contain numerous faculty and staff committed to various traditions who are willing to dialogue with others who are also interested. Public universities also frequently have assigned campus priests, ministers, rabbis who regard intellectual encounter with their own and other traditions as their special calling. Although I am not aware that secular humanists have the functional equivalent of campus pastors, there are certainly numerous adherents to secular humanism on any faculty who are both equipped and willing to enter into the kind of discussions advocated here. Traditions have their own magazines and publishing houses that allow interested parties to tap into the intellectual resources of the tradition. I have quoted only a few of these magazines and publications in this book.

If all of this sounds like hard work, it is because it is hard work. Being an emotivist looks to be an easier course. However, every once in a while one wonders, "Ought a rational person to feel this way?" Unless one pushes the question aside immediately, seeking the answer may plunge one back into the issues raised by this book.

Notes

[1]Two classic works on the positive effects of social conflict are Ralf Dahrendorf, *Class and Class Conflict in Industrial Society.* and Lewis Coser, *The Functions of Social Conflict.* Dahrendorf's thesis is that society is held together not by value consensus but by cross cutting conflict in a social world where individuals and groups are divided on some issues but in agreement regarding other issues. Karl Marx had predicted that social classes would become internally homogeneous with respect to all important issues. There would be unity within classes and alienation between classes. According to Dahrendorf, Marx's revolution did not occur because this internal homogeneity did not occur. People have interests and values that cut across class lines. Tremendous conflict exists but it cuts across the various associations that characterize modern democratic societies.

[2]For a good and readable introduction to Dooyeweerd's thought see L. Kalsbeek, *Contours of A Christian Philosophy.* This book contains a useful introduction to the Kuyperian movement by Bernard Zylstra. Zylstra for many years taught at The Institute for Christian Studies in Toronto, Canada There are two works by Dooyeweerd himself that give a readable introduction to his thought. *In the Twilight of Western Thought* is a compilation of a series of lectures that Dooweweerd gave in the United States in 1959-60. Dooyeweerd's *Roots of Western Culture* is a series of newspaper articles written for a Dutch audience after the close of W.W.II. The Netherlands had, of course, been occupied by the Nazi's during most all of the second world war and the post W.W.II period was a time of profound cultural and spiritual crisis. *Roots of Western Culture* is written for an audience composed of non-professional philosophers with deep concern over the direction of Dutch culture. The level of sophistication of these articles stands in sharp contrast to anything one could imagine in the current debate about cultural direction in the contemporary American scene.

[3]See Richard J. Mouw and Sander Griffioen, *Pluralism and Horizons: An Essay in Christian Public Philosophy* and James W. Skillen, *Recharging The American Experiment: Principled Pluralism for Genuine Civic Community.*

Glossary

A posteriori. After, dependent upon, or based on experience. The opposite of a priori.

A priori. Prior, before, or not based on experience.

Absolutism. Frequently used to define the opposite of both cultural and Individual relativism. Used in this book as a synonym for universalism. Absolutists believe that there is at least one value that applies everywhere and at all times.

Act utilitarianism. The view that the criterion for moral action consists in every act being for the greatest good of the greatest number. Act utilitarianism is contrasted with rule utilitarianism.

Analytic. To analyze is to define by mentally taking apart the meaning of a term or concept. An analytic statement is one that is most appropriately defined by this method. This is the opposite of a synthetic statement that synthesizes or brings together two concepts that are not identical. "A bachelor is an unmarried male" is an analytic statement since it affirms a relationship between two concepts, 'bachelor' and 'unmarried male,' that by analysis are shown to mean the same thing. "Jones is a bachelor," is a synthetic statement since it affirms a relationship (synthesizes or pulls together) between two entities 'Jones' and 'bachelor,' that do not by definition mean the same thing.

Analytic apriori. A statement that can be shown to be true or false by definition and is known independently of empirical investigation. Analytic apriori statements tell us about how we have come to define terms. They do not tell us about the world.

Anthropology. Theory of human nature. From 'logos' which means 'word' or 'theory of' and 'Anthropos' which is one of the Greek words for man.

Aristippus. An egoistic, quantitative hedonist who emphasized intensity of pleasure as the good.

Artificial Identity of Interest. The view that where human beings have desires or interests that place them in conflict, it is possible to arrange social reality so that they have an identity or harmony of interests. Artificial Identity of Interests is contrasted with those situations where human beings have a Natural Identity of Interest and no special social engineering is necessary to make their interests compatible. Bentham believed that where a Natural Identity of Interest did not already exist, that it was possible through legislation to create an Artificial Identity of Interests.

Autonomy: Autonomy means being free because one is a law giver for one's self.

Axiology. Theory of value. From 'logos' and 'axios' which is Greek for value. Ethics (theory of moral value), political philosophy (theory of the good political order), and aesthetics (theory of that which is good in art and the realm of beauty) are all aspects of axiology.

Bentham. An egoistic (both psychological and ethical), a quantitative hedonist, and a utilitarian who affirmed the hedonic calculus as a scientific means of predicting and controlling human behavior.

Burden of proof. A phrase used to define which side in an argument has the responsibility to maintain its case. For example, in a court of law an individual is assumed innocent until proved guilty. The "burden of proof" is thus upon the prosecution to prove the guilt of the accused. The defense does not have to prove innocence, but only has to prove that the prosecution has not made her case. In the debate between cultural relativists and universalists, each side will attempt to argue that the other has the "burden of proof."

Categorical Imperative. A categorical imperative is a command that has no exceptions. "You must do act x."

Cultural relativism. The philosophical position that there are no values that are not the creation of some culture. Thus, the values in any particular culture are either the creation of that culture or have been appropriated from some other culture. There is no moral standard above the culture.

Deconstructionism. A philosophical position applied especially to the interpretation of literary texts. Very much in vogue in literary criticism. Deconstructionists affirm that there is no correct interpretation of any text or more broadly, of any cultural creation. The text doesn't have a single meaning. In the reading of the text a meaning is constructed in the relationship between the text and the individual interpreter. Therefore to get beyond the distortions imposed by past interpretations we must take apart these constructions or de-construct the text. All cultural phenomena are constructs which must not be understood as static entities having a definite meaning. cultural study therefore must be seen as a dynamic process that must be deconstructed.

Deontology. Deontological ethical theories affirm that consequences are irrelevant to the rightness or wrongness of an action. For deontology, the good is based on the right. Deontological theories are non-consequentialist.

Determinism. The view that all events including human behavior is neither random nor freely chosen. Human beings do not have freedom of the will.

Egoism. The position that all persons are always 100% selfish (psychological egoism) or the position that all persons always ought to be 100% selfish (ethical egoism).

Emotivism. The ethical theory that affirms that all ethical, aesthetic, or religious statements are simply expressions of emotions. Emotivism does not exclude statements about what people believe regarding ethics, religion, or aesthetics. For example, we can test whether or not a certain percentage of a given population believe in the existence of God, the wrongfulness of murder, or the beauty of a particular work of art. This is the work of the sociologist, or scientific pollster. "Jones believes murder is wrong," is a meaningful statement. It is not meaningful, however, to affirm that Jones is either right or wrong in his affirmation.

Empirical. Descriptive. Empirical statements are statements about the way things are constituted or the way people do behave and are contrasted with normative statements which are statements about the way things ought to be constituted or the way people ought to behave.

Epicurus. An egoistic quantitative hedonist who emphasized duration of pleasure as the good. Epicurus was a materialist in cosmology who relied exclusively on reason for knowledge about reality.

Epistemology. Theory of knowledge. Theory about how we know the most basic things about reality. From 'logos' and 'episteme' which is one of the Greek words for knowledge.

Ethics. The study of moral behavior and the theory value. The study of ethics deals with theories about how we determine what is morally right and morally wrong and theories about how we determine what is of moral and non-moral value in persons and human relationships. For example: "Love is the highest virtue." is a statement about moral value. "That car is worth $18,000." is a statement about economic value but makes no explicit claims about moral value. There are various sub-disciplines within the field of ethics, including business ethics, medical ethics, ecological ethics, etc.

Fact/Value distinction. The position that empirical or scientific facts can be clearly distinguished from values. Thus, scientific statements like "Slavery existed in the United States before the Civil War" can be distinguished from value statements like "Slavery is always morally wrong."

Fundamentalism. Historically refers to Protestants objecting to liberal theological movements which they regarded as denying the fundamentals of the Christian faith and attempting to define and affirm what they regarded as the fundamental beliefs necessary for anyone to be accurately described as Christian. Critics have come to use the term to describe any religious group (including Jews, Muslims, Hindus and others) whom they regard as extremely conservative, narrow, and radical in their beliefs.

Hedonic Calculus. Associated with Bentham who affirmed that pleasure must be measured by several criteria that included: intensity, duration, certainty, propinquity, fecundity, purity, and extent. Bentham affirmed that the hedonic calculus allowed its user to measure in exact terms the desirability of any act, principle, or proposed law. This could be done by assigning a weight to all of the relevant variables and calculating the sum total of pleasure for each activity or rule.

Hedonic Paradox. J.S. Mill observed that greater pleasure will be achieved if we directly pursue something other than pleasure. This is a paradox only if one assumes that pleasure is the good.

Hedonism. The philosophical position that affirms that pleasure is the highest good or the only good thing. Psychological hedonism is the psychological theory of personality that affirms that pleasure is the only thing that human beings do seek. Ethical hedonism is the ethical philosophical position   that pleasure is the only thing that human beings ought to seek.

Heteronomy: Heteronomy means rule from a source external to the individual. It is the opposite of autonomy.

Hypothetical Imperative. A hypothetical imperative is a constraint that can be avoided. "If you want to skate well, you must practice." The constraint of practice can be avoided by rejecting the goal of skating well.

Individual relativism. The philosophical position that there are no values that transcend or morally bind the individual other than his or her own choice.

Innernacy of Scripture. This is the view held by fundamentalists that the Bible is without error in all statements that it contains.   Inerrancy is often confused by critics of fundamentalism with the view that the Bible is "literally" true. Fundamentalists have never maintained that the Bible does not contain figurative language.   Thus, they do not maintain that all Biblical propositions are 'literally' true.

Laissez faire.   Literally "Let alone" or "Let be."   Refers to laissez faire economic theory that assumes that government should let the economy alone because it will function best for all citizens if interference is avoided. For example: It may be argued that 'laissez faire economic theory' is for the greatest good for the greatest number (utilitarianism) because there is a natural identity of Interests among all social economic classes.

Logical Positivism. A philosophical movement dedicated to the application of logical analysis and scientific method to all areas of knowledge. Has its origins in the so called Vienna Circle in the 1920's. Emotivism in ethics is an outgrowth of this movement.

Marginal Cost of Charity. This is a variant on the concept of 'marginal utility'. For any individual, the marginal utility (usefulness or desirability) decreases with the number of that item possessed. My second   hot   fudge sundae (on the same day) has less utility for me than my first.   After the second, the utility of hot fudge sundaes may approach zero. The cost to me of engaging in the charitable act of giving away my fourth hot fudge sundae is also close to zero. As far as I know, the concept of the 'marginal cost of charity' does not appear elsewhere in academic discussions. It is a useful concept, however, in explaining how an egoist can be 'charitable'.

Mill, James. Disciple and friend of Jeremy Bentham and the father of John Stuart Mill.

Mill, John Stuart. An Altruistic, qualitative, hedonist, and a utilitarian. Mill's altruism and insistence on qualitative distinctions among pleasures distinguished him from Bentham (and Aristippus and Epicurus) who affirmed both egoism and quantitative hedonism. His utilitarianism aligned him with Bentham but distinguished him once again from Aristippus and Epicurus neither of whom were utilitarians.

Natural Identity of Interest. The assumption held by Bentham (especially in economic life) that social reality is such that there is a natural harmony among various individuals and interest groups. Since the harmony is already present naturally (without government intervention), there is no need for the government to intervene. 'Natural identity of interest' is the chief perspective used to defend a free market economy and laissez faire economic theory. This assumption as applied to a capitalist social economic structure is the opposite of the theory of Karl Marx that assumes that there is a natural conflict of interest between the capitalist and labor classes.

Normative Morally binding or obligatory. A normative statement is a statement about the way persons or institutions ought to behave or be constituted. Usually contrasted with an empirical or descriptive statement which is a statement about the way persons or institutions are constituted or do behave.

Ontology: Theory of being. From 'logos' and 'ontos' which is Greek for being.

Philosophy. Literally, love of wisdom, from 'sophia' which is Greek for wisdom and 'phileo' which is one of the Greek words for love. Generally refers to the study of ultimate reality or ultimate principles defining the study of reality. Branches of philosophy include ethics, social philosophy, aesthetics (philosophy of beauty), ontology, epistemology and philosophy of the various disciplines. these include philosophy of law, philosophy of history, philosophy of the social sciences, philosophy of the natural sciences, philosophy of education, etc.

Qualitative hedonism. This is the position taken by J.S. Mill that pleasure is the only good but that there are qualitative distinctions among pleasures.

Some pleasures are intrinsically better than others quite apart from the amount of pleasure experienced.

Quantitative hedonism. This is the position taken by Aristippus, Epicurus, and Bentham that pleasure is the good but all pleasures are of the same kind. Therefore, there is no kind or type pleasure that is better than another. There is only more or less pleasure.

Rule utilitarianism. The view that the criterion for moral action consists in obeying rules result in the greatest good for the greatest number. One ought to obey the rule that leads to the greatest good for the greatest number even if the particular act in involved does not lead to the greatest good. Rule utilitarianism is contrasted with act utilitarianism.

Secular humanism. The position that human nature (not God or some supernatural spiritual reality) is the ultimate value in the universe. Society should be governed by principles capable of rational scientific explanation and not presumed supernatural or sacred principles.

Situation Ethics. Frequently held to be the relativistic position that all values are relative to the concrete situation in which individual decisions are made. Joseph Fletcher who wrote the book *Situation Ethics*, that made the phrase famous, held there was one and only one absolute value in Christian ethics which was the value of 'agape love.' He was thus not a relativist but an absolutist or universalist with a very short list (only one) of absolutes.

Subjectivism. The ethical position that ethical statements are 'statements about' the subjective feelings of the speaker. It is distinguished from the emotivist position that holds that ethical statements are 'expressions' of the subjective feelings of the speaker. Statements about how I feel can be true or false. Expressions of my feelings can be neither true nor false.

Synthetic. The opposite of analytic. See definition of analytic above.

Synthetic a posteriori. A statement that pulls together two different concepts and can be proved true or false only be empirical investigation. Synthetic a posteriori propositions give us information about the empirical world but give us only probable knowledge.

Teleology. Teleological ethical theories affirm that an action is right if it maximizes the good. The right is based on the good. Utilitarianism is a teleological (consequentalist) theory since it affirms that an action is right if it maximizes the greatest good consequences for the greatest number.

Theology. Theory of the nature of God. From 'logos' and 'theos' which is Greek for God. Theology is more broadly defined as the study of the doctrines or teachings of religious groups. Thus, we may speak of Christian theology but also of Muslim theology.

Universalism. The position that holds that there is at least one value or standard that applies to all persons and cultures, everywhere and at all times. The opposite of relativism whether individual or cultural. Used in this book as synonym for absolutism.

Utilitarianism. The ethical position that affirms that choosing the right action or rule among possible alternatives is done by assessing which of those actions or rules would be for the greatest good of the greatest number.

Weltanschauung. Refers to a total world and life view. Egoistic, hedonistic, utilitarianism is a perspective put forth as a world and life view encompassing all areas of life. Fundamentalism and secular humanism are also examples of alternative weltanschauungs. Rawls' is explicit in his attempt to develop a political theory that would allow for a variety of weltanschauungs.

Study Guide:

The following sample questions will test the students grasp of some of the basic concepts introduced in the various chapters.

Chapter I

1. The following statements have direct implications for ontology.
   A. There is a rational order in the universe.
   B. Matter does not exist.
   C. So called spiritual reality is an illusion.
   D. A & C above.
   E. All of the above.

2. The following statements have direct implications for epistemology.
   A. God has revealed himself in scripture.
   B. There is no such thing as supernatural revelation.
   C. Human beings can be understood through scientific method.
   D. A & C above.
   E. All of the above.

3. The following statements have direct implications for axiology.
   A. Murder is wrong.
   B. The sky is beautiful tonight.
   C. There are no moral absolutes.
   D. Human beings are the supreme value in the universe.
   E. All of the above.

4. *"Equality is a fundamental principle of justice because respect for humanity is the ultimate principle of moral value."*
   The author of the above statement is giving an argument which is most consistent with:
   A. Christianity.
   B. Islam.
   C. Secular humanism.
   D. Judaism.
   E. Hinduism.

5. *"All knowledge about is derived from application of reason and the scientific method."*
   The author of the above statement is making an assertion which has most direct implications for which one of the following:
   A. Ontology.
   B. Ethics
   C. Epistemology

Culture War and Ethical Theory

D.   Anthropology
E.   Theology

6. Fundamentalists and secular humanists necessarily disagree at the level
    of:
    A.   Case application.
    B.   Principle
    C.   Rules
    D.   All of the above.
    E.   None of the above.

7. Secular humanists and fundamentalists necessarily disagree on the level
    of:
    A.   Principle.
    B.   Base.
    C.   Rules.
    D.   A and B above.
    E.   All of the above.

8. The use of the term 'culture war' has exclusively been used to refer to:
    A.   Violent conflict concerning basic values.
    B.   Cases of genocide.
    C.   American political conflict.
    D.   Christian/Islamic conflict
    E.   None of the above.

9. Which of the following would seem to qualify best for the term 'culture
    war'.
    A.   The American Revolution.
    B.   WW I
    C.   The presidential elections of 1992.
    D.   The American Indian wars.
    E.   The American Civil War.

10. Culture wars are most likely under the following conditions:
    A.   There is disagreement at the base level.
    B.   There is disagreement at the rule level.
    C.   All parties agree on the basic principles involved.
    D.   There is disagreement at the level of case application.
    E.   B and D above.

Study Guide Chapter I: Answer key: 1. Since A, B, and C all make claims
about the nature of ultimate reality, they are all correct. Thus, the fully correct
answer is E or all of the above. All of the other answers would be at least
partially correct. 2. A, B, and C all make assertions relevant to how we know
and are all correct. Thus, E is the fully correct answer and the others are all
partially correct. 3. Axiology refers to theories of value. A, C and D have

reference to moral *values. B makes reference to* aesthetic *values. Therefore the correct answer is E or all of the above. All of the other answers are partially correct. 4. In this case, there is only one correct answer which is C for secular humanism. All the other perspectives would hold that here is some higher value to the universe than humanity. 5. The correct answer is C for epistemology since the emphasis is on knowledge and ways of knowing. 6. The correct answer is E or none of the above. 7. The correct answer is B. Fundamentalists assume that God provides the Base for their ethical views. Secular humanists assume that humanity is the ultimate value in the universe. 8. The correct answer is E or none of the above since the term "culture war" has been widely used to mean allot of different things. 9. The correct answer is D since the American Indian Wars. Refer to the discussion above. 10. A is correct. Culture wars occur over fundamental values.*

1. *Respond to the following argument. Jones is a professor of English. English is one of the disciplines identified with the humanities. Therefore Jones is a secular humanist.*

2. *What is the point of studying ethical theories?*

3. *Write a brief statement identifying your own epistemology, ontology, anthropology, and ethics. How are your views regarding these various aspect of your own philosophy related to each other?*

4. *To what extent was the American Civil War a culture war?*

5. *To what extent was WW II a culture war?*

Chapter II

1. *Moral absolutists or universalists:*
   A. *Believe that ethical assertions are meaningless.*
   B. *Believe that all values must be applied the same way no matter what the culture.*
   C. *Believe that at least one value is normative for all cultures in all times.*
   D. *All of the above.*
   E. *None of the above*

2. *The following statements would be agreed to by most cultural relativists:*
   A. *Cultural relativism is supported by the social sciences.*
   B. *Cultural relativism is good because it leads to tolerance.*
   C. *Moral absolutism is bad because it leads to intolerance.*
   D. *A & B above.*
   E. *All of the above.*

3.   *Cultural relativists hold which of the following?*
     A.   *There are some values common to all cultures.*
     B.   *Relativism leads to intolerance.*
     C.   *Values are not derived from culture.*
     D.   *All of the above.*
     E.   *None of the above.*

4.   *The following sources of value are excluded by cultural relativists.*
     A.   *Biblical revelation from a transcendent God.*
     B.   *Mystical union with a transcendent God.*
     C.   *Unique characteristics of human nature which transcend all cultures.*
     D.   *A & B above.*
     E.   *All of the above.*

5.   *The following are probably true of cultural relativists.*
     A.   *All cultural relativists with respect to values are cultural relativists with respect to science*
     B.   *Some cultural relativists with respect to values are cultural relativists with respect to science.*
     C.   *No cultural relativist with respect to values is a cultural relativist with respect to science.*
     D.   *Cultural relativism with respect to science would mean that scientific method is not necessarily the best means for understanding reality.*
     E.   *B & D above.*

6.   *Which of the following statements are true?*
     A.   *All Fundamentalists are cultural relativists.*
     B.   *No Fundamentalists are cultural relativists.*
     C.   *All Secular Humanists are cultural relativists.*
     D.   *B & C above.*
     E.   *None of the above.*

7.   *The following statements would be agreed to by many if not most cultural relativists:*
     A.   *All values are derived from some culture.*
     B.   *All values are mediated through but not necessarily derived from some culture.*
     C.   *Since there are no values which are common to all cultures, there are no values which ought to be common to all cultures.*
     D.   *A & C above.*
     E.   *None of the above.*

8.   *Critics of cultural relativists are likely to maintain the following:*
     A.   *Relativism with respect to case application does not count as evidence for relativism on   level of principles.*
     B.   *Cultural relativists are not in a position to criticize social values.*

    C. *Jesus, Gandhi, Socrates, and Martin Luther King Jr. all believed in universal values.*
    D. *All of the above.*
    E. *None of the above.*

9. *Which of the following are arguments or statements consistent with cultural relativism?*
    A. *All values are relative to the individual.*
    B. *Duration of pleasure is the ultimate good.*
    C. *The ultimate good is that which contributes to the greatest good of the greatest number.*
    D. *All of the above.*
    E. *None of the above.*

10. *Which of the following are arguments or statements necessarily inconsistent with cultural relativism?*
    A. *The Bible is true.*
    B. *God is love.*
    C. *The ultimate sanction of all morality is a sympathy with mankind.*
    D. *A & B above*
    E. *All of the above.*

Answer key: 1. The correct answer is C. Absolutists or universalists think ethical assertions are meaningful and they recognize that values must be applied differently in different contexts. 2. The correct answer is E. 3. The correct answer is E. 4. The correct answer is E. Cultural relativism excludes all non-cultural sources of truth. 5. The correct answer is E. B is true because although some cultural relativists accept cultural relativity with respect to science not all do. D is true since it seems to follow from the assertion of the cultural relativity of the Western scientific method. 6. B is true. No fundamentalists are cultural relativists. Some secular humanists, however, believe in absolute or universal norms. 7. D is true. A is one of the fundamental tenets of cultural relativism. C is one of the most common arguments given by cultural relativists in defense of their position. 8. D is correct. 9. E is correct. "All values are relative to the individual," expresses the basic tenant of "individual" relativism but not "cultural" relativism. D and C refer to an ultimate good that transcends culture. 10. E is true. The assertions under A, B and C assert the existence of culturally transcendent norms.

1. *Discuss and critically evaluate the arguments for and against cultural relativism. Define your own position about values in relationship to cultural relativism.*

2. *What is the significance of the fact-value distinction for the defense or criticism of cultural relativism?*

3. *What if any, is the relationship of deconstructionism to cultural relativism?*

4. *Discuss the relationship of cultural relativism to cultural conflict.*

Chapter III

1. *Which of the following is an analytic a priori proposition?*
    A.   The sun will rise tomorrow.
    B.   All circles are round.
    C.   Jones is a bachelor.
    D.   All good men and women ought to adopt Ayer's theory of language.
    E.   Jesus is the son of God.

2. *Which of the following is not an analytic a priori proposition?*
    A.   All triangles have three sides.
    B.   All bachelors are unmarried males.
    C.   The red hat is red.
    D.   Jones' hat is red.
    E.   The square table has four sides.

3. *Which of the following is not a synthetic a posteriori proposition?*
    A.   Lenoir-Rhyne is a Lutheran school affiliated with the Evangelical Lutheran Church in America.
    B.   Chemistry is a difficult subject.
    C.   Murder is morally wrong.
    D.   Most people have negative feelings about child abuse.
    E.   Philosophy is difficult for some and easy for others.

4. *Which of the following propositions would Ayer accept as meaningful?*
    A.   All circles are not round.
    B.   The moon is beautiful.
    C.   God is love.
    D.   Stealing is wrong.
    E.   Abortion on demand is morally right.

5. *Which of the following propositions would Ayer reject as not meaningful?*
    A.   The moon is made of green cheese.
    B.   Some bachelors are married.
    C.   Life is good.
    D.   Man is a mammal.
    E.   No dog is a man.

6. *Which of the following propositions would Ayer accept as meaningful?*
    A.   All men ought to accept a theory of language that conforms to scientific discourse.

B. The world would be morally a better place in which to live if all ethicists were emotivists.

C. Most people think all non-scientific assertions are not meaningful.

D. Love is the ultimate.

E. When in Rome one ought to do as the Romans do.

7. Which of the following is an argument or statement against emotivism?

A. Emotivism leaves us with no basis for making moral judgments.

B. It is generally accepted that natural science theories contain many non-analytic and non-synthetic a posteriori statements.

C. The English language does not by definition exclude ethical assertions.

D. A & B above.

E. All of the above.

8. Cultural relativists and emotivists would agree on which of the following?

A. It cannot be consistently maintained that there are moral absolutes

B. Since there are no moral absolutes one ought to obey the norms of one's culture.

C. There is no basis for asserting values that transcend the culture.

D. A & C above.

E. All of the above.

9. Emotivism in ethical theory:

A. Asserts that pleasurable emotions are the good.

B. Is not the position of Ayer.

C. Asserts that so called ethical assertions are merely expressions of emotions.

D. Denies that 'ought' type statements are meaningful assertions.

E. C and D above.

10. Emotivists and cultural relativists would agree that:

A. Analytic a priori statements are meaningful.

B. Synthetic a posteriori statements are meaningful.

C. Value statements are meaningful.

D. A & B above.

E. All of the above.

Answer key: 1. B since circles are by definition round. 2. D since the color of Jone's hat can be determined only by observation. 3. C since "Murder is morally wrong is a value statement." 4. A is obviously false but it is an analytic a priori proposition and hence meaningful. 5. C is not meaningful (according to Ayer) because it is a value statement. 6. C is probably false but this could be tested by social scientists. 7. E is correct. They may not all be good arguments. B is probably a false statement. They are, however, all arguments against emotivism. 8. D is correct. The emotivist denies that there are arguments for or against transcendent values. The cultural relativists denies that there are good grounds for affirming the existence of transcendent values. 9. E is correct. 10. D is correct.

1. Distinguish between the position of the emotivist and the cultural relativist.
2. Why or why not are fundamentalists and secular humanists emotivists?
3. Discuss and critically evaluate emotivism as a philosophical position and theory of language.
4. Discuss and critically evaluate emotivism as a cultural phenomena.
5. Distinguish between emotivism and subjectivism.
6. Discuss the relationship of emotivism to cultural conflict.

Chapter IV

1. The following are statements or arguments in favor of Aristippus' philosophy:
   A. Mental pleasures last longer.
   B. The good act is that which contributes to the greatest pleasure of the greatest number.
   C. Intensity of pleasure is the criteria for the good.
   D. A & C above.
   E. All of the above.

2. All ethical hedonists assert:
   A. Mental pleasure is better than physical pleasure.
   B. Mental pleasure is intrinsically better than physical pleasure.
   C. All persons ought to seek only pleasure.
   D. Mental pleasures are better than physical pleasures because they last longer.
   E. All the above.

3. Which of the following statements would be rejected by a psychological egoistic hedonist?
   A. All persons seek pleasure.
   B. All persons seek their own pleasure.
   C. All persons seek only their own pleasure.
   D. All persons always seek only their own pleasure.
   E. None the above.

4. An ethical egoistic hedonist would probably assert:
   A. Since psychological egoistic hedonism is true, ethical egoistic hedonism is true.

B.   All persons ought to seek only their own pleasure.
C.   Some times everyone should love other persons.
D.   Agape love is probably possible and obligatory.
E.   A & B above.

5. *Aristippus believed:*
    A.   Mental pleasures were best.
    B.   Mental pleasures were best because they are intrinsically better than physical pleasures.
    C.   Intense pleasures are the best.
    D.   Physical pleasures are the best.
    E.   C & D above.

6. *Epicurus believed:*
    A.   Intense pleasures are the best.
    B.   Physical pleasures are the best.
    C.   Mental pleasures are the best because they last longer.
    D.   Mental pleasures are best because they are intrinsically better than physical pleasures.
    E.   C & D above.

7. *Epicurus believed:*
    A.   The world is made up of atoms falling in a void.
    B.   The Christian God is true.
    C.   Political activity is likely to be pleasurable.
    D.   The Gods are out to destroy human beings.
    E.   None of the above.

8. *The following variables were taken into account by Bentham's hedonic calculus.*
    A.   Intensity of pleasure.
    B.   Duration of pleasure.
    C.   Purity of pleasure.
    D.   Fecundity of pleasure.
    E.   All of the above.

9. *The following are statements or arguments against the philosophy of J.S. Mill.*
    A.   It is better to be a man dissatisfied than a pig satisfied.
    B.   It is better to be Socrates dissatisfied than a fool satisfied.
    C.   Sympathy for our fellow creatures is the ultimate sanction for morality.
    D.   A & C above.
    E.   None of the above.

10. *The following are statements or arguments in favor of the philosophy of J.S. Mill*

A.   *It is better to be a man dissatisfied than a pig satisfied.*
B.   *It is better to be Socrates dissatisfied than a fool satisfied.*
C.   *Sympathy for our fellow creatures is the ultimate sanction for morality.*
D.   *A & C above.*
E.   *All of the above.*

Answers key: 1. C is correct. Aristippus was a quantitative hedonist who emphasized intensity of pleasure. 2. C is correct. Ethical hedonists differ among themselves on all of the other issues. 3. E is correct. D is the fullest expression of the psychological egoistic position and incorporates all of the other assertions. 4. E is correct. Egoistic hedonism excludes love as a motive. 5. E is correct. Aristippus believed that physical pleasures are the best because they are most intense. 6. C is the only correct answer. Epicurus argued for mental pleasure on the basis of quantity alone. 7. A is correct. 8. E is correct. 9. E is correct. A, B, and C all affirm Mill's philosophy. 10. E is correct.

1.   *What is the importance of the concepts of the 'artificial and natural identity of interest's to Bentham's theory?*

2.   *How is the hedonic calculus related to Bentham's utilitarianism?*

3.   *Discuss the chief ways in which the hedonism of J.S. Mill differs from that of Bentham.*

4.   *Describe a possible utilitarian position that is not hedonistic.*

5.   *How do the positions of Aristippus, Epicurus, Bentham and J. S. Mill function in similar and different ways as means of dealing with cultural conflict?*

6.   *What is the significance of the 'marginal cost of charity?'*

7.   *Discuss Bentham's vision of the social sciences, social justice and happiness.*

Chapter V

1.   *Which of the following statements are consistent with the philosophy of Epicurus?*
     A.   *You should not commit adultery because God will punish you for it.*
     B.   *You should not commit adultery because it will provide only short term pleasure.*
     C.   *You should not commit adultery because it is likely to lead to intense emotional involvement and disrupt your life.*
     D.   *B & C above.*
     E.   *All of the above.*

2. Which of the following statements are consistent with the philosophy of J.S. Mill?
   A. If adultery feels right for you, then it is right for you.
   B. If a rule allowing adultery could be shown to be for the greatest good of the greatest number, then it would be a good rule.
   C. Adulterous relationships are wrong since they usually do not emphasize the qualitatively best pleasures.
   D. B & C above.
   E. All of the above.

3. Which of the following designations apply to J. S. Mill?
   A. Altruism, psychological hedonism, qualitative hedonism, utilitarianism.
   B. Egoism, quantitative hedonism, utilitarianism.
   C. The hedonic calculus
   D. A & C above.
   E. None of the above.

4. "I agree with the statement 'Thou shalt not commit adultery' because this statement is an analytic a priori statement since "adultery" by definition is an illegitimate sexual relationship."
   The author of the above statement is giving an argument which is most consistent with:
   A. Fundamentalism.
   B. A non-fundamentalist Christianity.
   C. emotivism.
   D. A rule utilitarianism.
   E. Deontology.

5. "I agree with the statement 'Thou shalt not commit adultery' because I belong to a religious sub-culture which regards adultery as wrong."
   The author of the above statement is giving an argument which is most consistent with
   A. emotivism.
   B. cultural relativism.
   C. rule utilitarianism.
   D. act utilitarianism.
   E. fundamentalism.

6. "I agree with the statement 'Thou shalt not commit adultery' because both the Bible and natural law indicate that adultery is wrong.
   The author of the above statement is giving an argument which is most consistent with:
   A. teleology.
   B. utilitarianism.
   C. deontology.

D.   *egoistic hedonism.*

E.   *altruistic hedonism.*

7.   *"Equality is a fundamental principle of justice because the greatest good for the greatest number will be realized by its institutionalization."*
     The author of the above statement is giving an argument which is consistent with:

A.   *A teleological ethic.*

B.   *Bentham.*

C.   *J.S. Mill.*

D.   *utilitarianism.*

E.   *All of the above.*

8.   *"All knowledge about 'the good' is derived from application of reason and the scientific method."*
     The above assertion is consistent with:

A.   *Bentham.*

B.   *J.S. Mill.*

C.   *Epicurus.*

D.   *Secular humanism.*

E.   *All of the above.*

9.   *The following are statements or arguments in favor of Bentham's philosophy.*

A.   *Intensity of pleasure is always best.*

B.   *Identity of interest" is an ambiguous phrase.*

C.   *Sympathy is the basic motivation to be moral.*

D.   *All of the above.*

E.   *None of the above.*

10. *The following are statements or arguments against psychological egoism.*

A.   *All men seek self-realization.*

B.   *Frequently our selfish motives are hidden even from ourselves.*

C.   *"x always seeks self-realization" and "x is always selfish" are not identical in meaning.*

D.   *B & C above.*

E.   *All of the above.*

Answer key: 1. D is correct. Epicurus was committed to long term pleasure and avoidance of pain. 2. D is correct. Mill's criterion for a good rule is stated in B and Mill was committed to quality of pleasure. 3. A is correct. 4. C is correct. 5. B is correct. 6. C is correct. The author might defend his adherence to natural law and the Bible in a way consistent with some of the theories. Here, however, he simply refers to the "right" authority. 7. E. The statement is a utilitarian argument. Bentham and Mill are utilitarians. All utilitarians are teleologists. 8. E. 9. E. A excludes the other criteria of the hedonic calculus. *B is part of an argument against Bentham. C is consistent with Mill but not Bentham. 10. C. A and B are statements in favor of psychological egoism.*

1. *Discuss and critically evaluate the arguments for and against psychological egoism.*

2. *Discuss and critically evaluate the arguments for and against ethical egoism.*

3. *Discuss and critically evaluate the arguments for and against psychological hedonism.*

4. *Discuss and critically evaluate the arguments for and against ethical hedonism.*

5. *Compare and contrast the arguments against adultery likely to be advanced by Bentham and a fundamentalist.*

6. *Discuss the strengths and weaknesses of utilitarianism.*

7. *Compare and contrast the ethical theories of Bentham and J.S. Mill.*

Chapter VI

1. *Kant and Bentham would have agreed that:*
   A. *Acting for the sake of duty is the most important ethical goal.*
   B. *Acting according to duty is most important.*
   C. *It is equally important to act for the sake of duty and according to duty.*
   D. *All of the above.*
   E. *None of the above.*

2. *Kant believed that:*
   A. *A feeling of benevolence is the ultimate ground of morality.*
   B. *Agreed with J.S. Mill that duty not benevolence is the ultimate ground for morality.*
   C. *Would agree with Freud that a sense of duty is the sublimation of our aggressive instinct.*
   D. *All of the above.*
   E. *None of the above.*

3. *Kant was:*
   A. *A deontologist because he rejected consequences as a criterion for the good.*
   B. *A teleologist because he rejected consequences as a criterion for the good.*
   C. *Like Mill a teleologist.*
   D. *All of the above.*
   E. *None of the above.*

4. *Kant was:*
   A.   *A teleologist like Aristotle.*
   B.   *A deontologist like Aristotle because he maintained that happiness was the good.*
   C.   *A deontologist like Bentham.*
   D.   *All of the above.*
   E.   *None of the above.*

5. *Kant argues it is wrong to commit suicide because:*
   A.   *It is irrational to end your life out of a motive of self love.*
   B.   *You should continue to live out of love for your neighbor.*
   C.   *God forbids it.*
   D.   *All of the above.*
   E.   *None of the above.*

6. *Kant argues that you should not refuse to help others when they are in need because:*
   A.   *If you don't help others they won't help you.*
   B.   *You would not be willing to affirm the existence of a society in which no one helped anyone else.*
   C.   *A feeling of benevolence for humanity directs us to help others.*
   D.   *All of the above.*
   E.   *None of the above.*

7. *Kant argues that you should not waste your talents because:*
   A.   *You can't will that the wasting of talents should be made into a universal law.*
   B.   *If you waste your talents that will increase the probability that others will also.*
   C.   *If you develop your talents you are likely to enhance your happiness.*
   D.   *All of the above.*
   E.   *None of the above.*

8. *Kant argues that you should keep your promises because:*
   A.   *You will be more likely to be successful in business and love if people trust you.*
   B.   *To will universal promise breaking is logically contradictory.*
   C.   *To will universal promise breaking is logically possible but would not work empirically.*
   D.   *All of the above.*
   E.   *None of the above.*

9. *Kant argues that the categorical imperative enjoins respect for persons because:*
   A.   *To respect rationality is to respect what is sacred in persons and the universe.*

B.   *We should act as if we are making universal law in a kingdom of beings who are ends in themselves.*

C.   *To never treat people simply as means is to show respect for the reason within them.*

D.   *All of the above.*

E.   *None of the above.*

10. Kant argues that if we determine what is right on empirical grounds:

A.   *We will be irrational.*

B.   *We will be controlled by our passions.*

C.   *We will not be autonomous persons.*

D.   *All of the above.*

E.   *None of the above.*

Answer key: *1. E is correct. 2. E is correct. Kant did not found his ethics on feeling while J.S. Mill did. He, of course, respected 'duty' in contrast to Freud. 3. A is correct. 4. E is correct. Kant was a deontologist. In this he differed from both Bentham and Aristotle. He did not think that happiness was the ultimate good. 5. A is correct. 6. B is correct. One cannot make not helping others into a universal law. 7. A is correct. The reason is similar to 6 above. 8. B is the only correct answer. 9. D is correct. 10. D is correct.*

1.   *Compare Kant's view of what it means to be free with that of Bentham. Which view is most adequate?*

2.   *To what extent is the Kantian ethic compatible with the Biblical ethic?*

3.   *Compare, contrast and critically evaluate the view of Kant and A.J. Ayer.*

4.   *Compare Kant's view of individualism with that of Bentham.*

5.   *Compare, contrast and critically evaluate the views of Kant and J.S. Mill.*

6.   *To what extent is Kant's ethic compatible or incompatible with a secular humanist ethic?*

7.   *Discuss Kant's ethic in the context of contemporary cultural conflict.*

8.   *Compare, contrast and critically evaluate the views of Kant and cultural relativism.*

Chapter VII

1.   *John Rawls and Bentham would probably agree that:*
A. *Human beings are altruistic.*
B. *The greatest good of the greatest number is the criterion for a just social order.*
C. *Social justice requires the affirmation of a totally teleological ethic.*
D. *All of the above.*
E. *None of the above.*

2. *John Rawls in his* A Theory of Justice *rejects slavery because:*
    A. *Slavery is not for the greatest good of the greatest number.*
    B. *Slavery is not a social arrangement which Western culture accepts.*
    C. *Slavery is inefficient.*
    D. *All of the above.*
    E. *None of the above.*
3. *Rawls believes that an adequate conception of justice:*
    A. *Is founded on agape love.*
    B. *Is founded on egoism.*
    C. *Is founded on a commitment to qualitative pleasures as the good.*
    D. *All of the above.*
    E. *None of the above*
4. *Rawls would probably:*
    A. *Reject slavery because it denies the equal liberty principle.*
    B. *Reject a closed aristocracy even if it benefited the least advantaged.*
    C. *Reject the doubling of the wealth of a nation if it failed to benefit the least advantaged.*
    D. *All of the above.*
    E. *None of the above*
5. *For Rawls to accept unequal distribution of primary goods:*
    A. *Inequality must benefit the least advantaged.*
    B. *There must be equality of opportunity.*
    C. *There must be equality under the law.*
    D. *All of the above.*
    E. *None of the above.*
6. *Rawls accepts unequal distribution of primary goods:*
    A. *Only if it benefits the least advantaged.*
    B. *Only if there is agreement on ultimate good.*
    C. *Only if average utility is increased.*
    D. *B & C above.*
    E. *None of the above.*
7. *John Rawls affirms:*
    A. *Equality before the law*
    B. *Equality of opportunity*
    C. *Equal distribution of wealth, under every and all circumstances.*
    D. *A & B above.*
    E. *All of the above.*

8. *John Rawls is:*
    A. *Like Kant, a teleologist.*
    B. *Like J.S. Mill, a deontologist.*
    C. *Like Bentham an egoist.*
    D. *Like Epicurus, committed to atheism.*
    E. *None of the above.*
9. *Rawls and Kant would probably agree that:*
    A. *Persons should never be treated as means.*
    B. *Persons should never be treated simply as means.*
    C. *Rational autonomy is a desirable goal for human beings.*
    D. *All of the above.*
    E. *B & C above.*
10. *John Rawls:*
    A. *Places equality of opportunity above equal liberty.*
    B. *Places equal liberty above equality of opportunity.*
    C. *Rejects utilitarianism because all utilitarians are hedonists.*
    D. *A & C above.*
    E. *B & C above.*

Answer key: *1. E is correct. Rawls regards his ethic as partially deontological. 2. E is correct. 3. E is correct. 5. D is correct. 6. A is correct. 7. D is correct. 8. E is correct. 9. E is correct. 10. B is correct.*

1. *Compare, contrast, and critically evaluate the theories of justice of Rawls and Bentham.*
2. *Compare contrast and critically evaluate the theories of personality of Kant and Rawls.*
3. *Compare, contrast and critically evaluate the theories of justice of Rawls and utilitarianism.*
4. *Compare, contrast, and critically evaluate Rawls' theory and that .cultural relativism.*
5. *Discuss the relationship of Rawls' theory to the problem of cultural conflict.*
6. *Discuss Rawls' position on egoism.*
7. *Discuss Rawls' position on hedonism.*
8. *Compare, contrast and critically evaluate the theories of Rawls and J.S. Mill.*

Chapter VIII

1. The Enlightenment is characterized by which of the following?
    A. Belief in universal laws of reason.
    B. The rejection of the authority of tradition.
    C. The rejection of the ultimate authority of revelation.
    D. A and B above.
    E. All of the above.

2. The Enlightenment is best represented by which of the following?
    A. Islamic fundamentalism.
    B   Deconstructionism
    C. MacIntyre's philosophy.
    D. B and C above.
    E. None of the above.

3. The Enlightenment is best represented by which of the following?
    A. Freud
    B   Sartre.
    C. Kant.
    D. Hitler's national socialism.
    E. Mussolini's fascism.

4. Which of the following are committed to a rule ethic?
    A.   Kant.
    B. J. S. Mill.
    C. Alasdair MacIntyre.
    D. A and B above.
    E. All of the above.

5. Which of the following statements are true?
    A. Philosophers committed to rule ethics have no place for virtues in their systems.
    B.   Philosophers committed to virtue ethics have no place for rules in their systems.
    C.. Philosophers committed to virtue ethics allow for a secondary focus on rules.
    D. Philosophers committed to rule ethics allow for a secondary focus on virtues.
    E.   C and D above.

6. Which of the following are best characterized by commitment to virtue ethics?
    A. Plato.
    B. Aristotle.
    C. Alasdair MacIntyre.
    D. A and C above.
    E. All of the above.

7. Alasdair MacIntyre:
    A. Is a cultural relativist.
    B. Is a cultural relativist because he is committed to the Enlightenment ideal.
    C. Is a cultural relativist because he affirms that values are necessarily linked to tradition.
    D. All of the above.
    E. None of the above.

8. Alasdair MacIntyre:
    A. Is a deconstructionist.
    B. Agrees with Kant about the possibility of synthetic apriori propositions.
    C.. Agrees with Ayer about the distinction between fact and values.
    D. All of the above.
    E. None of the above.

9. By teleological explanation, MacIntyre means:
    A. The emotivist fact/value distinction should be rejected.
    B. The goodness of a person or an action must be understood in terms of ultimate purpose.
    C. Every action must be evaluated in terms of its telos or end.
    D. A and B above.
    E. All of the above.

10. MacIntyre believes that:
    A. Emotivism is an adequate ethical theory.
    B. The Enlightenment was destined to break down into emotivism.
    C. Kant has the better of the argument over against A.J.Ayer.
    D. .Aristotle's approach to ethics is to be preferred to that of Rawls.
    E. B and D above.

1. Discuss and critically evaluate MacIntyre's relationship to the Enlightenment.
2. Discuss and critically evaluate the relationship of rule versus virtue ethics.

3. *Discuss the relationship of culture wars to the place of tradition in society.*
4. *Discuss and critically evaluate MacIntyre's relationship to cultural relativism.*
5. *Discuss and critically evaluate MacIntyre's relationship to emotivism.*
6. *Discuss and critically evaluate MacIntyre's relationship to utilitarianism.*
7. *Discuss and critically evaluate MacIntyre's relationship to Kant.*
8. *Discuss and critically evaluate MacIntyre's relationship to Rawls.*
9. *Discuss and critically evaluate MacIntyre's views on the relationship to ethics of teleological and mechanistic explanation.*
10. *Discuss and critically evaluate MacIntyre's relationship to secular humanism and fundamentalism.*
11. *Explain what MacIntyre means by knowing another tradition as a second first language.*
12. *How is MacIntyre's work related to the so called culture wars? To what extent does he provide or fail to provide a viable solution to the problems raised by contemporary debate in American culture*

Works Cited

Aristotle. *The Nicomachean Ethics* Trans. J. A. K. Thomson. Baltimore: Penguin Books, 1953.

Augustine. *The City of God. Trans. Marcus Dodds, D.D. New York: The Modern Library, 1950.*

Ayer, Alfred Jules. *Language, Truth and Logic* New York: Dover Publications, Inc., 1935.

Bellah, Robert, Richard Madsen, William M. Sullivan, Ann Swidler, Steven M Tipton. *Habits of the Heart: Individualism and Commitment in American Life.* New York: Harper and Row Publishers, 1985.

Bennett, William. *The Book of Virtues, A Treasury of Great Moral Stories.* New York: Simon and Schuster, 1993.

_____. *The De-valuing of America.* New York: Summit Books, 1992.

Birnbaum, Jeffrey H. "The right Hand of God: The Gospel According to Ralph." *Time Magazine,* 15 May, 1995.

Brandt, Richard. "Ethical Relativism," in *Ethical Issues In Business,* ed. by Thomas Donaldson and Patricia H. Werhane. Englewood Cliffs, New Jersey: Prentice Hall, Inc., 1979.

Cohen, Norman J., Ed. *The Fundamentalist Phenomenon, A View From Within, A Response From Without.* Grand Rapids: William B. Eerdmans Publishing Company, 1990.

Coser, Lewis A. *The Masters of Sociological Thought.* 2nd. ed. New York: Harcourt, Brace , Janovich, Inc., 1971, 1977.

_____. *The Functions of Social Conflict.* New York: The Free Press, 1959.

Dahrendorf, Ralf. *Class and Class Conflict in Industrial Society.* Stanford California: Stanford University Press, 1959.

*Dooyeweerd, Herman. A New Critique of Theoretical Thought Vol. I-IV. T*rans. David H. Freeman and William S. Young Philadelphia: The Presbyterian and Reformed Publishing Company, 1953.

_____. *In the Twilight of Western Thought: Studies in the Pretended Autonomy of Theoretical Thought.* Philadelphia: The Presbyterian and Reformed Publishing Company, 1960.

_____.*Roots of Western Culture: Pagan, Secular, and Christian Options.* Trans. John Kraay. Ed. Mark Vander Vennen and Bernard Zylstra. Toronto: Wedge Publishing Foundation, 1979.

Eisenstadt, S.N. Ed. *The Protestant Ethic and Modernization.* New York: Basic Books, 1968.

Ethics Vol. 99 No. 4, July 1989 and Volume 105 No. 1, October 1994. Chicago: The University of Chicago Press.

Exodus 20:12-17. New International Version.

Galations 3:19-25, 5:14, 5:22-23. NIV.

Galston, William A. "Pluralism and Social Unity." *Ethics, Vol. 99, N0. 4,* July 1989. Chicago: The University of Chicago Press.

Gouldner, Alvin. *The Coming Crisis in Western Sociology.* New York: Basic Books, 1970.

Fletcher, Joseph. *Situation Ethics* Philadelphia: The Westminster Press, 1966.

Frankena, William K. *Ethics.* Second Edition. Englewood Cliffs, New Jersey: Prentice Hall, Inc.

Halevy, Elie. *The Growth of Philosophic Radicalism.* trans. Mary Morris. Boston: The Beacon Press, 1955.

Holmes, Arthur F. *Ethics: Approaching Moral Decisions.* Downers Grove, Illinois: Intervarsity Press, 1984.

Hunter, James Davison. *Before the Shooting Starts: Searching for Democracy in America's Culture War.* New York: The Free Press, 1994.

_____. *Culture Wars: The Struggle to Define America.* New York: Basic Books, 1991.

Kalsbeek, L. *Contours of A Christian Philosophy: An Introduction to Herman Dooyeweerd's Thought.* Bernard and Josina Zylstra, Ed. with an Introduction by Bernard Zylstra. Toronto: Wedge Publishing Foundation, 1975.

Kant, Immanuel. *Religion Within The Limits Of Reason Alone.* Trans. Theodore M. Greene and Hoyt H. Hudson. New York: Harper and Brothers, 1960.

_____. *The Critique of Pure Reason,* trans. Norman Kemp Smith New York: St. Martin's Press, Inc., 1961.

_____. *Foundations of the Metaphysics of Morals* Trans. Lewis White Beck. New York: The Bobbs-Merrill Company, Inc., 1959.

Kuhn. Thomas. *The Structure of Scientific Revolutions.* Second Edition Enlarged. International Encyclopedia of Unified Science II, No. 2. Chicago: University of Chicago Press, 1970.

Kurtz, Paul. *A Secular Humanist Declaration.* drafted by Paul Kurtz and Endorsed by 58 Prominent Scholars and Writers. Reprinted From *Free Inquiry* Magazine, Vol. 1 #1, Winter, 1980.

Loconte, Joe "The Battle to Define America Turns Violent." *Christianity Today.* October 25, 1993.

MacIntyre, Alasdair. *After Virtue* Notre Dame, Indiana: University of Notre Dame Press, 1984.

_____. *Three Rival Versions of Moral Inguiry: Encyclopedia, Genealogy and Tradition.* Notre Dame, Indiana: Notre Dame University Press, 1990.

_____. *Whose Justice? Which Rationality?* Notre Dame, Indiana: University of Notre Dame Press, 1988.

Marsden, George M. *Understanding Fundamentalism and Evangelicalism.* Grand Rapids: William B. Eerdmans   Publishing Company, 1991.

Matthew 22:35-40. NIV.

Mill, John Stuart. "Utilitarianism." in *The English Philosophers From Bacon To Mill* 902ff. New York: The Modern Library, 1939.

Mouw, Richard J. and Griffioen, Sander. *Pluralism and Horizons: An Essay in Christian Public Philosophy.* Grand Rapids, Michigan: William B. Eerdmans Publishing Company, 1993.

Mulhull Stephen and Swift, Adam. *Liberals and Communitarians.* Cambridge, Mass.: Blackwell Publishers, 1992.

Parsons, Talcott. *Societies: Evolutionary and Comparative Perspectives.* Englewood Cliffs, N. J. Prentice Hall, Inc., 1966.

_____. *The Structure of Social Action.* New York: The Free Press of Glencoe, 1937.

_____. *The System of Modern Societies.* Englewood Cliffs, N. J. Prentice Hall, Inc., 1971.

Parsons, Talcott and Winston White. "The Link Between Character and Society." in Parsons, Talcott. *Social Structure and Personality.* New York: The Free Press of Glencoe, 1964.

Passmore, John. *A Hundred Years of Philosophy.* Harmondsworth, Middlesex, England: Penguin Books, 1968.

Paton, H.J. *The Categorical Imperative* Chicago: The University of Chicago Press, 1948.

Plato. *Republic, Great Dialogues of Plato.* Trans. by W.H.D. Rouse. New York: Mentor Books, *1956.*

Rawls, John. *A Theory of Justice.* Cambridge, Mass.: Harvard University Press, 1971.

_____. "Kantian Constructivism in Moral Theory," *The Journal of Philosophy, Volume LXXVII,* NO. 9, September 1980.

_____. "Justice as Fairness: Political not Metaphysical" *Philosophy and Public Affairs, Vol. 14, NO. 3,* 1985.

_____. *Political Liberalism.* New York: Columbia University Press, 1993.

Riesman, David. *The Lonely Crowd.* New Haven Connecticut: Yale University Press, 1950, 1953, 1961.

Rorty, Richard. "Does Academic Freedom Have Philosophical Presuppositions?" Academe: Bulletin of the American Association of University Professors, November/December 1994, Volume 80, Number 6, pp. 52-63.

_____. *Philosophy and the Mirror of Nature.* Princeton, New Jersey: Princeton University Press, 1979.

Sartre, John Paul. *Being and Nothingness.* Trans. Hazel Barnes. New York: Philosophical Library, Inc. 1956.

_____. "Existentialism." Trans. Hazel Barnes, in *Existentialism and Human Emotions.* New York: Philosophical Library, Inc., 1957.

Silber, John R. "The Ethical Significance of Kant's Religion." Forward to
   Kant, Immanuel. *Religion Within The Limits Of Reason Alone.* Trans.
   Theodore M. Greene and Hoyt H. Hudson. New York: Harper and Brothers,
   1960.
Skillen, James W. *Recharging The American Experiment: Principled
   Pluralism for Genuine Civic Community* Grand   Rapids, Michigan: Baker
   Books, 1994.
Skinner, B.F. *Beyond Freedom and Dignity.* New York: Bantam Books, 1971.
   _____. *Walden Two.* New York: The MacMillan company, 1948.
Tawney, R.H. *Religion and The Rise of Capitalism.* New York: Harcourt,
   Brace and Company, Inc., 1926.
Weber, Max. *The Protestant Ethic and the Spirit of Capitalism.* Trans. Talcott
   Parsons. New York: Charles Scribner's Sons, 1958.
Woodbridge, John D. "Culture War Casualties: How Warfare Rhetoric is
   Hurting the Work of the Church." *Christianity Today,* March 6, 1995.

Index